TRAUMA

For Ron Eyerman

TRAUMA

A Social Theory

JEFFREY C. ALEXANDER

polity

First published in 2012 by Polity Press

Polity Press
65 Bridge Street
Cambridge CB2 1UR, UK

Polity Press
350 Main Street
Malden, MA 02148, USA

ISBN-13: 978-0-7456-4911-5 (hardback)
ISBN-13: 978-0-7456-4912-2 (paperback)

A catalog record for this book is available from the British Library.

Typeset in 10.5 on 12 pt Sabon
by Servis Filmsetting Ltd, Stockport, Cheshire
Printed and bound in Great Britain by the MPG Books Group

For further information on Polity, visit our website: www.politybooks.com

CONTENTS

PREFACE AND ACKNOWLEDGMENTS

This book has its origins in the ferment of an intellectual project begun in Palo Alto almost fifteen years ago under the auspices of the Center for Advanced Studies in the Behavioral Sciences. Ron Eyerman, Bernhard Giesen, Neil Smelser, and Piotr Sztmpka were co-creators, and our different lines of shared thinking eventually formed the chapters of *Cultural Trauma and Collective Identity* (Alexander, Eyerman, Giesen, Smelser, and Sztompka 2004). The cultural trauma project has continued in the years since, with many new contributors (see, e.g., Goodman 2009; Eyerman, Alexander, and Breese 2011). From the beginning of this project until today it has been my privilege to collaborate closely with Ron Eyerman, whose theoretical and empirical investigations into cultural trauma (Eyerman 2001, 2008, and 2011) have been immensely stimulating to my own, and with whom I have directed (along with Philip Smith) the Yale Center for Cultural Sociology. I dedicate this volume to Ron Eyerman with gratitude for the generosity of his thinking, collegiality, and friendship. And, as so often before, I also wish to record my indebtedness to Nadine Amalfi for her editorial assistance in the preparation of this volume.

The chapters that follow have been revised in small or large part for publication here. I thank the following publishers for permission to reprint:

University of California Press for "Towards a Theory of Cultural Trauma." In J. C. Alexander et al., *Cultural Trauma and Collective Identity*. 2004. (Chapter 1)

Oxford University Press for "On the Social Construction of Moral Universals: The 'Holocaust' from Mass Murder to Trauma Drama." In J. C. Alexander (ed.) *Remembering the Holocaust: A Debate*. 2009. (Chapter 2)

Paradigm Publishers for "Trauma Construction and Moral Restriction: The Ambiguity of the Holocaust for Israel" (with Shai Dromi). In R. Eyerman et al. (eds) *Narrating Trauma: On the Impact of Collective Suffering*. 2011. (Chapter 3)

Peking University Press for "Remembrance of Things Past: Cultural Trauma, The Nanking Massacre, and Chinese Identity" (with Rui Gao). In *Peking–Yale University Conference Publication on Tradition and Modernity: Comparative Perspectives*. 2007. (Chapter 4)

Routledge for "Postcolonialism, Trauma, and Civil Society: A New Understanding." In S. Koniordos et al. (eds) *Conflict, Citizenship and Civil Society*. 2009. (Chapter 5)

Springer for "Globalization as Collective Representation: The New Dream of a Cosmopolitan Civil Sphere." In I. Rossi (ed.) *Frontiers of Globalization Research: Theoretical and Methodological Approaches*. 2007. (Chapter 6)

"The essence of drama: what will happen, who suffer, who not suffer, what turn be determined, what crisis created, what issue found?"

— Henry James

INTRODUCTION

That groups visit grave injuries on one another is an historical certainty central to social theory. Exactly how these injuries are felt and configured, and how such feelings and figurations affect social perceptions of grievance and the conflicts that ensue, have not been deeply conceptualized. In theorizing group conflict, the object of injury is typically conceived as an interest denied or a capacity suppressed, and the response of the dominated subject understood either as resignation or rebellion. Such conceptions of injury, interest, capacity, and response are thin. They assume a narrowness of reference and a clarity of perception which, for better and for worse, simply do not exist.

With this book, I aim to thicken these conceptions. We need to blow up the idea of self-interest to encompass collective identity, as something not given but culturally conceived, whose boundary expands and contracts. Instead of dominated interest, we need to think about social suffering, about emotions and existential threats to ethical convictions. We must also reconsider agency. It is not a great coil of energy waiting to explode. Formed in the forge of social suffering, it too must be culturally conceived.

Instead of interest and capacity, this book offers a social theory of collective trauma. It explains how collective agency develops, or fails to develop, in response to the experience of social suffering. Religion, nation, race, ethnicity, gender, class – each of these dimensions can be a medium for inflicting social pain. What this suffering is exactly, who delivered it, and who was on the receiving end – the answers to these questions are not objectively known but established through a trauma process. And concern with moral responsibility marks every step along the way. How can agents be punished and victims

1

compensated? How can social conditions be repaired to prevent such pain from happening again?

These chapters investigate social suffering on a broad scale. They address exploitation and violence, war and genocide, the massacre of innocents, and intense and often heinous religious, economic, ethnic, and racial strife. It is not their focus on such gruesome topics, however, that makes this book distinctive. Rather, it is a particular approach to social suffering's causes and effects. While sensitive to the materiality and pragmatics of social suffering, these studies reject materialist and pragmatic approaches for one centered inside a cultural sociology.

Material forces are deeply implicated in social suffering, and the strategic calculations and practical considerations surrounding traumatic events have significant effects on social organization. I am concerned, however, to trace the manner in which these causes and effects are crucially mediated by symbolic representations of social suffering, with understanding how a cultural process channels powerful human emotions, and to what effect. These symbolic-cum-emotional forces are carried by social groups whose actions transform the worlds of morality, materiality, and organization. Intellectuals, artists, politicians, and social movement leaders create narratives about social suffering. Projected as ideologies that create new ideal interests, trauma narratives can trigger significant repairs in the civil fabric. They can also instigate new rounds of social suffering.

I approach symbolic-cum-emotional representation as a collective process centering on meaning making. The cultural construction of collective trauma is fuelled by individual experiences of pain and suffering, but it is the threat to collective rather than individual identity that defines the suffering at stake. Individual suffering is of extraordinary human, moral, and intellectual import; in itself, however, it is a matter for ethics and psychology. My concern is with traumas that become collective. They can become so if they are conceived as wounds to social identity. This is a matter of intense cultural and political work. Suffering collectivities – whether dyads, groups, societies, or civilizations – do not exist simply as material networks. They must be imagined into being. The pivotal question becomes not who did this to me, but what group did this to us? Intellectuals, political leaders, and symbol creators of all kinds make competing claims. They identify protagonists and antagonists and weave them into accusatory narratives projected to audiences of third parties.

Which narrative wins out is a matter of performative power. The emotional experience of suffering, while critical, is not primordial. To find the meaning of suffering, it must be framed against background expectations. But effective performance depends upon more than creating powerful symbols. It is a matter also of material resources and demographics, which affect, even if they do not determine, what can be heard and who might listen. Who can command the most effective platform to tell the trauma story? Some stories are repressed by ruthless states, while others are materially sustained. Some stories are enriched by long-standing background representations; others seem so counterintuitive *vis-à-vis* established traditions as scarcely to be believed. Some trauma narratives address homogeneous audiences, others face fragmented and divided audiences; for others, there is nobody listening at all.

When social groups do construe events as gravely endangering, suffering becomes a matter of collective concern, cultural worry, social panic, gut-wrenching fear, catastrophic anxiety. *Individual* victims react to traumatic injury with repression and denial, gaining relief when these psychological defenses are overcome, bringing pain into consciousness so they are able to mourn. For *collectivities*, it is different. Rather than denial, repression, and "working through," it is a matter of symbolic construction and framing, of creating stories and characters, and moving along from there. A "we" must be constructed via narrative and coding, and it is this collective identity that experiences and confronts the danger. Hundreds and thousands of individuals may have lost their lives, and many more might experience grievous pain. Still, the construction of a shared cultural trauma is not automatically guaranteed. The lives lost and pains experienced are individual facts; shared trauma depends on collective processes of cultural interpretation.

Massive deaths from war can be seen as morally justified sacrifice. Americans who sent soldiers to triumphal victory in the First and Second World Wars did not experience collective trauma, despite the tens of thousands of deaths to men and women they loved and lost and the postwar "shell shock" so many individual soldiers experienced after they returned. Neither did Germans experience trauma during their early Blitzkriegs. Far from endangering American and German collective identities, these military confrontations actually seemed to reinforce them. It is only when narratives of triumph are challenged, when individual deaths seem worthless or polluted, when those who have fallen are seen not as sacrificing for a noble cause but as wasted victims of irresponsible chicanery, that wars become traumatic indeed (Giesen 2004; Heins 2011; Eyerman et al. 2011).

To transform individual suffering into collective trauma is cultural work. It depends upon speeches, rituals, marches, meetings, plays, movies, and storytelling of all kinds. Carrier groups tie their material and ideal interests to particular scripts about who did what to whom, and how society must respond if a collective identity is to be sustained. These constructions have the potential to trigger horrific group conflict, but they can also become the platform for amelioration and reconciliation. Lost wars, economic depressions, even mass murders can be understood according to drastically varying accounts and imply sharply antithetical social prescriptions. But, even the most compelling trauma narratives must reach outside themselves. The spiral of signification is mediated by institutional structures and uneven distributions of wealth and power. Are we struggling over the nature of collective trauma in the field of party conflict, in a court of law, in the mass media, or on a theatrical stage? Do cultural entrepreneurs have access to the means of symbolic production? Once again: Power and resources are critical, even if they alone will not decide.

Collective traumas are reflections of neither individual suffering nor actual events, but symbolic renderings that reconstruct and imagine them. Rather than descriptions of what is, they are arguments about what must have been and what should be. From the perspective of a cultural sociology, the contrast between factual and fictional statements is not an Archimedean point. The truth of a cultural script depends not on its empirical accuracy, but on its symbolic power and enactment. Yet, while the trauma process is not rational, it is intentional. It is people who make traumatic meanings, in circumstances they have not themselves created and which they do not fully comprehend.

Trauma scripts are performed in the theatres of everyday collective life. In the wake of the Sabra and Shatila massacres after Israeli's 1982 Lebanon War, it was not only the public war of words between right-wing Likud officials and their Peace Now critics that allowed the Holocaust narrative to be extended to Palestinians for the first time. It was the extraordinary and unprecedented ritual of the "400,000 Protest," the spectacle of hundreds of thousands of patriotic but outraged Israelis massively protesting against the massacres in a Tel Aviv square (Chapter 3).

The relative independence of collective trauma narration from individual experience and historical event, the intervening agency of culture creators, the performative impact of textual enactment – these social facts explain why and how trauma-dramas have such extraordinarily powerful effects on the organization and structure of our social worlds. Would Mao's communism have achieved sustained legitimacy, despite its political repression and disastrous economic policies, if class-trauma had not been so strenuously narrated as to suppress humiliating memories of Japan's Rape of Nanjing (Chapter 4)? Would the new states of India and Pakistan have been able to project progressive postcolonial identities if the massacres of Partition had been narrated in a manner that thrust the responsibility of their founding fathers into public view (Chapter 5)? Would the horrors of the twentieth century have looked the same if they had not been haunted by the construction of post-Holocaust morality (Chapter 2)? Would globalization have become central to the contemporary imagination if the trauma of Cold War had not triggered utopian hopes for a civil repair (Chapter 6)?

Simply to ask these questions is to see how cultural constructions of collective trauma have often played out in world-historical ways. The trauma process is a dangerous game. It can lead to utopian heights or to depths of despair. Yet, while the actual outcome of any particular trauma process is contingent, the challenges it confronts can be clearly foreseen. Illuminating these cultural structures and social processes cannot prevent massive social suffering. But a social theory of trauma might allow victims, audiences, and even perpetrators to gain enough critical distance to prevent some of its most horrific results.

— 1 —

CULTURAL TRAUMA: A SOCIAL THEORY

Cultural trauma occurs when members of a collectivity feel they have been subjected to a horrendous event that leaves indelible marks upon their group consciousness, marking their memories forever and changing their future identity in fundamental and irrevocable ways.

As I develop it here, cultural trauma is first of all an empirical, scientific concept, suggesting new meaningful and causal relationships between previously unrelated events, structures, perceptions, and actions. But this new scientific concept also illuminates an emerging domain of social responsibility and political action. It is by constructing cultural traumas that social groups, national societies, and sometimes even entire civilizations not only cognitively identify the existence and source of human suffering but may also take on board some significant responsibility for it. Insofar as they identify the cause of trauma in a manner that assumes such moral responsibility, members of collectivities define their solidary relationships in ways that, in principle, allow them to share the suffering of others. Is the suffering of others also our own? In thinking that it might in fact be, societies expand the circle of the "we." By the same token, social groups can, and often do, refuse to recognize the existence of others' trauma, or place the responsibility for it on people other than themselves. Because of their failure they cannot achieve a moral stance. Refusing to participate in the process of trauma creation, social groups restrict solidarity, leaving others to suffer alone.

Ordinary Language and Reflexivity

One of the great advantages of this new theoretical concept is that it partakes so deeply of everyday life. In the last century, first in Western societies and then, soon after, throughout the rest of the world, people spoke continually about being traumatized by an experience, by an event, by an act of violence or harassment, or even, simply, by an abrupt and unexpected, and sometimes not even particularly malevolent, experience of social transformation and change.[1] People also have continually employed the language of trauma to explain what happens, not only to themselves, but to the collectivities to which they belong as well. We often speak of an organization being traumatized when a leader departs or dies, when a governing regime falls, when an organization suffers an unexpected reversal of fortune. Actors describe themselves as traumatized when the environment of an individual or a collectivity suddenly shifts in an unforeseen and unwelcome manner.

We know from ordinary language, in other words, that with the idea of trauma we are on to something widely experienced and intuitively understood. Such rootedness in the life-world is the soil that nourishes every social scientific concept. The trick is to gain reflexivity, to move from the sense of something commonly experienced to the sense of strangeness that allows us to think sociologically. For trauma is not something naturally existing; it is something constructed by society.

In this task of making trauma strange, its embeddedness in everyday life and language, so important for providing an initial intuitive understanding, now presents itself as a challenge to be overcome. The scholarly approaches to trauma developed thus far have actually been distorted by the powerful, commonsense understandings of trauma that have emerged in everyday life. Indeed, it might be said that these commonsense understandings constitute a kind of "lay trauma theory" in contrast to which a more theoretically reflexive approach to trauma must be erected.

Lay Trauma Theory

According to lay theory, traumas are naturally occurring events that shatter an individual or collective actor's sense of well-being. In other words, the power to shatter – the "trauma" – is thought to emerge from events themselves. The reaction to such shattering events – "being traumatized" – is experienced as an immediate and

7

unreflexive response. According to the lay perspective, the trauma experience occurs when the traumatizing event interacts with human nature. Human beings need security, order, love, and connection. If something happens that sharply undermines these needs, it hardly seems surprising, according to the lay theory, that people will be traumatized as a result.[2]

Enlightenment Thinking

There are "Enlightenment" and "psychoanalytic" versions of this lay trauma theory. The Enlightenment understanding suggests that trauma is a kind of rational response to abrupt change, whether at the individual or social level. The objects or events that trigger trauma are perceived clearly by actors, their responses are lucid, and the effects of these responses are problem solving and progressive. When bad things happen to good people, they become shocked, outraged, indignant. From an Enlightenment perspective, it seems obvious, perhaps even unremarkable, that political scandals are cause for indignation; that economic depressions are cause for despair; that lost wars create a sense of anger and aimlessness; that disasters in the physical environment lead to panic; that assaults on the human body lead to intense anxiety; that technological disasters create concerns, even phobias, about risk. The responses to such traumas will be efforts to alter the circumstances that caused them. Memories about the past guide this thinking about the future. Programs for action will be developed, individual and collective environments will be reconstructed, and eventually the feelings of trauma will subside.

This Enlightenment version of lay trauma theory informs Arthur Neal in his *National Trauma and Collective Memory*. In explaining whether or not a collectivity is traumatized, Neal points to the quality of the event itself. National traumas have been created, he argues, by "individual and collective reactions to a volcano-like event that shook the foundations of the social world" (Neal 1998: ix). An event traumatizes a collectivity because it is "an extraordinary event," an event that has such "an explosive quality" that it creates "disruption" and "radical change . . . within a short period of time" (Neal 1998: 3, 9–10). These objective empirical qualities "command the attention of all major subgroups of the population," triggering emotional response and public attention because rational people simply cannot react in any other way (Neal 1998: 9–10). "Dismissing or ignoring the traumatic experience is not a reasonable option," Neal asserts; neither is "holding an attitude of benign neglect" or "cynical indifference" (Neal 1998: 4, 9–10). It is precisely because actors are reasonable that traumatic events typically lead to progress: "The very fact that a disruptive event has occurred" means that "new opportunities emerge for innovation and change" (Neal 1998: 18). It is hardly surprising, in other words, that "permanent changes were introduced into the [American] nation as a result of the Civil War, the Great Depression, and the trauma of World War II" (Neal 1998: 5).

Despite what I will later call the naturalistic limitations of such an Enlightenment understanding of trauma, what remains singularly important about Neal's approach is its emphasis on the collectivity rather than the individual, an emphasis that sets it apart from the more individually oriented psychoanalytically informed approaches discussed below. In focusing on events that create trauma for national, not individual, identity, Neal follows the sociological model developed by Kai Erikson in *Everything in its Path*. This heart-wrenching account of the effects on a small Appalachian community of a devastating flood was constrained by a naturalistic perspective, yet it laid the groundwork for a distinctively sociological approach by thematizing the difference between collective and individual trauma. Both the attention to collectively emergent properties and the naturalism with which such collective traumas are conceived are evident in the following passage.

> By individual trauma I mean a blow to the psyche that breaks through one's defenses so suddenly and with such brutal force that one cannot react to it effectively . . . By collective trauma, on the other hand, I mean a blow to the basic tissues of social life that damages the bonds attaching people together and impairs the prevailing sense of communality. The collective trauma works its way slowly and even insidiously into the awareness of those who suffer from it, so it does not have the quality of suddenness normally associated with "trauma." But it is a form of shock all the same, a gradual realization that the community no longer exists as an effective source of support and that an important part of the self has disappeared: . . . "We" no longer exist as a connected pair or as linked cells in a larger communal body. (Erikson 1976: 153–4)

As Smelser suggests (2004), following, lay trauma theory began to enter ordinary language and scholarly discussions alike in the efforts to understand the kind of "shell shock" that affected so many soldiers during the First World War, and it became expanded and elaborated in relation to other wars that followed in the course of the twentieth century. When Glen Elder (1974) created life-course analysis to trace the cohort effects on individual identity of these and other cataclysmic

:s in the twentieth century, he and his students adopted a
ightenment mode of trauma. Similar understandings have
ned approaches in other disciplines, for example, the vast
phy devoted to the far-reaching effects on nineteenth-
century Europe and the United States of the "trauma" of the French
Revolution. Elements of the lay Enlightenment perspective have also
informed contemporary thinking about the Holocaust and responses
to other episodes of mass murder in modern times.

Psychoanalytic Thinking

Such realist thinking continues to permeate everyday life and scholarly thought alike. Increasingly, however, it has come to be filtered
through a psychoanalytic perspective that has become central to
both commonsense and academic thinking. This approach places
a model of unconscious emotional fears and cognitively distorting
mechanisms of psychic defense between the external shattering event
and the actor's internal traumatic response. When bad things happen
to good people, according to this version of lay theory, they can
become so frightened that they can actually repress the experience
of trauma itself. Rather than activating direct cognition and rational
understanding, the traumatizing event becomes distorted in the
actor's imagination and memory. The effort to accurately attribute
responsibility for the event and the progressive effort to develop an
ameliorating response are undermined by displacement. This psychoanalytically mediated perspective continues to maintain a naturalistic
approach to traumatic events, but it suggests a more complex understanding about the human ability to perceive them consciously. The
truth about the experience is perceived, but only unconsciously. In
effect, truth goes underground, and accurate memory and responsible action are its victims. Traumatic feelings and perceptions, then,
come not only from the originating event but also from the anxiety
of keeping it repressed. Trauma will be resolved not only by setting
things right in the world, but also by setting things right in the self.[3]
According to this perspective, the truth can be recovered, and psychological equanimity restored, only, as the Holocaust historian Saul
Friedlander (1979) once put it, "when memory comes."

This phrase actually provides the title of Friedlander's memoir
about his childhood during the Holocaust years in Germany and
France. Recounting, in evocative literary language, his earlier experiences of persecution and displacement, Friedlander suggests that
conscious perception of highly traumatic events can emerge only after

10

psychological introspection and "working through" allows actors to recover their full capacities for agency (Friedlander 1979, 1992). Emblematic of the intellectual framework that has emerged over the last three decades in response to the Holocaust experience, this psychoanalytically informed theorizing particularly illuminated the role of collective memory, insisting on the importance of working backward through the symbolic residues that the originating event has left upon contemporary recollection.[4]

Much as these memory residues surface through free association in psychoanalytic treatment, they appear in public life through the creation of literature. It should not be surprising, then, that literary interpretation, with its hermeneutic approach to symbolic patterns, has been offered as a kind of academic counterpart to the psychoanalytic intervention. In fact, the major theoretical and empirical statements of the psychoanalytic version of lay trauma theory have been produced by scholars in the various disciplines of the humanities. Because within the psychoanalytic tradition it has been Lacan who has emphasized the importance of language in emotional formation, it has been Lacanian theory, often in combination with Derridean deconstruction, that has informed these humanities-based studies of trauma.

Perhaps the most influential scholar in shaping this approach has been Cathy Caruth, in her own collection of essays, *Unclaimed Experience: Trauma, Narrative, and History* and in her edited collection, *Trauma: Explorations in Memory* (Caruth 1995, 1996).[5] Caruth focuses on the complex permutations that unconscious emotions impose on traumatic reactions, yet, at the same time, she roots her analysis in the power and objectivity of the originating traumatic event. "Freud's intuition of, and his passionate fascination with, traumatic experiences," she asserts, related traumatic reactions to "the unwitting reenactment of an event that one cannot simply leave behind" (Caruth 1995: 2). The event cannot be left behind because "the breach in the mind's experience," according to Caruth, "is experienced too soon." This abruptness prevents the mind from fully cognizing the event. It is experienced "too unexpectedly . . . to be fully known and is therefore not available to consciousness." Buried in the unconscious, the event is experienced irrationally, "in the nightmares and repetitive actions of the survivor." The psychoanalytic version of lay trauma theory goes beyond the Enlightenment one: "Trauma is not locatable in the simple violent or original event in an individual's past, but rather in the way its very unassimilated nature – the way it was precisely *not known* in the first instance – returns to haunt the

11

survivor later on." When Caruth describes these traumatic symptoms, however, she returns to the theme of objectivity, suggesting that they "tell us of a reality or truth that is not otherwise available" (Caruth 1995: 3–4, italics added).[6]

The enormous influence of this psychoanalytic version of lay trauma theory can be seen in the manner in which it has informed the efforts by Latin American scholars to come to terms with the traumatic brutalities of their late-twentieth century dictatorships. Many of these discussions, of course, are purely empirical investigations of the extent of repression or normative arguments that assign responsibilities and demand reparations. Yet, there is an increasing body of literature that addresses the effects of the repression in terms of the traumas it caused.

The aim is to restore collective psychological health by lifting societal repression and restoring memory. To achieve this, social scientists stress the importance of finding – through public acts of commemoration, cultural representation, and public political struggle – some collective means for undoing repression and allowing the pent-up emotions of loss and mourning to be expressed. While thoroughly laudable in moral terms, and without doubt also very helpful in terms of promoting public discourse and enhancing self-esteem, this advocacy literature typically is limited by the constraints of lay commonsense. Both the traumatized feelings of the victims and the actions that should be taken in response are treated as unmediated, commonsense reactions to the repression itself. Elizabeth Jelin and Susana Kaufman, for example, directed a large-scale project on "Memory and Narrativity" sponsored by the Ford Foundation, involving a team of investigators from different South American countries. In a powerful report on their initial findings, "Layers of Memories: Twenty Years After in Argentina,"[7] they contrast the victims' insistence on recognizing the reality of traumatizing events and experiences with the denials of the perpetrators and their conservative supporters, denials that insist on looking to the future and forgetting the past: "The confrontation is between the voices of those who call for commemoration, for remembrance of the disappearances and the torment, for denunciation of the repressors, and those who make it their business to act as if nothing has happened here." Jelin and Kaufman call these conservative forces the "bystanders of horror" who claim they "did not know" and "did not see." But because the event which triggered the traumatizing repression was real, they argue, such denials will not work: "The personalized memory of people cannot be erased or destroyed by decree or by force." The efforts to memorialize the victims of the repression are presented as efforts to restore the objective reality of the brutal events, to separate them from the unconscious distortions of memory: "Monuments, museums and memorials are ... attempts to make statements and affirmations [to create] a materiality with a political, collective, public meaning [and] a physical reminder of a conflictive political past" (5–7).

The Naturalistic Fallacy

It is through these Enlightenment and psychoanalytic approaches that trauma has been translated from an idea in ordinary language into an intellectual concept in the academic languages of diverse disciplines. Both perspectives, however, share the naturalistic fallacy of the lay understanding from which they derive. It is from the rejection of this naturalistic fallacy that my argument in this volume precedes. First and foremost, I maintain that events do not, in and of themselves, create collective trauma. Events are not inherently traumatic. Trauma is a socially mediated attribution. The attribution may be made in real time, as an event unfolds; it may also be made before the event occurs, as an adumbration, or after the event has concluded, as a post-hoc reconstruction. Sometimes, in fact, events that are deeply traumatizing may not actually have occurred at all; such imagined events, however, can be as traumatizing as events that have actually occurred.

This notion of an "imagined" traumatic event seems to suggest the kind of process that Benedict Anderson (1991) describes in *Imagined Communities*. Anderson's concern, of course, is not with trauma per se, but with the kinds of self-consciously ideological narratives of nationalist history. Yet these collective beliefs often assert the existence of some national trauma. In the course of defining national identity, national histories are constructed around injuries that cry out for revenge. The twentieth century was replete with examples of angry nationalist groups, and their intellectual and media representatives, asserting they were injured or traumatized by agents of some putatively antagonistic ethnic and political group, which must then be battled against in turn. The Serbians inside Serbia, for example, contended that ethnic Albanians in Kosovo did them traumatic injury, thus providing justification for their own "defensive" invasion and ethnic cleansing (Spasić 2011). The type case of such militarist construction of primordial national trauma was Adolf Hitler's grotesque assertion that the international Jewish conspiracy had been responsible for Germany's traumatic losses in the First World War.

But what Anderson means by "imagined" does not quite point to what I have in mind, for he employs the concept to reference the illusory, nonempirical quality of the original event. Anderson is horrified by the ideology of nationalism, and his analysis of imagined national communities partakes of ideology critique. As such, it applies the kind of Enlightenment perspective that mars lay trauma theory. It is not that traumas are never constructed from nonexistent events. Certainly they are. But it is too easy to accept the imagined dimension of trauma when the reference is primarily to claims like these, which point to events that either never did occur or to events whose representation involve exaggerations that serve obviously aggressive and harmful political forces. My own approach to the idea of "imagined" is more like what Durkheim meant in *The Elementary Forms of Religious Life* when he wrote of the "religious imagination." Imagination is intrinsic to the very process of representation. It seizes upon an inchoate experience from life, and forms it, through association, condensation, and aesthetic creation, into some specific shape.

Imagination informs trauma construction just as much when the reference is to something that has actually occurred as to something that has not. It is only through the imaginative process of representation that actors have the sense of experience. Even when claims of victimhood are morally justifiable, politically democratic, and socially progressive, these claims still cannot be seen as automatic, or natural, responses to the actual nature of an event itself. To accept the constructivist position in such cases may be difficult, for the claim to verisimilitude is fundamental to the very sense that a trauma has occurred. Yet, while every argument about trauma claims ontological reality, as cultural sociologists we are not primarily concerned with the accuracy of social actors' claims, much less with evaluating their moral justification. We are concerned only with how and under what conditions the claims are made, and with what results. It is neither ontology nor morality, but epistemology, with which we are concerned.

Traumatic status is attributed to real or imagined phenomena, not because of their actual harmfulness or their objective abruptness, but because these phenomena are believed to have abruptly, and harmfully, affected collective identity. Individual security is anchored in structures of emotional and cultural expectations that provide a sense of security and capability. These expectations and capabilities, in turn, are rooted in the sturdiness of the collectivities of which individuals are a part. At issue is not the stability of a collectivity in the material or behavioral sense, although this certainly plays a part. What is at stake, rather, is the collectivity's identity, its stability in terms of meaning, not action.

Identity involves a cultural reference. Only if the patterned meanings of the collectivity are abruptly dislodged is traumatic status attributed to an event. It is the challenge to meaning that provides the sense of shock and fear, not the events themselves. Whether or not the structures of meaning are destabilized and shocked is not the result of an event but the effect of a sociocultural process. It is the result of an exercise of human agency, of the successful imposition of a new system of cultural classification. This cultural process is deeply affected by power structures and by the contingent skills of reflexive social agents.

The Social Process of Cultural Trauma

At the level of the social system, societies can experience massive disruptions that do not become traumatic. Institutions can fail to perform. Schools may fail to educate, failing miserably even to provide basic skills. Governments may be unable to secure basic protections and may undergo severe crises of delegitimation. Economic systems may be profoundly disrupted, to the extent that their allocative functions fail even to provide basic goods. Such problems are real and fundamental, but they are not, by any means, necessarily traumatic for members of the affected collectivities, much less for the society at large. For traumas to emerge at the level of the collectivity, social crises must become cultural crises. Events are one thing; representations of these events are quite another. Trauma is not the result of a group experiencing pain. It is the result of this acute discomfort entering into the core of the collectivity's sense of its own identity. Collective actors "decide" to represent social pain as a fundamental threat to their sense of who they are, where they came from, and where they want to go.

Claim Making: The Spiral of Signification

The gap between event and representation can be conceived as the trauma process. Collectivities do not make decisions as such; rather, it is agents who do (Sztompka 1991a, 1993a; Alexander 1987; Alexander, Giesen, Munch, and Smelser 1987).[8] The persons who

15

ɔose collectivities broadcast symbolic representations – char-
rizations – of ongoing social events, past, present, and future.
. _ ?y broadcast these representations as members of a social group.
These group representations can be seen as claims about the shape
of social reality, its causes, and the responsibilities for action such
causes imply. The cultural construction of trauma begins with such a
claim (Thompson 1998).[9] It is a claim to some fundamental injury, an
exclamation of the terrifying profanation of some sacred value, a narrative about a horribly destructive social process, and a demand for
emotional, institutional, and symbolic reparation and reconstitution.

Carrier Groups

Such claims are made by what Max Weber, in his sociology of religion, called carrier groups (Weber 1978: 468–517).[10] Carrier groups
are the collective agents of the trauma process. Carrier groups have
both ideal and material interests; they are situated in particular places
in the social structure; and they have particular discursive talents
for articulating their claims – for "meaning making" – in the public
sphere. Carrier groups may be elites, but they may also be denigrated
and marginalized classes. They may be prestigious religious leaders or
groups whom the majority has designated as spiritual pariahs. Carrier
groups can be generational, representing the perspectives and interests
of a younger generation against an older one. It can be national, pitting
one's own nation against a putative enemy. It can be institutional, representing one particular social sector or organization against others in
a fragmented and polarized social order (Alexander 2011).

Audience and Situation: Social Performance

The trauma process can be likened, in this sense, to performative
speech acts (Austin 1962; Alexander, Giesen, and Mast 2006).

> Speaker: the carrier group
> Audience: the public, putatively homogeneous but sociologically
> fragmented
> Situation: the historical, cultural, and institutional environment within
> which the performance unfolds

The goal of performative actions is to project the trauma claim to the
audience-public persuasively. In doing so, the carrier group makes use
of the particularities of the historical situation, the symbolic resources
at hand, and the opportunities provided by institutional structures.

16

Initially, the performance of trauma is projected to members of the carrier group itself. If successful, the members of this originating collectivity become convinced that they have been traumatized by a singular event. Only with this success can the audience for the traumatic claim be broadened to include other publics within the "society at large."

Cultural Classification: The Creation of Trauma as a New Master Narrative

Bridging the gap between event and representation depends upon what Kenneth Thompson has called, in reference to moral panics, a "spiral of signification" (Thompson 1998: 20–4).[11] Representation of trauma depends on constructing a compelling framework of cultural classification. In one sense, this is simply telling a new story. Yet this storytelling is, at the same time, a complex and multivalent symbolic process that is contingent, contested, and sometimes highly polarizing. For the wider audience to become persuaded that they, too, have become traumatized by an experience or an event, the carrier group needs to engage in successful meaning making work.

Four critical representations are essential to the creation of a new master narrative. While I will place these four dimensions of representations into an analytical sequence, I do not mean to suggest temporality. In social reality, these representations unfold in an interlarded manner that is continuously cross-referential. The causality is symbolic and aesthetic, not sequential or developmental but "value-added" (Smelser 1962).

These are the questions to which a successful process of collective representation must provide compelling answers:

(1) *The nature of the pain.* What actually happened – to the particular group and to the wider collectivity of which it is a part?
   - Did the denouncement of the Vietnam War leave a festering wound on the American psyche, or was it incorporated in a more or less routine way? If there was a shattering wound, of what exactly did it consist? Did the American military lose the Vietnam War, or did the Vietnam trauma consist of the pain of having the nation's hands "tied behind its back"?[12]
   - Did hundreds of ethnic Albanians die in Kosovo, or was it tens and possibly even hundreds of thousands? Did they die because of starvation or displacement in the course of a civil war, or were they deliberately murdered?

17

- Was slavery a trauma for African Americans? Or was it, as some revisionist historians have claimed, merely a coercive, and highly profitable, mode of economic production? If the latter, then slavery did not produce traumatic pain. If the former, it involved brutal and traumatizing physical domination.
- Was the internecine ethnic and religious conflict in Northern Ireland "civil unrest and terrorism," as Queen Elizabeth II once described it, or a "bloody war," as claimed by the IRA (quoted in Maillot 2000)?
- Were there less than a hundred persons who died at the hands of Japanese soldiers in Nanjing, China, in 1938, or were there 300,000 victims? Did these deaths result from a one-sided "massacre" or a "fierce contest" between opposing armies? (Chang 1997: 206; and Chapter 4, below).

(2) *The nature of the victim.* What group of persons were affected by this traumatizing pain? Were they particular individuals or groups, or "the people" in general? Did a singular and delimited group receive the brunt of the pain, or were several groups involved?

- Were German Jews the primary victims of the Holocaust, or did the victim group extend to the Jews of the Pale, European Jewry, or the Jewish people as a whole? Were the millions of Polish people who died at the hands of German Nazis also victims of the Holocaust? Were Communists, socialists, homosexuals, and disabled persons also victims of the Nazi Holocaust?
- Were Kosovar Albanians the primary victims of ethnic cleansing, or were Kosovar Serbs also significantly or even equally victimized?
- Are African Americans the victims of the brutal, traumatizing conditions in the desolate inner cities of the United States, or are the victims of these conditions members of an economically defined "underclass"?
- Were Native Americans the victims of European colonizers, or were the victims particularly situated, and particularly "aggressive," Indian nations?
- Are non-Western nations the victims of globalization, or is it only the least developed, or the least equipped, among them?

(3) *Relation of the trauma victim to the wider audience.* Even when the nature of the pain has been crystallized and the identity of the victim established, there remains the highly significant question of the relation of the victim to the wider audience. To what

18

extent do the members of the audience for trauma representations experience identification with the immediately victimized group? Typically, at the beginning of the trauma process, most audience members see little if any relation between themselves and the victimized group. Only if the victims are represented in terms of valued qualities shared by the larger collective identity will the audience be able to symbolically participate in the experience of the originating trauma.

- Roma ("Gypsies") are acknowledged by many contemporary Central Europeans as trauma victims, the bearers of a tragic history. Yet insofar as large numbers of Central Europeans represent Roma people as deviant and uncivilized, they have not made that tragic past their own.
- Influential groups of German and Polish people have acknowledged that Jews were victims of mass murder, but they have often refused to experience their own national collective identities as being affected by the Jews' tragic fate.
- Did the police brutality that traumatized black civil rights activists in Selma, Alabama, in 1965, create identification among the white Americans who watched the events on their televisions in the safety of the nonsegregated North? Is the history of white American racial domination relegated to an entirely separate time, or is it conceived, by virtue of the reconstruction of collective memory, as a contemporary issue?

(4) *Attribution of responsibility.* In creating a compelling trauma narrative, it is critical to establish the identity of the perpetrator – the "antagonist." Who actually injured the victim? Who caused the trauma? This issue is always a matter of symbolic and social construction.

- Did "Germany" create the Holocaust, or was it the Nazi regime? Was the crime restricted to special SS forces, or was the Werhmacht, the entire Nazi army, also deeply involved? Did the crime extend to ordinary soldiers, to ordinary citizens, to Catholic as well as Protestant Germans? Was it only the older generation of Germans who were responsible, or were later generations responsible as well (Giesen 2004)?

Institutional Arenas

This representational process creates a new master narrative of social suffering. Such cultural (re)classification is critical to the process by which a collectivity becomes traumatized.[13] But it does not unfold in what Habermas would call a transparent speech situation (Habermas 1984).[14] The notion of transparency is a normative ideal essential to the democratic functioning of the public sphere, not an empirical description. In actual social practice, social performances never unfold in an unmediated way. Linguistic action is powerfully mediated by the nature of the institutional arenas and stratification hierarchies within which it occurs.

Religious. If the trauma process unfolds inside the religious arena, its concern will be to link trauma to theodicy. The Torah's story of Job, for example, asks: Why did God allow this evil? The answers to such questions will generate searching discussions about whether and how human beings strayed from divinely inspired ethics and sacred law, or whether the existence of evil means that God does not exist.

Aesthetic. Insofar as meaning making work takes place in the aesthetic realm, it will be channeled by specific genres and narratives that aim to produce imaginative identification and emotional catharsis.

In the early representations of the Holocaust, for example, *The Diary of Anne Frank* played a vital role, and in later years an entirely new genre called "survivor literature" developed (Hayes 1999). In the aftermath of ethnocide in Guatemala, in which 200,000 Mayan Indians were killed and entire villages destroyed, an ethnographer recorded how, in the town of Santa Maria Tzeja, theater was "used to publicly confront the past":

> A group of teenagers and . . . a North American teacher and director of the community's school write a play that documents what Santa Maria Tzeja has experienced. They call the play "There Is Nothing Concealed That Will Not Be Disclosed (Matthew 10: 26)," and the villagers themselves perform it. The play not only recalls what happened in the village in a stark, unflinching manner but also didactically lays out the laws and rights that the military violated. The play pointedly and precisely cites articles of the Guatemalan constitution that were trampled on, not normally the text of great drama. But, in Guatemala, reading the constitution can be a profoundly dramatic act. Performances inevitably led to moving, at times heated, discussions. [The production] had a cathartic impact on the village. (Manz 2002: 292–309)

As this example suggests, mass media are significant, but not necessary, in the aesthetic arena. In the aftermath of the NATO bombing that forced Yugoslavian Serbs to abandon their violent, decade-long domination of Albanian Kosovo, Serbian films provided mass channels for reexperiencing the period of suffering even while they narrated the protagonists, victims, and the very nature of the trauma in strikingly different ways.

> It is hard to see why anyone who survived 78 traumatic days of air-strikes in 1999 would want to relive the experience in a theater, bringing back memories as well of a murderous decade that ended in October with the fall of President Slobodan Milosevic. Yet Yugoslavia's feature film industry has done little else in the past year but turn out NATO war movies [some of which] have begun to cut through the national façade that Milosevic's propagandists had more than 10 years to build. [In one movie, the protagonist recounts] "It is dead easy to kill . . . They stare at you, weep and wail, and you shoot 'em and that's the end-end of story. Later, of course, they all come back and you want to set things right, but it's too late. That's why the truth is always returning to judge men." (Watson 2001: AI–6)

Legal. When the cultural classification enters the legal realm, it will be disciplined by the demand to issue a definitive judgment of legally binding responsibilities and to distribute punishments and material reparations. Such a demonstration may have nothing at all to do with the perpetrators themselves accepting responsibility or a broader audience identifying with those who suffered as the trauma-drama plays out.

In regard to binding definitions of war crimes and crimes against humanity, the 1945 Nuremberg Trials were critical. They created revolutionary new law and resulted in dozens of successful prosecutions, yet they did not, by any means, succeed in compelling the German people themselves to recognize the existence of Nazi traumas, much less their responsibility for them. Nonetheless, the legal statutes developed at Nuremberg were elaborated in the decades following, laying the basis for dozens of highly publicized lawsuits that in later years created significant dramaturgy and unleashed profound moral effects. These trials for "crimes against humanity" implicated not only individuals but also national organizations.

Because neither postwar Japanese governments nor some influential Japanese publics have recognized the war crimes committed by Japan's imperial war policies, much less taken moral responsibility for them (Hashimoto 2011), no suit seeking damages for imperial atrocities has, until recently, ever made any substantial headway in Japan's courts. In explaining why one suit against the imperial government's biological warfare unit finally did make substantial progress, observers pointed to the specificity and autonomy of the legal arena.

As a member of the Japanese biological warfare outfit, known as United 73 I, Mr Shinozuka was told that if he ever faced capture by the Chinese, his duty to Emperor Hirohito was to kill himself rather than compromise the secrecy of a program that so clearly violated international law ... Now, 55 years later, he is a hale 77–year old. But still haunted by remorse, he has spoken – providing the first account before a Japanese court by a veteran about the workings of the notorious unit ... That this case, now in its final stages, has not been dismissed like so many others is due in part to painstaking legal research and to cooperation over strategy by some of Japan's leading lawyers. Lawyers who have sued the government say the fact that this case has become the first in which a judge has allowed the extensive introduction of evidence instead of handing down a quick dismissal may also attest to an important shift under way on the issue of reparations. (French 2000: A3)

Scientific. When the trauma process enters the scientific world, it becomes subject to evidentiary stipulations of an altogether different kind, creating scholarly controversies, "revelations," and "revisions." When historians endeavor to define an historical event as traumatic, they must document, by acceptable scholarly methods, the nature of the pain, the victims, and responsibility. In doing so, the cultural classification process often triggers explosive methodological controversies.

- What were the causes of the First World War? Who was responsible for initiating it? Who were its victims?
- Did the Japanese intend to launch a "sneak" attack on Pearl Harbor, or was the late-arriving message to Washington, DC, by the Japanese imperial government delayed by inadvertence and diplomatic confusion?
- The German "Historichstreit" controversy captured international attention in the 1980s, questioning the new scholarly conservatives' emphasis on anti-Communism as a motivation for the Nazi seizure of power and its anti-Jewish policies. In the 1990s, Daniel Goldhagen's *Hitler's Willing Executioners* was attacked by mainstream historians for overemphasizing the uniqueness of German anti-Semitism.

Mass media. When the trauma process enters the mass media, it gains opportunities and at the same time becomes subject to distinctive kinds of restriction. Mediated mass communication allows traumas to be expressively dramatized and permits some of the competing interpretations to gain enormous persuasive power over others. At the same time, however, these representational processes become subject to the restrictions of news reporting, with their demands for concision, ethical neutrality, and perspectival balance. Finally, there is the competition for readership that often inspires the sometimes exaggerated and distorted production of "news" in mass circulation newspapers and magazines. As an event comes to be reported as a trauma, a particular group as "traumatized," and another group as the perpetrators, politicians and other elites may attack the media, their owners, and often the journalists whose reporting established the trauma facts.

- During the late 1960s, American television news brought evocative images of terrible civilian suffering from the Vietnam War into the living rooms of American citizens. These images were seized upon by antiwar critics. The conservative American politician Vice-President Spiro Agnew initiated virulent attacks against the "liberal" and "Jewish dominated" media for their insistence that the Vietnamese civilian population was being traumatized by the American-dominated war.

State bureaucracy. When the trauma process enters into the state bureaucracy, it can draw upon the governmental power to channel the representational process. Decisions by the executive branches of governments to create national commissions of inquiry, votes by parliaments to establish investigative committees, the creation of state-directed police investigations and new directives about national priorities – all such actions can have decisive effects on handling and channeling the spiral of signification that marks the trauma process (Smelser 1962).[15] In the last decade, blue ribbon commissions have become a favored state vehicle for such involvement. By arranging and balancing the participation on such panels, forcing the appearance of witnesses, and creating carefully choreographed public dramaturgy, such panels tilt the interpretative process in powerful ways, expanding and narrowing solidarity, creating or denying the factual and moral basis for reparations and civic repair.

- Referring to hundreds of thousands of Mayan Indians who died at the hands of Guatemalan counterinsurgency forces between 1981 and 1983, an ethnographer of the region asserts that, "without question, the army's horrific actions ripped deep psychological wounds into the consciousness of the inhabitants of this village [who were also] involved in a far larger trauma" (Manz 2002:

23

293–4). Despite the objective status of the trauma, however, and the pain and suffering it had caused, the ability to collectively recognize and process it was inhibited because the village was "a place hammered into silence and accustomed to impunity" (ibid.). In 1994, as part of the negotiation between the Guatemalan government and the umbrella group of insurgent forces, a Commission for Historical Clarification (CEH) was created to hear testimony from the affected parties and to present an interpretation. Five years later, its published conclusion declared that "agents of the State of Guatemala . . . committed acts of genocide against groups of Mayan people" (ibid.). According to the ethnographer, the report "stunned the country." By publicly representing the nature of the pain, defining victim and perpetrator, and assigning responsibility, the trauma process was enacted within the governmental arena: "It was as if the whole country burst into tears, tears that had been repressed for decades and tears of vindication" (ibid.).

- In the middle 1990s, the post-apartheid South African government established a Truth and Reconciliation Commission. Composed of widely respected blacks and whites, the group called witnesses and conducted widely broadcast hearings about the suffering created by the repression that marked the preceding Afrikaner government. The effort succeeded to a significant degree in generalizing the trauma process beyond racially polarized audiences, making it into a shared experience of the new, more solidary, and more democratic South African society. Such a commission could not have been created until blacks became enfranchised and became the dominant racial power.

- By contrast, the post-fascist Japanese government has never been willing to create official commissions to investigate the war crimes committed by its imperial leaders and soldiers against non-Japanese during the Second World War. In regard to the Japanese enslavement of tens and possibly hundreds of thousands of "comfort women," primarily Korean, who provided sexual services for imperial soldiers, the Japanese government finally agreed in the late 1990s to disperse token monetary reparations to the Korean women still alive. Critics have continued to demand that an officially sanctioned commission hold public hearings regarding the trauma, a dramaturgical and legally binding process that the Japanese government, despite its ambiguous and brief public apology to the "comfort women," has never been willing to allow. It is revealing of the significance of such a governmental arena that these critics eventually mounted an unofficial tribunal themselves.

Last week in Tokyo, private Japanese and international organizations convened a war tribunal that found Japan's military leaders, including Emperor Hirohito, guilty of crimes against humanity for the sexual slavery imposed on tens of thousands of women in countries controlled by Japan during World War II. The tribunal has no legal power to exact reparations for the survivors among those so-called comfort women. But with its judges and lawyers drawn from official international tribunals for the countries that once were part of Yugoslavia and for Rwanda, it brought unparalleled moral authority to an issue scarcely discussed or taught about in Japan. (French 2000: A3)

Stratificational Hierarchies

The constraints imposed by institutional arenas are mediated by the uneven distribution of material resources and the social networks that provide differential access to them. The following questions illustrate this problem.

- Who owns the newspapers? To what degree are journalists independent of political and financial control?
- Who controls the religious orders? Are they internally authoritarian, or can congregants exercise independent influence?
- Are courts independent? What is the scope of action available to entrepreneurial legal advocates?
- Are educational policies subject to mass movements of public opinion, or are they insulated by bureaucratic procedures at more centralized levels?
- Who exercises controls over the government?

As I indicated earlier, local, provincial, and national governments deploy significant power over the trauma process. What must be considered here is that these bodies might occupy a position of dominance over the traumatized parties themselves. In these cases, the commissions might whitewash the perpetrators' actions rather than dramatize them.

- In the 1980s, the conservative US and British governments of Ronald Reagan and Margaret Thatcher initially did little to dramatize the dangers of the virulent AIDS epidemic because they did not wish to create sympathy or identification with the homosexual practices their ideologies so stigmatized. This failure allowed the epidemics to spread more rapidly. Finally, the Thatcher government launched a massive public education campaign about the dangers of HIV. The effort quickly took the steam out of the moral panic over the AIDS epidemic that had swept through British society and helped launch appropriate public health measures (Thompson 1998).

- In 2000, reports surfaced in American media about a massacre of several hundreds of Korean civilians by American soldiers at No Gun Ri early in the Korean War. Statements from Korean witnesses, and newfound testimony from some American soldiers, suggested the possibility that the firings had been intentional, and allegations about racism and war crimes were made. In response, President Clinton assigned the US Army itself to convene its own official, in-house investigation. While a senior army official claimed that "we have worked closely with the Korean government to investigate the circumstances surrounding No Gun Ri," the power to investigate and interpret the evidence clearly rested with the perpetrators of the trauma alone. Not surprisingly, when its findings were announced several months later, the US Army declared itself innocent of the charges that had threatened its good name:

> We do not believe it is appropriate to issue an apology in this matter. [While] some of those civilian casualties were at the hand[s] of American solider[s] , that conclusion is very different from the allegation that was made that this was a massacre in the classic sense that we lined up innocent people and gunned them down. (*New York Times* 2000: A5)

Identity Revision, Memory, and Routinization

"Experiencing trauma" can be understood as a sociological process that defines a painful injury to the collectivity, establishes the victim, attributes responsibility, and distributes the ideal and material consequences. Insofar as traumas are so experienced, and thus imagined and represented, the collective identity will shift. This reconstruction means that there will be a searching re-remembering of the collective past, for memory is not only social and fluid but also deeply connected to the contemporary sense of the self. Identities are continuously constructed and secured not only by facing the present and future but also by reconstructing the collectivity's earlier life.

Once the collective identity has been so reconstructed, there will eventually emerge a period of "calming down." The spiral of signification flattens out, affect and emotion become less inflamed, preoccupation with sacrality and pollution fades. Charisma becomes routinized, effervescence evaporates, and liminality gives way to re-aggregation. As the heightened and powerfully affective discourse of trauma disappears, the "lessons" of the trauma become objectified in monuments, museums, and collections of historical artifacts.[16] The new collective identity will be rooted in sacred places and structured in ritual routines. In the late 1970s, the ultra-Maoist Khmer Rouge (DK) government was responsible for the deaths of more than one-third of Cambodia's citizens. The murderous regime was deposed in 1979. While fragmentation, instability, and authoritarianism in the decades following prevented the trauma process from fully playing itself out, the processes of reconstruction, representation, and working through produced significant commemoration, ritual, and reconstruction of national identity.

> Vivid reminders of the DK's [Khmer Rouge] horrors are displayed in photographs of victims, paintings of killings, and implements used for torture at the Tuol Sleng Museum of Genocidal Crimes, a former school that had become a deadly interrogation center . . . as well as in a monumental display of skulls and bones at Bhhoeung Ek, a former killing field where one can still see bits of bone and cloth in the soil of what had been mass graves. The PRK [the new Cambodian government] also instituted an annual observance called The Day of Hate, in which people were gathered at various locales to hear invectives heaped on the Khmer Rouge. State propaganda played on this theme with such slogans as: "We must absolutely prevent the return of this former black darkness" and "We must struggle ceaselessly to protect against the return of the . . . genocidal clique." These formulaic and state-sanctioned expressions were genuine and often expressed in conversations among ordinary folk. (Ebihara and Ledgerwood 2002: 282–3)

With routinization, the trauma process, once so vivid, can become subject to the technical, sometimes desiccating attention of specialists who detach affect from meaning. This triumph of the mundane is often noted with regret by audiences that had been mobilized by the trauma process, and it is sometimes forcefully opposed by carrier groups. Often, however, it is welcomed with a sense of public and private relief. Intended to remember and commemorate the trauma process, efforts to institutionalize the lessons of the trauma will eventually prove unable to evoke the strong emotions, the sentiments of betrayal, and the affirmations of sacrality that once were so powerfully associated with it. No longer deeply preoccupying, the reconstructed collective identity remains, nevertheless, a fundamental resource for resolving future social problems and disturbances of collective consciousness.

The inevitability of such routinization processes by no means neutralizes the extraordinary social significance of cultural traumas. Their creation and routinization have, to the contrary, the most profound normative implications for the conduct of social life. By allowing members of wider publics to participate in the pain of others, cultural traumas broaden the realm of social understanding and sympathy, and they provide powerful avenues for new forms of social incorporation.[17]

The elements of the trauma process I have outlined here can be thought of as social structures, if we think of this term in something other than its materialist sense. Each element plays a role in the social construction and deconstruction of a traumatic event. Whether any of these structures actually come into play is not itself a matter of structural determination. It is subject to the contingencies of human agency and historical time. A war is lost or won. A new regime has entered into power or a discredited regime remains stubbornly in place. Hegemonic or counter publics may be empowered and enthusiastic or undermined and exhausted by social conflict and stalemate. Such contingent historical factors exercise powerful influence on whether a consensus will be generated that allows the cultural classification of trauma to be set firmly in place.

Trauma Creation and Practical-Moral Action: The Non-Western Relevance

In this chapter, I have elaborated a middle-range theory that models the complex causes propelling the trauma process. In illustrating this analytical argument, I have referred to traumatic situations in Western and non-Western, developed and less developed societies – in Northern Ireland and Poland, the United Kingdom and Cambodia, Japan and Yugoslavia, South Africa, Guatemala, and Korea.

It would be a serious misunderstanding if trauma theory were restricted in its reference to Western social life. True, it has been Western societies that have recently provided the most dramatic apologias for traumatic episodes in their national histories. But it has been the non-Western regions of the world, and the most defenseless among them, that have been subjected to some of the most terrifying traumatic injuries. Hinton has suggested that "while the behaviors it references have an ancient pedigree, the concept of genocide . . . is thoroughly modern" (Hinton 2002: 25). Nonetheless, by the latter half of the twentieth century this modern framework had thoroughly penetrated non-Western societies: "In the mass media, the victims of genocide are frequently condensed into an essentialized portrait of the universal sufferer, an image that can be . . . (re)broadcast to global audiences who see their own potential trauma reflected in this simulation of the modern subject" (Hinton 2002: 21–2).

Genocide is more likely to occur in collective arenas that are neither legally regulated, democratic, nor formally egalitarian (Kuper 1981). So, it is hardly surprising that, in the last half century, the most dramatic and horrifying examples of mass murder have emerged from within the more fragmented and impoverished areas of the non-Western world: the Hutu massacre of more than 500,000 Tutsis in fewer than three weeks in Rwanda, the Guatemalan military's ethnocide of 200,000 Mayan Indians during the dirty civil war in the early 1980s, the Maoist Khmer Rouge's elimination of almost a third of Cambodia's entire population in its revolutionary purges in the late 1970s. The tragic reasons for these recent outpourings of mass murder in the non-Western world cannot be our concern here. A growing body of social scientific work is devoted to this question (e.g., Kleinman, Das, and Lock 1997). What cultural trauma theory helps us understand, instead, is a central paradox, not about the causes of genocide but its after-effects: Why have these genocidal actions, so traumatic to their millions of immediate victims, so rarely branded themselves on the consciousness of the wider populations? Why have these horrendous phenomena of mass suffering not become compelling, publicly available narratives of collective suffering to their respective nations, let alone to the world at large? The reasons, I suggest, can be found in the complex patterns of the trauma process I have outlined here.

Several years before the Nazi massacre of the Jews, which eventually branded Western modernity as the distinctive bearer of collective trauma in the twentieth century, the most developed society outside the West had itself already engaged in systematic atrocities (see Chapter 4, below). In early December 1937, invading Japanese soldiers slaughtered as many as 300,000 Chinese residents of Nanjing, China. Under orders from the highest levels of the imperial government, they carried out this massacre in six of the bloodiest weeks of modern history, without the technological aids later developed by the Nazis in their mass extermination of the Jews. By contrast with the Nazi massacre, this Japanese atrocity was not hidden from the rest of the world. To the contrary, it was carried out under the eyes of critical and highly articulate Western observers and reported upon massively by respected members of the world's press. Yet, in the sixty years that have elapsed since that time, the memorialization of the "Rape of Nanjing" has never extended beyond the regional confines of China, and, until recently, barely beyond the confines of Nanjing itself. The trauma contributed scarcely at all to the collective identity of the People's Republic of China, let alone to the self-conception of the postwar democratic government of Japan. As the most recent narrator of the massacre puts it, "Even by the standards of history's most destructive war, the Rape of Nanjing represents one of the worst instances of mass extermination" (Chang 1997: 5). Yet, though extraordinarily traumatic for the contemporary residents of Nanjing, it became "the forgotten Holocaust of World War II," and it remains an "obscure incident" today (ibid.: 6), the very existence of which is routinely and successfully denied by some of Japan's most powerful and esteemed public officials.

As I have suggested in this introductory chapter, such failures to recognize collective traumas, much less to incorporate their lessons into collective identity, do not result from the intrinsic nature of the original suffering. This is the naturalistic fallacy that follows from lay trauma theory. The failure stems, rather, from an inability to carry through what I have called a trauma process. In Japan and China, just as in Rwanda, Cambodia, and Guatemala, claims have certainly been made for the central relevance of such "distant sufferings" (Boltanski 1999).[18] But for both social structural and cultural reasons, carrier groups have not emerged with the resources, authority, or interpretive competence to powerfully disseminate these trauma claims. Sufficiently persuasive narratives have not been created, or they have not been successfully broadcast to wider audiences. Because of these failures, the perpetrators of these collective sufferings have not been compelled to accept moral responsibility, and the lessons of these social traumas have been neither memorialized nor ritualized. New definitions of moral responsibility have not been generated. Social solidarities have not been extended. More primordial and more particularistic collective identities have not been changed.

However tortuous the trauma process, however, it can allow collectivities to define new forms of moral responsibility and to redirect the course of political action. Collective traumas have no geographical or cultural limitations. They emerge when collectivities experience themselves as having sustained grave injuries, and when they draw, for better and for worse, on the moral lessons that seem to emanate from them.

— 2 —

HOLOCAUST AND TRAUMA: MORAL UNIVERSALISM IN THE WEST

How did a specific and situated historical event, an event marked by ethnic and racial hatred, violence, and war, become transformed into a generalized symbol of human suffering and moral evil, a universalized symbol whose very existence has created historically unprecedented opportunities for ethnic, racial, and religious justice, for mutual recognition, and for global conflicts becoming regulated in a more civil way?[1] This cultural transformation has been achieved because the originating historical event, traumatic in the extreme for a delimited particular group, has come over the last sixty years to be redefined as a traumatic event for all of humankind.[2] Now free-floating rather than situated – universal rather than particular – this traumatic event vividly "lives" in the memories of contemporaries whose parents and grandparents never felt themselves even remotely related to it.

In what follows, I explore the social creation of a cultural fact and the effects of this cultural fact on social and moral life.

In the beginning, in April 1945, the Holocaust was not the "Holocaust." In the torrent of newspaper, radio, and magazine stories reporting the discovery by American infantrymen of the Nazi concentration camps, the empirical remains of what had transpired were typified as "atrocities." Their obvious awfulness, and indeed their strangeness, placed them for contemporary observers at the borderline of the category of behavior known as "man's inhumanity to man." Nonetheless, qua atrocity, the discoveries were placed side-by-side – metonymically and semantically – with a whole series of other brutalities that were considered to be the natural results of the ill wind of this second, very unnatural, and most inhuman world war.

31

The first American reports on "atrocities" during that Second World War had not, in fact, even referred to actions by German Nazis, let alone to their Jewish victims, but to the Japanese army's brutal treatment of American and other allied prisoners of war after the loss of Corregidor in 1943. On January 27, 1944, the United States released sworn statements by military officers who had escaped the so-called Bataan Death March. In the words of contemporary journals and magazines, these officers had related "atrocity stories" revealing "the inhuman treatment and murder of American and Filipino soldiers who were taken prisoner when Bataan and Corregidor fell." In response to these accounts, the US State Department had lodged protests to the Japanese government about its failure to live up to the provisions of the Geneva Prisoners of War Convention (*Current History*, March 1944: 249). Atrocities, in other words, were a signifier specifically connected to war. They referred to war-generated events that transgressed the rules circumscribing how national killing could normally be carried out.[3] Responding to the same incident, *Newsweek*, in a section entitled "The Enemy" and under the headline "Nation Replies in Grim Fury to Jap Brutality to Prisoners," reported that "with the first impact of the news, people had shuddered at the story of savage *atrocity* upon Allied prisoners of war by the Japanese" (February 7, 1944: 19, italics added).[4]

It is hardly surprising, then, that it was this nationally specific and particular war-related term that was employed to represent the grisly Jewish mass murders discovered by American GIs when they liberated the Nazi camps.[5] Through April 1945, as one camp after another was discovered, this collective representation was applied time after time.[6] When, toward the end of that month, a well-known Protestant minister explored the moral implications of the discoveries, he declared that, no matter how horrifying and repulsive, "it is important that the full truth be made known so that a clear indication may be had of the nature of the enemy we have been dealing with, as well of as a realization *of the sheer brutalities that have become the accompaniment of war.*" The *New York Times* reported this sermon under the headline "Bonnell Denounces German Atrocities" (April 23, 1945: 23, italics added). When alarmed members of the US Congress visited Buchenwald, the *Times* headlined that they had witnessed first hand the "*War Camp Horror*" (April 26, 1945: 12, italics added). When a few days later the US Army released a report on the extent of the killings in Buchenwald, the *Times* headlined it an "Atrocity Report" (April 29, 1945: 20). A few days after that, under the headline "Enemy Atrocities in France Bared," the *Times* wrote that a just-released report had shown that "in France, German brutality was not limited to the French underground or even to the thousands of hostages whom the Germans killed for disorders they had nothing to do with, but was practiced almost systematically against entirely innocent French people" (May 4, 1945: 6).

The Nazis' anti-Jewish mass murders had once been only putative atrocities. From the late 1930s on, reports about them had been greeted with widespread public doubt about their authenticity. Analogies to the allegations about German atrocities during the First World War that later had been thoroughly discredited, they were dismissed as a kind of Jewish moral panic. Only three months before the GI's "discovery" of the camps, in introducing a first-hand report on Nazi mass murder from a Soviet-liberated camp in Poland, *Collier's* magazine acknowledged: "A lot of Americans simply do not believe the stories of Nazi mass executions of Jews and anti-Nazi Gentiles in eastern Europe by means of gas chambers, freight cars partly loaded with lime and other horrifying devices. These stories are so foreign to most Americans' experience of life in this country that they seem incredible. Then, too, some of the atrocity stories of World War I were later proved false" (January 6, 1945: 62).[7] From April 3, 1945, however, the date when the GIs first liberated the concentration camps, all such earlier reports were retrospectively accepted as facts, as the realistic signifiers of Peirce rather than the "arbitrary" symbols of Saussure. That systematic efforts at Jewish mass murder had occurred, and that the numerous victims and the few survivors had been severely traumatized, the American and world-wide audience now had little doubt.[8] Their particular and unique fate, however, even while it was widely recognized as representing the grossest of injustices, did not itself become a traumatic experience for the audience to which the mass media's collective representations were transmitted – that is, for those looking on, either from near or from far. Why this was not so defines my initial explanatory effort here.

For an audience to be traumatized by an experience that they themselves do not directly share, symbolic extension and psychological identification are required. This did not occur. For the American infantry who first made contact, for the general officers who supervised the rehabilitation, for the reporters who broadcast the descriptions, for the commissions of Congress and influentials who quickly traveled to Germany to conduct on-site investigations, the starving, depleted, often weird-looking and sometimes weird-acting Jewish camp survivors seemed like a foreign race. They could just as well have been from Mars, or from hell. The identities and characters

33

of these Jewish survivors rarely were personalized through interviews or individualized through biographical sketches; rather, they were presented as a mass, and often as a mess, a petrified, degrading, and smelly one, not only by newspaper reporters but also by some of the most powerful general officers in the Allied High Command. This depersonalization made it more difficult for the survivors' trauma to generate compelling identification.

Possibilities for universalizing the trauma were blocked not only by the depersonalization of its victims but also by their historical and sociological specification. As I have indicated, the mass murders semantically were immediately linked to other "horrors" in the bloody history of the century's second great war and to the histori-cally specific national and ethnic conflicts that underlay it. Above all, it was never forgotten that these victims were Jews. In retrospect, it is bitterly ironic, but it is also sociologically understandable, that the American audience's sympathy and feelings of identity flowed much more easily to the non-Jewish survivors, whether German or Polish, who had been kept in better conditions and looked more "normal," more composed, more human. Jewish survivors were kept for weeks and sometimes even for months in the worst areas and under the worst conditions of what had become, temporarily, displaced persons' camps. American and British administrators felt impatient with many Jewish survivors, even personal repugnance for them, sometimes resorting to threats and even to punishing them.[9] The depth of this initial failure of identification can be seen in the fact that when American citizens and their leaders expressed opinions and made decisions about national quotas for emergency postwar immi-gration, displaced German citizens ranked first, Jewish survivors last.

How could this have happened? Was it not obvious to any human observer that this mass murder was fundamentally different from the other traumatic and bloody events in a modern history already dripping in blood, that it represented not simply evil but "radical evil," in Kant's remarkable phrase (Kant 1960),[10] that it was unique? To understand why none of this was obvious, to understand how and why each of these initial understandings and behaviors was radically changed, and how this transformation had vast repercus-sions for establishing not only new moral standards for social and political behavior but also unprecedented, if still embryonic, regula-tory controls, it is important to see the inadequacy of commonsense understandings of traumatic events.

There are two kinds of commonsense thinking about trauma, forms of thinking that constitute what I called in Chapter 1 "lay

34

trauma theory." These commonsensical forms of reasoning have deeply informed thinking about the effects of the Holocaust. They are expressed in the following strikingly different conceptualizations of what happened after the revelations of the mass killings of Jews.

- *The Enlightenment version.* The "horror" of onlookers provoked the postwar end of anti-Semitism in the United States. The commonsense assumption here is that because people have a fundamentally "moral" nature – as a result of their rootedness in Enlightenment and religious traditions – they will perceive atrocities for what they are and react to them by attacking the belief systems that provided legitimation.
- *The psychoanalytic version.* When faced with the horror, Jews and non-Jews alike reacted not with criticism and decisive action but with silence and bewilderment. Only after two or even three decades of repression and denial were people finally able to begin talking about what happened and to take actions in response to this knowledge.

Enlightenment and psychoanalytic forms of lay trauma thinking have permeated academic efforts at understanding what happened after the death-camp revelations. One or the other version has informed not only every major discussion of the Holocaust but also virtually every contemporary effort to investigate trauma more generally, efforts that are, in fact, largely inspired by Holocaust debates.[11]

What is wrong with this lay trauma theory is that it is "naturalistic," either in the naively moral or the naively psychological sense. Lay trauma theory fails to see that there is an interpretive grid through which all "facts" about trauma are mediated, emotionally, cognitively, and morally. This grid has a supraindividual, cultural status; it is symbolically structured and sociologically determined. No trauma interprets itself: Before trauma can be experienced at the collective (not individual) level, there are essential questions that must be answered, and answers to these questions change over time.

The Cultural Construction of Trauma

Coding, Weighting, Narrating

Elie Wiesel, in a moving and influential statement in the late 1970s, asserted that the Holocaust represents an "ontological evil." From a

sociological perspective, however, evil is epistemological, not ontological. For a traumatic event to have the status of evil is a matter
of its *becoming* evil. It is a matter of how the trauma is known, how
it is coded.[12] "At first glance it may appear a paradox," Diner has
noted – and certainly it does – but, considered only in and of itself,
"Auschwitz *has* no appropriate narrative, only a set of statistics"
(Diner 2000: 178). Becoming evil is a matter, first and foremost, of
representation. Depending on the nature of representation, a traumatic event may be regarded as ontologically evil, or its badness, its
"evilness," may be conceived as contingent and relative, as something
that can be ameliorated and overcome. This distinction is theoretical,
but it is also practical. In fact, decisions about the ontological versus
contingent status of the Holocaust were of overriding importance in
its changing representation.

If we can deconstruct this ontological assertion even further, I
would like to suggest that the very existence of the category "evil"
must be seen not as something that naturally exists but as an arbitrary construction, the product of cultural and sociological work.
This contrived binary, which simplifies empirical complexity to two
antagonistic forms and reduces every shade of gray between, has been
an essential feature of all human societies but especially important in
those Eisenstadt (1982) has called the Axial Age civilizations. This
rigid opposition between the sacred and profane, which in Western
philosophy has typically been constructed as a conflict between nor-
mativity and instrumentality, not only defines what people care about
but also establishes vital safeguards around the shared normative
"good." At the same time it places powerful, often aggressive barriers against anything that is construed as threatening the good, forces
defined not merely as things to be avoided but as sources of horror
and pollution that must be contained at all costs.

The Material "Base":
Controlling the Means of Symbolic Production

Yet if this grid is a kind of functional necessity, how it is applied very
much depends on who is telling the story, and how. This is first of all
a matter of cultural power in the most mundane, materialist sense:
Who controls the means of symbolic production?[13] It was certainly
not incidental to the public understanding of the Nazis' policies of
mass murder, for example, that for an extended period of time it was
the Nazis themselves who were in control of the physical and cultural
terrain of their enactment. This fact of brute power made it much

more difficult to frame the mass killings in a distinctive way. Nor is it incidental that, once the extermination of the Jews was physically interrupted by Allied armies in 1945, it was America's "imperial republic" – the perspective of the triumphant, forward-looking, militantly and militarily democratic New World warrior – that directed the organizational and cultural responses to the mass murders and their survivors. The contingency of this knowledge is so powerful that it might well be said that, if the Allies had not won the war, the "Holocaust" would never have been discovered.[14] Moreover, if it had been the Soviets and not the Allies who "liberated" most of the camps, and not just those in the Eastern sector, what was discovered in those camps might never have been portrayed in a remotely similar way.[15] It was, in other words, precisely and only because the means of symbolic production were not controlled by a victorious postwar Nazi regime, or even by a triumphant communist one, that the mass killings could be called the Holocaust and coded as evil.

Creating the Culture Structure

Still, even when the means of symbolic production came to be controlled by "our side," even when the association between evil and what would become known as the Holocaust trauma was assured, this was only the beginning, not the end. After a phenomenon is coded as evil, the question that immediately follows is: How evil is it? In theorizing evil, this refers to the problem not of coding but of weighting. For there are degrees of evil, and these degrees have great implications in terms of responsibility, punishment, remedial action, and future behavior. Normal evil and radical evil cannot be the same.

Finally, alongside these problems of coding and weighting, the meaning of a trauma cannot be defined unless we determine exactly what the "it" is. This is a question of narrative: What were the evil and traumatizing actions in question? Who was responsible? Who were the victims? What were the immediate and long-term results of the traumatizing actions? What can be done by way of remediation or prevention?

What these theoretical considerations suggest is that even after the physical force of the Allied triumph and the physical discovery of the Nazi concentration camps, the nature of what was seen and discovered had to be coded, weighted, and narrated. This complex cultural construction, moreover, had to be achieved immediately. History does not wait; it demands that representations be made, and they will be. Whether or not some newly reported event is startling, strange, terrible, or inexpressibly weird, it must be "typified," in the sense of Husserl and Schutz – that is, it must be explained as a typical and even anticipated example of some thing or category that was known about before.[16] Even the vastly unfamiliar must somehow be made familiar. To the cultural process of coding, weighting, and narrating, in other words, what comes before is all-important. Historical background is critical, both for the first "view" of the traumatic event and, as "history" changes, for later views as well. Once again, these shifting cultural constructions are fatefully affected by the power and identity of the agents in charge, by the competition for symbolic control, and by the structures of power and distribution of resources that condition it.

Background Constructions

Nazism as the Representation of Absolute Evil

What was the historical structure of "good and evil" within which, on April 3, 1945, the "news" of the Nazi concentration camps was first confirmed to the American audience? To answer this question, it is first necessary to describe what came before. In what follows I will venture some observations, which can hardly be considered definitive, about how social evil was coded, weighted, and narrated during the interwar period in Europe and the United States.

In the deeply disturbing wake of the First World War, there was a pervasive sense of disillusionment and cynicism among mass and elite members of the Western "audience," a distancing from protagonists and antagonists that, as Paul Fussell has shown, made irony the master trope of that first postwar era.[17] This trope transformed "demonology" – the very act of coding and weighting evil – into what many intellectuals and lay persons alike considered to be an act of bad faith. Once the coding and weighting of evil were de-legitimated, however, good and evil became less distinct from one another and relativism became the dominant motif of the time. In such conditions, coherent narration of contemporary events becomes difficult if not impossible. Thus it was that, not only for many intellectuals and artists of this period but for many ordinary people as well, the startling upheavals of these interwar years could not easily be sorted out in a conclusive and satisfying way.

It was in the context of this breakdown of representation that racism and revolution, whether fascist or communist, emerged as compelling frames, not only in Europe but also in the United States. Against a revolutionary narrative of dogmatic and authoritarian modernism on the Left, there arose the narrative of reactionary modernism, equally revolutionary but fervently opposed to rationality and cosmopolitanism.[18] In this context, many democrats in Western Europe and the United States withdrew from the field of representation itself, becoming confused and equivocating advocates of disarmament, nonviolence, and peace "at any price." This formed the cultural frame for isolationist political policy in both Britain and the United States.

Eventually the aggressive military ambition of Nazism made such equivocation impossible to sustain. While racialism, relativism, and narrative confusion continued in the United States and Britain until the very beginning of the Second World War, and even continued well into it, these constructions were countered by increasingly forceful and confident representations of good and evil that coded liberal democracy and universalism as unalloyed goods and Nazism, racism, and prejudice as deeply corrosive representations of the polluting and profane.

From the late 1930s on, there emerged a strong, and eventually dominant, anti-fascist narrative in Western societies. Nazism was coded, weighted, and narrated in apocalyptic, Old Testament terms as "the dominant evil of our time." Because this radical evil aligned itself with violence and massive death, it not merely justified but also compelled the risking of life in opposing it, a compulsion that motivated and justified massive human sacrifice in what came later to be known as the last "good war."[19] That Nazism was an absolute, unmitigated evil, a radical evil that threatened the very future of human civilization, formed the presupposition of America's four-year prosecution of the world war.[20]

The representation of Nazism as an absolute evil emphasized not only its association with sustained coercion and violence but also, and perhaps even especially, the way Nazism linked violence with ethnic, racial, and religious hatred. In this way, the most conspicuous example of the practice of Nazi evil – its policy of systematic discrimination, coercion, and, eventually, mass violence against the Jews – was initially interpreted as "simply" another horrifying example of the subhumanism of Nazi action.

Interpreting Kristallnacht: Nazi Evil as Anti-Semitism

The American public's reaction to Kristallnacht demonstrates how important the Nazis' anti-Jewish activities were in crystallizing

39

the polluted status of Nazism in American eyes. It also provides a prototypical example of how such representations of the evils of anti-Semitism were folded into the broader and more encompassing symbolism of Nazism. *Kristallnacht* refers, of course, to the rhetorically virulent and physically violent expansion of the Nazi repression of Jews that unfolded throughout German towns and cities on November 9 and 10, 1938. These activities were widely recorded. "The morning editions of most American newspapers reported the *Kristallnacht* in banner headlines," according to one historian of that fateful event, "and the broadcasts of H. V. Kaltenborn and Raymond Gram Swing kept the radio public informed of Germany's latest adventure" (Diamond 1969: 198). Exactly why these events assumed such critical importance in the American public's continuing effort to understand "what Hitlerism stood for" (201) goes beyond the simple fact that violent and repressive activities were, perhaps for the first time, openly, even brazenly, displayed in direct view of the world public sphere. Equally important was the altered cultural framework within which these activities were observed. For *Kristallnacht* occurred just six weeks after the now infamous Munich agreements, acts of appeasing Hitler's expansion that were understood, not only by isolationists but also by many opponents of Nazism, indeed by the vast majority of the American people, as possibly reasonable accessions to a possibly reasonable man (197). In other words, *Kristallnacht* initiated a process of understanding fuelled by symbolic contrast, not simply observation.

What was interpretively constructed was the cultural difference between Germany's previously apparent cooperativeness and reasonableness – representations of the good in the discourse of American civil society – and its subsequent demonstration of violence and irrationality, which were taken to be representations of anti-civil evil. Central to the ability to draw this contrast was the ethnic and religious hatred Germans demonstrated in their violence against Jews. If one examines the American public's reactions, it clearly is this anti-Jewish violence that is taken to represent the evil of Nazism. It was with reference to this violence that the news stories of the *New York Times* employed the rhetoric of pollution to further code and weight Nazi evil: "No foreign propagandist bent upon blackening the name of Germany before the world could outdo the tale of beating, of blackguardly assaults upon defenseless and innocent people, which degraded that country yesterday" (quoted in Diamond 1969: 198). The *Times*'s controversial columnist Anne O'Hare McCormick wrote that "the suffering [the Germans] inflict on others, now that they are

40

on top, passes all understanding and mocks all sympathy," and she went on to label *Kristallnacht* "the darkest day Germany experienced in the whole post-war period" (quoted in Diamond 1969: 199). The *Washington Post* identified the Nazi activities as "one of the worst setbacks for mankind since the Massacre of St. Bartholomew" (quoted in Diamond 1969: 198–9).

This broadening identification of Nazism with evil, simultaneously triggered and reinforced by the anti-Jewish violence of *Kristallnacht*, stimulated influential political figures to make more definitive judgments about the antipathy between American democracy and German Nazism than they had up until that point. Speaking on NBC radio, Al Smith, former New York governor and democratic presidential candidate, observed that the events confirmed that the German people were "incapable of living under a democratic government" (quoted in Diamond 1969: 200). Following Smith on the same program, Thomas E. Dewey, soon to be New York governor and future presidential candidate, expressed the opinion that "the civilized world stands revolted by the bloody pogrom against a defenseless people . . . by a nation run by madmen" (quoted in Diamond 1969: 201). Having initially underplayed America's official reaction to the events, four days later President Franklin Roosevelt took advantage of the public outrage by emphasizing the purity of the American nation and its distance from this emerging representation of violence and ethnic hatred: "The news of the past few days from Germany deeply shocked public opinion in the United States . . . I myself could scarcely believe that such things could occur in a twentieth century civilization" (quoted in Diamond 1969: 205).

Judging from these reactions to the Nazi violence of *Kristallnacht*, it seems only logical that, as one historian has put it, "most American newspapers or journals" could "no longer . . . view Hitler as a pliable and reasonable man, but as an aggressive and contemptible dictator [who] would have to be restrained" (quoted in Diamond 1969: 207). What is equally striking, however, is that in almost none of the American public's statements of horror is there explicit reference to the identity of the victims of *Kristallnacht* as Jews. Instead they are referred to as a "defenseless and innocent people," as "others," and as a "defenseless people" (quoted in Diamond 1969: 198, 199, 201). In fact, in the public statement just quoted, President Roosevelt goes well out of his way to separate his moral outrage from any link to a specific concern for the fate of the Jews. "Such news from *any part* of the world," the President insists, "would inevitably produce similar profound reaction among Americans in *any part* of the nation"

41

(Diamond 1969: 205, italics added). In other words, despite the centrality of the Nazis' anti-Jewish violence to the emerging American symbolization of Nazism as evil, there existed – at that point in historical and cultural time – a reluctance for non-Jewish Americans to identify with Jewish people as such. Jews were highlighted as vital representations of the evils of Nazism: their fate would be understood only in relation to the German horror that threatened democratic civilization in America and Europe. This failure of identification would be reflected seven years later in the distancing of the American soldiers and domestic audience from the traumatized Jewish camp survivors and their even less fortunate Jewish compatriots whom the Nazis had killed.

Anti-Anti-Semitism: Fighting Nazi Evil by Fighting for the Jews

It was also during the 1930s, in the context of the Nazi persecution of German Jews, that an historically unprecedented attack on anti-Semitism emerged in the United States. It was not that Christians suddenly felt genuine affection for, or identification with, those whom they had vilified for countless centuries as the killers of Christ.[21] It was that the logic of symbolic association had dramatically and fatefully changed. Nazism was increasingly viewed as the vile enemy of universalism, and the most hated enemies of Nazism were the Jews. The laws of symbolic antinomy and association thus were applied. If Nazism singled out the Jews, then the Jews must be singled out by democrats and anti-Nazis. Anti-Semitism, tolerated and condoned for centuries in every Western nation, and for the preceding fifty years embraced fervently by proponents of American "nativism," suddenly became distinctly unpopular in progressive circles throughout the United States (Gleason 1981; Higham 1984).[22]

What I will call "anti-anti-Semitism"[23] became particularly intense after the United States declared war on Nazi Germany. The nature of this concern is framed in a particularly clear manner by one leading historian of American Jewry: "The war saw the merging of Jewish and American fates. Nazi Germany was the greatest enemy of both Jewry and the United States" (Shapiro 1992: 16). For the first time, overtly positive representations of Jewish people proliferated in popular and high culture alike. It was during this period that the phrase "Judeo-Christian tradition" was born. It appeared as Americans tried to fend off the Nazi enemy that threatened to destroy the sacred foundations of Western democratic life (Silk 1984).

Mass Murder under the Progressive Narrative

Nazism marked a traumatic epoch in modern history. Yet, while coded as evil and weighted in the most fundamental, *weltgeschichte* (world-historical) terms, it was narrated inside a framework that offered the promise of salvation and triggered actions that generated confidence and hope.[24] What I will call the "progressive narrative" proclaimed that the trauma created by social evil would be overcome, that Nazism would be defeated and eliminated from the world, that it would eventually be relegated to a traumatic past whose darkness would be obliterated by a new and powerful social light. The progressivity of this narrative depended on keeping Nazism situated and historical, which prevented this representation of absolute evil from being universalized and its cultural power from being equated, in any way, shape, or form, with the power possessed by the good. In narrative terms, this asymmetry, this insistence on Nazism's anomalous historical status, assured its ultimate defeat. In popular consciousness and in dramas created by cultural specialists, the origins of Nazism were linked to specific events in the interwar period and to particular organizations and actors within it, to a political party, to a crazy and inhuman leader, to an anomalous nation that had demonstrated militaristic and violent tendencies over the previous one hundred years.

Yes, Nazism had initiated a trauma in modern history, but it was a liminal trauma presenting "time out of time," in Victor Turner's sense.[25] The trauma was dark and threatening, but it was, at the same time, anomalous and, in principle at least, temporary. As such, the trauma could and would be removed via a just war and a wise and forgiving peace.[26] The vast human sacrifices demanded by the winds of war were measured and judged in terms of this progressive narrative and the salvation it promised. The blood spilled in the war sanctified the future peace and obliterated the past. The sacrifice of millions could be redeemed and the social salvation of their sacred souls achieved, not by dwelling in a lachrymose manner on their deaths but by eliminating Nazism, the force that had caused their deaths, and by planning the future that would establish a world in which there could never be Nazism again.

Framing Revelations about the Jewish Mass Murder

While initially received with surprise, and always conceived with loathing, the gradual and halting but eventually definitive revelations of Nazi plans for displacing, and quite possibly murdering, the entirety of European Jewry actually confirmed the categorizing of evil already in place: the coding, weighting, and narrating of Nazism as an inhuman, absolutely evil force. What had been experienced as an extraordinary trauma by the Jewish victims was experienced by the audience of others as a kind of categorical vindication.[27] In this way, and for this reason, the democratic audience for the reports on the mass murders experienced distance from, rather than identification with, the trauma's victims. The revelations had the effect, in some perverse sense, of normalizing the abnormal.

The empirical existence of Nazi plans for the "Final Solution," as well as extensive documentation of their ongoing extermination activities, had been publicly documented by June 1942 (Dawidowicz 1982; Laqueur 1980; Norich 1998–9). In July of that year more than twenty thousand persons rallied in Madison Square Garden to protest the Nazis' war against the Jews. Though he did not attend in person, President Franklin Roosevelt sent a special message that what he called "these crimes" would be redeemed by the "final account-ing" following the Allied victory over Nazism. In March 1943 the American Jewish Congress announced that 2 million Jews had already been massacred and that millions more were slated for death. Its detailed descriptions of the "extermination" were widely reported in the American press.[28] Dawidowicz shows that, by March 1944, when the Germans occupied Hungary and their intention to liqui-date its entire Jewish population became known, "Auschwitz was no longer an unfamiliar name" (Dawidowicz 1982).

Yet it was this very familiarity that seemed to undermine the sense of astonishment that might have stimulated immediate action. For Auschwitz was typified in terms of the progressive narrative of war, a narrative that made it impossible to denormalize the mass killings, to make the Holocaust into the "Holocaust." As I indicated in my earlier reconstruction of the discourse about atrocity, what eventu-ally came to be called the Holocaust was reported to contemporaries as a war story, nothing less but nothing more. In private conferences with the US president, Jewish leaders demanded that Allied forces make special efforts to target and destroy the death camps. In describ-ing these failed efforts to trigger intervention, a leading historian explains that the leaders "couldn't convince a preoccupied American President and the American public of the significance of Auschwitz for their time in history" (Feingold 1974: 250). In other words, while Auschwitz was coded as evil, it simply was not weighted in a sufficiently dire way.

In these symbolically mediated confrontations, attention was not focused on the mass killings in and of themselves. What was definitely not illuminated or asserted was the discovery of an evil unique in human history. The evil of that time had already been discovered, and it was Nazism, not the massive killing of European Jews. The trauma that this evil had created was a second world war. The trauma that the Jews experienced in the midst of their liquidation was represented as one among a series of effects of Nazi evil. When the London *Times* reported Adolf Hitler's death, on May 2, 1945 – in the month following the death-camp revelations – its obituary described the German dictator as "the incarnation of absolute evil" and only briefly mentioned Hitler's "fanatical aversion to Jews" (quoted in Benn 1995: 102). As one historian has put it, "the processed mass murders became merely another atrocity in a particularly cruel war" (quoted in Benn 1995: 102).[29] The mass murders were explained, and they would be redeemed, within the framework of the progressive struggle against Nazism.

To understand fully the initial, frame-establishing encounter between Americans and the Jewish mass murder, it is vital to remember that narratives, no matter how progressive and future oriented, are composed of both antagonists and protagonists. The antagonists and their crimes were well established: The German Nazis had murdered the Jews in a gigantic, heinous atrocity of war. The protagonists were the American GIs, and their entrance into the concentration camps was portrayed not only as a discovery of such horrendous atrocities but also as another, culminating stage in a long and equally well-known sequence of "liberation," with all the ameliorating expectations that utopian term implies.

"When the press entered the camps of the western front," the cultural historian Barbie Zelizer writes, "it found that the most effective way to tell the atrocity story was as a chronicle of liberation" (1998: 63). In fact, Zelizer entitles her own detailed reconstruction of these journalist encounters "Chronicles of Liberation" (63–85). When readers of the *New York Times* and *Los Angeles Times* were confronted, on April 16, 1945, with the photo from Buchenwald of bunk beds stuffed to overflowing with haunted, pathetically undernourished male prisoners, they were informed that they were looking at "freed slave laborers" (183). On May 5, the *Picture Post* published a six-page spread of atrocity photos. Framing the heart-wrenching visual images, the theme of forward progress was palpable. One collective caption read: "These Were Inmates of Prison Camps Set Free in the Allied Advance: For Many We Came Too Late" (129). Photos of dead or tattered and starving victims were often juxtaposed with pictures of well-dressed, well-fed German citizens from the surrounding towns, pointedly linking the crime to the particular nature of the German people themselves. In a sidebar story entitled "The Problem That Makes All Europe Wonder," the *Picture Post* described "the horror that took place within the sight and sound of hundreds of thousands of seemingly normal, decent German people. How was it possible? What has happened to the minds of a whole nation that such things should have been tolerated for a day?" (quoted in Zelizer 1998: 128). The same photos often included a representative GI standing guard, passing judgment while looking on the scene. The text alongside another widely circulated photo in the *Picture Post* made the progressive answer to such questions perfectly plain. "It is not enough to be mad with rage. It is no help to shout about 'exterminating' Germany. Only one thing helps: the attempt to understand how men have sunk so far, and the firm resolve to face the trouble, the inconvenience and cost of seeing no nation gets the chance to befoul the world like this again" (quoted in Zelizer 1998: 129). It was within this highly particularized progressive narrative that the first steps toward universalization actually took place. Because the Jewish mass killings came at the chronological conclusion of the war, and because they without doubt represented the most gruesome illustration of Nazi atrocities, they came very quickly to be viewed not merely as symptoms but also as emblems and iconic representations of the evil that the progressive narrative promised to leave behind. As the novelist and war correspondent Meyer Levin wrote of his visit to Ohrdruf, the first camp American soldiers liberated, "it was as though we had penetrated at last to the center of the black heart, to the very crawling inside of the vicious heart" (quoted in Abzug 1985: 19). On the one hand, the trauma was localized and particularized – it occurred in this war, in this place, with these persons. On the other hand, the mass murder was universalized. Within months of the initial revelations, indeed, the murders frequently were framed by a new term, *genocide*, a crime defined as the effort to destroy an entire people, which, while introduced earlier, during the war period itself, came to be publicly available and widely employed only after the discovery of the Nazi atrocities.[30]

In response to this new representation, the scope of the Nuremberg War Crimes Tribunal was enlarged. Conceived as a principal vehicle for linking the postwar Allied cause to progressive redemption, the trials were now to go beyond prosecuting the Nazi leaders for crimes of war to considering their role in the mass murder of the Jewish people. Justice Robert Jackson, the chief American prosecutor, promised that the trial would not only prosecute those responsible for the war but also would present "undeniable proofs of incredible events" – the Nazi crimes (quoted in Benn 1995: 102). The first three counts of the twenty-thousand-word indictment against the twenty-three high-ranking Nazi officials concerned the prosecution of the war itself. They charged conspiracy, conducting a war of aggression, and violating the rules of war. The fourth count, added only in the months immediately preceding the October trial in Nuremberg, accused the Nazi leaders of something new, namely of "crimes against humanity." This was the first step toward universalizing the public representation of the Jewish mass murder. From the perspective of the present day, however, it appears as a relatively limited one, for it functioned to confirm the innocent virtue and national ambitions of one particular side. In its first report on the indictments, for example, the *New York Times* linked the Jewish mass murder directly to the war itself and placed its punishment within the effort to prevent any future "war of aggression." Under the headline "The Coming War Trials," the paper noted that "the authority of this tribunal to inflict punishment is directly from victory in war" and that its goal was "to establish the principle that no nation shall ever again go to war, except when directly attacked or under the sanction of a world organization" (October 9, 1945: 20). The Nuremberg trials were not, in other words, perceived as preventing genocide or crimes against humanity as such. At that time the commission of such crimes could not be conceived apart from the Nazis and the recently concluded aggressive war.

The force of the progressive narrative meant that while the 1945 revelations confirmed the Jewish mass murder, they did not create a trauma for the postwar audience. Victory and the Nuremburg war trials would put an end to Nazism and alleviate its evil effects. Postwar redemption depended on putting mass murder "behind us," moving on, and getting on with the construction of the new world.

From the end of the war until the early 1960s, a "can-do," optimistic spirit pervaded America. Those who had returned from the war were concerned with building a family and a career, not with dwelling on the horrors of the past ... It did not seem to be an appropriate time to focus on a painful past, particularly a past which seemed to be of no direct concern to this country. This event had transpired on another continent. It had been committed by another country against "another" people. What relevance did it have for Americans? (Lipstadt 1996: 195–214).

[As for] the terms in which Americans of the mid-1950s were prepared to confront the Holocaust: a terrible event, yes, but ultimately not tragic or depressing; an experience shadowed by the specter of a cruel death, but at the same time not without the ability to inspire, console, uplift ... Throughout the late 1940s and well into the 50s, a prevalent attitude was to put all of "that" behind one and get on with life. (Rosenfeld 1995: 37–8)

After the War, American Jewry turned – with great energy and generosity – to liquidating the legacy of the Holocaust by caring for the survivors [who] were urged to put the ghastly past behind them, to build new lives in their adopted homes ... When a proposal for a Holocaust memorial in New York City came before representatives of the leading Jewish organizations in the late 1940s, they unanimously rejected the idea: it would, they said, give currency to the image of Jews as "helpless victims," an idea they wished to repudiate. (Novick 1994: 160)

It was neither emotional repression nor good moral sense that created the early responses to the mass murder of the Jews. It was, rather, a system of collective representations that focused its beam of narrative light on the triumphant expulsion of evil. Most Americans did not identify with the victims of the Jewish trauma. Far from being implicated in it, Americans had defeated those responsible for the mass murders and righteously engaged in restructuring the social and political arrangements that had facilitated them. This did not mean that the mass murder of Jews was viewed with relativism or equanimity. According to the progressive narrative, it was America's solemn task to redeem the sacrifice of this largest of all categories of Nazi victims. In postwar America, the public redeemed the sacrifices of war by demanding the thorough denazification not only of German but also of American society. As Sumner Welles eloquently framed the issue a month after the GIs had entered the Nazi death camps,

The crimes committed by the Nazis and by their accomplices against the Jewish people are indelible stains upon the whole of our modern civilization ... They are stains which will shame our generation in the eyes of generations still unborn. For we and our governments, to which we have entrusted power during these years between the Great Wars, cannot shake off the responsibility for having permitted the growth of world conditions which made such horrors possible. The democracies cannot lightly attempt to shirk their responsibility. No recompense can be offered the dead ... But such measure of recompense as can be offered surely constitutes the moral obligation of the free peoples of the earth as soon as their victory is won. (Welles 1945: 511)

Purifying America and Redeeming the Murder of the Jews

Propelled by the logic of this progressive understanding of redemption, in America's immediate postwar years the public legitimation of anti-Semitism was repeatedly attacked and some of its central institutional manifestations destroyed. The long-standing anti-anti-Semitism framing the progressive narrative, and crystallized during the interwar years by leading figures in the American intellectual and cultural elite, culminated in the immediate postwar period in a massive shift of American public opinion on the Jewish question (Stember 1966). Only days after the hostilities ceased, in response to an appeal from the National Council of Christians and Jews, the three candidates for mayor of New York City pledged to "refrain from appeals to racial and religious divisiveness during the campaign." One of them made explicit the connection of this public anti-anti-Semitism to the effort to remain connected to, and enlarge on, the meaning of America's triumph in the anti-Nazi war.

> This election will be the first held in the City of New York since our victory over nazism and Japanese fascism. It will therefore be an occasion for a practical demonstration of democracy in action – a democracy in which all are equal citizens, in which there is not and never must be a second class citizenship and in which . . . the religion of a candidate must play no part in the campaign. (*New York Times*, October 1, 1945: 32)

In an influential article, Leonard Dinnerstein has documented the vastly heightened political activism of Jewish groups in the immediate postwar period from 1945 to 1948 (Dinnerstein 1981–2). He records how these newly surfaced and often newly formed groups held conferences, wrote editorials, and issued specific proposals for legal and institutional changes. By 1950, these activities had successfully exposed and often defeated anti-Jewish quotas and, more generally, created an extraordinary shift in the practical and cultural position of American Jews. During the same month that New York's mayoral candidates announced their anti-anti-Semitism, the *American Mercury* published an article, "Discrimination in Medical Colleges," replete with graphs and copious documentation, detailing the existence of anti-Jewish quotas in some of America's most prestigious professional institutions. While the specific focus was anti-Jewish discrimination, these facts were narrated in terms of the overarching promise of America and democracy. The story began with a vignette

49

about "Leo, a bright and personable American lad" who "dreamed of becoming a great physician."

> [He] made an excellent scholastic record [but] upon graduation . . . his first application for admission to a medical school . . . was mysteriously turned down. He filed another and another – at eighty-seven schools – always with the same heartbreaking result . . . not one of the schools had the courage to inform Leo frankly that he was being excluded because he was a Jew . . . The excuse for imposing a quota system usually advanced is that there ought to be some correlation between the number of physicians of any racial or religious strain and the proportion of that race or religion in the general population [but] the surface logic of this arithmetic collapses as soon as one subjects it to *democratic or sheerly human,* let alone scientific, tests. [It is] spurious and *un-American* arithmetic. (October, 1945: 391–9, italics added)[31]

Earlier that year, an "Independent Citizens Committee" had asked three hundred educators to speak out against restricting Jewish enrollment in the nation's schools. Ernest Hopkins, the president of Dartmouth College, refused, openly defending Dartmouth's Jewish quota on the grounds that German Nazism had been spurred because a large proportion of the German professions had become Jewish. A storm of public opprobrium followed Hopkins' remarks. The *New York Post* headlined, "Dartmouth Bars Jews 'To End Anti-Semitism,' Says Prexy." The next day, the rival tabloid, *PM,* placed Hopkins' picture side-by-side with the Nazi ideologue Alfred Rosenberg and accused the Dartmouth president of "spouting the Hitler–Rosenberg line" (quoted in "Sense or Nonsense?" *Time,* August 20, 1945: 92. In an article entitled "Anti-Semitism at Dartmouth," the *New Republic* brought a progressive perspective to the controversy by suggesting that it could bring "us a step nearer to amelioration of one of the outstanding blots on American civilization *today.*" Anti-Semitism belonged to the outmoded past that had been shattered by the anti-Nazi war: "We can *no longer* afford the luxury of these *obsolete* myths of racial differentiation, Mr Hopkins; if you don't believe it, ask Hitler" (August 20, 1945: 208–9, italics added).

In the years that followed, the fight against quotas continued to be informed by similar themes. In 1946, an educational sociologist wrote in the *American Scholar* that such restrictions were "in contradistinction to the *growing* realization which has come as a result of the war." Quotas must be abolished if postwar progress were to be made.

Today, our society as a whole sees the relationship between social welfare and prejudices which thwart the development of the capacities of individuals. This threat to the basic concepts of democracy is so plain that almost all of us, except the vested interests, have seen it. The question is whether or not the colleges and universities have seen it and are willing to bring their practices into line with *present day* insights, even though some of their most precious traditions be jeopardized. (Dodson 1946: 268, italics added)

Similar connections between the anti-Nazi war, anti-quotas, and the progress of anti-anti-Semitism informed another popular magazine article the following year: "It is extremely regrettable that *in 1946*, the children of [parents] who are returning from all parts of the world where they have been engaged in mortal combat to preserve democracy, are confronted with the same closed doors that greeted their 'alien' fathers" (Hart 1947: 61). In 1949, *Collier's* published an article describing the "scores of college men to whom fraternities" for "'fullblooded Aryans' are a little nauseating *in this day*." Quoting the finding of an Amherst College alumni committee that exclusive fraternities gave young men "a false and undemocratic sense of superiority," the article claimed that "the anti-discrimination movement is hopping from campus to campus" (Whitman 1949: 34–5).

While Jewish voluntary organizations had begun to organize in 1943–5, they entered the American public sphere as aggressive political advocates only after 1945, an intervention that marked the first time Jews had forcefully entered the civil sphere as advocates for their own rather than others' causes. In the prewar period, and even less in earlier times, such an explicit and aggressively Jewish public intervention would certainly have been repelled; in fact, it would only have made anti-Semitism worse. In the postwar period, however, despite their failure to identify with the Jewish victims of Nazism, the American non-Jewish audience was determined to redeem them. If, as Dinnerstein writes, Jewish groups intended to "mobilize public opinion against intolerance, and [thus to] utilize the courts and legislative bodies" (1981–2: 137) in their anti-Semitic fight they were able to carry on these political activities only because postwar public opinion had already been defined as committed to "tolerance."

Progress toward establishing civil relations between religious and ethnic groups was woven into the patriotic postwar narratives of the nation's mass-circulation magazines. *Better Homes and Gardens* ran such stories as "Do You Want Your Children to Be Tolerant?" "The old indifference and local absorption cannot continue. If we relapse into our *before-the-war* attitudes and limitations, war will burst upon us as suddenly and as unexpectedly as the atomic bomb fell upon the people of Hiroshima – and we shall be as helpless" (Buck 1947: 135, italics added).

In another piece in *Better Homes and Gardens* the same year, "How to Stop the Hate Mongers in Your Home Town," a writer observed: "I suspect that many a decent German burgher, hearing tales of Nazi gangs, likewise shrugged off the implications of uncurbed racial and religious persecution" (Carter 1947: 180). The following year, the *Saturday Evening Post* profiled "the story of the Jewish family of Jacob Golomb." The lengthy article concluded with the by now widely expected forward-looking line:

> As a family, the Golombs are more than just nice folks who lead busy, fruitful, decent lives; a family whose sons have sprung, in time of national emergency, with promptness to the defense of their country. As members of a race with a long history of persecution, they have kept the faith, since Abraham Golomb's time, that the United States really was, or *would soon be*, the land of the genuinely free. They are still convinced. (Perry 1948: 96, italics added)

Four years later, America's most popular photo magazine published "*Life* Goes to a Bar Mitzvah: A Boy Becomes a Man" (October 13, 1952: 170–6).

The anti-anti-Semitism theme also entered popular culture through the movies. In the 1945 box office hit *Pride of the Marines*, the Jewish protagonist Larry Diamond chided a friend for pessimism about the possibility of eliminating prejudice in the postwar years. He did so by connecting their present situation to the progressive ideals that had sustained their anti-Nazi war: "Ah, come on, climb out of your foxholes, what's a matter you guys, don't you think anybody learned anything since 1930? Think everybody's had their eyes shut and brains in cold storage?" (Short 1981: 161). Diamond goes on to remark that, if and when prejudice and repression dare to show their ugly heads in the postwar United States, he will fight to defeat them, just as he has learned to fight in the war: "I fought for me, for the right to live in the USA. And when I get back into civilian life, if I don't like the way things are going, OK it's my country; I'll stand on my own two legs and holler! If there's enough of us hollering we'll go places – Check?" (161). The narrative of progress is forcefully extended from the anti-Nazi war into the post-Nazi peace. Diamond had been "the pride of the marines," and the war's progressive narrative is fundamentally tied to assertions about the utopian telos of the United States. As the movie's closing music turns into "America the Beautiful," Diamond wraps it up this way: "One happy afternoon when God was feeling good, he sat down and thought of a rich beautiful country and he named it the USA. All of it, Al, the hills, the rivers, the lands, the whole works. Don't tell me we can't make it work in peace like we do in war. Don't tell me we can't pull together. Don't you see it guys, can't you see it?" (161–2).

Two years later, a movie promoting anti-anti-Semitism, *Gentleman's Agreement*, won the Academy Award for best motion picture, and another, *Crossfire*, had been nominated as well. Both are conspicuously progressive, forward-looking narratives. In the final dialogue of *Gentlemen's Agreement*, the film's future-oriented, utopian theme could not be more clear. "Wouldn't it be wonderful," Mrs Green asks Phil, "if it turned out to be everybody's century, when people all over the world, free people, found a way to live together? I'd like to be around to see some of that, even a beginning" (quoted in Short 1981: 180).[32]

As they had immediately before and during the war, "Jews" held symbolic pride of place in these popular-culture narratives because their persecution had been pre-eminently associated with the Nazi evil. In fact, it was not tolerance as such that the progressive narrative demanded but tolerance of the Jews.[33] Thus, despite their feelings of solidarity with their foreign co-religionists, Jewish leaders carefully refrained from publicly endorsing the wholesale lifting of anti-immigration quotas after 1945. They realized that the idea of immigration remained so polluted by association with stigmatized others that it might have the power to counteract the ongoing purification of Jewishness. In the preceding half-century, anti-immigration and anti-Semitism had been closely linked, and Jews did not want to pollute "Jewishness" with this identity again. While demonstrating their support in private, Jewish leaders resolutely refused to make any public pronouncements about lifting the immigration quotas (Dinnerstein 1981–2: 140).

What Dinnerstein has called the "turnabout in anti-Semitic feelings" represented the triumph over Nazism, not recognition of the Holocaust trauma. News about the mass murder, and any ruminations about it, disappeared from newspapers and magazines rather quickly after the initial reports about the camps' liberation, and the Nazis' Jewish victims came to be represented as displaced persons, potential immigrants, and potential settlers in Palestine, where a majority of Americans wanted to see a new, and redemptive, Jewish state. This interpretation suggests that it was by no means simply Realpolitik that led President Truman to champion, against his former French and British allies, the postwar creation of Israel, the new Jewish state. The progressive narrative demanded a future-oriented renewal. Zionists argued that the Jewish trauma could be redeemed, that Jews could both sanctify the victims and put the trauma behind them, only if they returned to Jerusalem. According to the Zionist world view, if Israel were allowed to exist, it would create a new race of confident and powerful Jewish farmer-warriors who would redeem the anti-Jewish atrocities by developing such an imposing military power that the massive murdering of the Jews would never, anywhere in the world, be allowed to happen again. In important respects, it was this convergence of progressive narratives in relation to the war and the Jewish mass killings that led the postwar paths of the United States and the state of Israel to become so fundamentally intertwined. Israel would have to prosper and survive for the redemptive telos of America's progressive narrative to be maintained.

These cultural–sociological considerations do not suggest that the postwar American fight against anti-Semitism was in any way morally inauthentic. It was triggered by grassroots feelings as deep as those that had motivated the earlier anti-Nazi fight. When one looks at these powerful new arguments against anti-Semitism, it is only retrospectively surprising to realize that the "atrocities" revealed in 1945 – the events and experiences that defined the trauma for European Jews – figure hardly at all. This absence is explained by the powerful symbolic logic of the progressive narrative, which already had been established in the prewar period. With the victory in 1945, the United States got down to the work of establishing the new world order. In creating a Nazi-free future, Jewishness came for the first time to be analogically connected with core American symbols of "democracy" and "nation."

In the course of this postwar transformation, American Jews also became identified with democracy in a more primordial and less universalistic way, namely as newly minted, patriotic representations of the nation. "After 1945," a leading historian of that period remarks, "other Americans no longer viewed the Jews as merely another of the many exotic groups within America's ethnic and religious mosaic. Instead, they were now seen as comprising one of the country's three major religions" (Shapiro 1992: 28). This patriotic–national definition was expressed by the Jewish theologian Will Herberg's insistence on the "Judeo-Christian" rather than

"Christian" identity of the religious heritage of the United States (53).[34] As I have indicated, what motivated this intense identification of anti-anti-Semitism with the American nation was neither simple emotional revulsion for the horrors of the Jewish mass killings nor commonsense morality. It was, rather, the progressive narrative frame. To end anti-Semitism, in President Truman's words, was to place America alongside "the moral forces of the world" (quoted in Shapiro 1992: 143). It was to redeem those who had sacrificed themselves for the American nation, and according to the teleology of the progressive narrative, this emphatically included the masses of murdered European Jews.

The critical point is this: What was a trauma for the victims was not a trauma for the audience.[35] In documenting this for the American case, I have examined the principal carrier group for the progressive narrative, the nation that in the immediate postwar world most conspicuously took the lead in "building the new world upon the ashes of the old." I have shown that the social agents, both Jewish and non-Jewish Americans, who took the lead in reconstructing a new moral order dedicated themselves to redeeming those who had been sacrificed to the anti-Nazi struggle, and most especially to the Jewish victims, by putting an end to anti-Semitism in the United States. The goal was focused not on the Holocaust but on the need to purge postwar society of Nazi-like pollution.

Jewish Mass Murder under the Tragic Narrative

I will now show how a different kind of narrative developed in relation to the Nazis' mass murder of the Jews, one that gave the evil it represented significantly greater symbolic weight. I will treat this new culture structure both as cause and as effect. After reconstructing its internal contours, I will examine the kind of "symbolic action" it caused and how these new meanings compelled the trauma of the mass murders to be seen in a radically different way, with significant consequences for social and political action that continue to ramify to the present day.[36] After completing this analytic reconstruction of the new cultural configuration, I will proceed to a concrete examination of how it was constructed in real historical time, looking at changes in carrier groups, moral contexts, and social structural forces. Finally, I will examine some of the long-term ramifications of the highly general, decontextualized, and universal status that the trauma of the Holocaust came to assume.

The New Culture Structure

Ever since Dilthey defined the method specific to the *Geisteswissenschaften* – literally "sciences of the spirit" but typically translated as "human sciences" – it has been clear that what distinguishes the hermeneutic from the natural scientific method is the challenge of penetrating beyond the external form to inner meaning of actions, events, and institutions. Yet to enter into this thicket of subjectivity is not to embrace impressionism and relativism. As Dilthey emphasized, meanings are governed by structures just as surely as are economic and political processes; they are just governed in different ways. Every effort at interpretive social science must begin with the reconstruction of this culture structure.[37]

Deepening Evil. In the formation of this new culture structure, the coding of the Jewish mass killings as evil remained, but its weighting substantially changed. It became burdened with extraordinary gravitas. The symbolization of the Jewish mass killings became generalized and reified, and in the process the evil done to the Jews became separated from the profanation of Nazism per se. Rather than seeming to "typify" Nazism, or even the nefarious machinations of any particular social movement, political formation, or historical time, the mass killings came to be seen as not being typical of anything at all. They came to be understood as a unique, historically unprecedented event, as evil on a scale that had never occurred before.[38] The mass killings entered into universal history, becoming a "world-historical" event in Hegel's original sense, an event whose emergence onto the world stage threatened, or promised, to change the fundamental course of the world.[39] In the introduction to an English collection of his essays on Nazi history and the Holocaust, the German-Israeli historian Dan Diner observes that "well into the 1970s, wide-ranging portraits of the epoch would grant the Holocaust a modest (if any) mention."[40] By contrast, "it now tends to fill the entire picture . . . The growing centrality of the Holocaust has altered the entire warp and woof of our sense of the passing century . . . The incriminated event has thus become the epoch's marker, its final and inescapable wellspring" (Diner 2000: 1).

The Jewish mass killings became what we might identify, in Durkheimian terms, as a sacred-evil, an evil that recalled a trauma of such enormity and horror that it had to be radically set apart from the world and all of its other traumatizing events. It became inexplicable in ordinary, rational terms. As part of the Nazi scheme of world domination, the Jewish mass killing was heinous, but at least it had been understandable. As a sacred-evil, set apart from ordinary evil things, it had become mysterious and inexplicable. One of the first to comment on, and thus to characterize, this postprogressive inexplicability was the Marxist historian Isaac Deutscher. This great biographer of Trotsky, who had already faced the consequences of Stalinism for the myth of communist progress, was no doubt precon-ditioned to see the tragic dimensions of the Holocaust. In 1968, in "The Jewish Tragedy and the Historian," Deutscher suggested that comprehending the Holocaust "will not be just a matter of time." What he meant was that there would not be progress.

> I doubt whether even in a thousand years people will understand Hitler, Auschwitz, Majdanek, and Treblinka better than we do now. Will they have a better historical perspective? On the contrary, posterity may even understand it all even less than we do. Who can analyze the motives and the interests behind the enormities of Auschwitz . . . We are confronted here by a huge and ominous mystery of the generation of the human character that will forever baffle and terrify mankind. (Deutscher 1968: 163)

For Deutscher, such a huge and mysterious evil, so resistant to the normal progress of human rationality, suggested tragedy and art, not scientific fact gathering. "Perhaps a modern Aeschylus and Sophocles could cope with this theme," he suggested, "but they would do so on a level different from that of historical interpretation and explana-tion" (1968: 164). Geoffrey Hartman, the literary theorist who has directed Yale University's Video Archive for the Holocaust since 1981 and has been a major participant in post-sixties discussions of the trauma, points to the enigma that, while no historical event has ever "been so thoroughly documented and studied," social and moral "understanding comes and goes; it has not been progressive." By way of explaining this lack of progress, Hartman suggests that

> The scholars most deeply involved often admit an "excess" that remains dark and frightful . . . Something in the . . . Shoah remains dark at the heart of the event . . . A comparison with the French Revolution is useful. The sequence *French Revolution: Enlightenment* cannot be matched by *Holocaust: Enlightenment*. What should be placed after the colon? "Eclipse of Enlightenment" or "Eclipse of God"? (Hartman 1996: 3–4)

To this day the Holocaust is almost never referred to without assert-ing its inexplicability. In the spring of 1999, a *New York Times* theater reviewer began his remarks on *The Gathering*, a newly opened drama, by asserting that "the profound, agonizing mystery of the Holocaust echoes through the generations and across international borders," presenting "an awesome human and theological enigma as an old century prepares to give way to a new millennium" (van Gelder 1999: 1).

This separateness of sacred-evil demanded that the trauma be renamed, for the concept of "mass murder" and even the notion of "genocide" now appeared unacceptably to normalize the trauma, to place it too closely in proximity to the banal and mundane. In contrast, despite the fact that the word *holocaust* did have a formally established English meaning – according to the *Oxford English Dictionary*, "something wholly burnt up" (Garber and Zuckerman 1989: 199) – it no longer performed this sign function in everyday speech. Rather, the term entered into ordinary English usage in the early 1960s as a proper rather than a common noun.[41] Only several years after the Nazis' mass murder did Israelis begin to employ the Hebrew word *shoah*, the term by which the Torah evoked the kind of extraordinary sufferings God had periodically consigned to the Jews. In the official English translation of the phrase "Nazi *shoah*" in the preamble to the 1948 Israeli Declaration of Independence, one can already find the reference to "Nazi holocaust"(Novick 1999: 132). With the decline of the progressive narrative, in other words, as *Holocaust* became the dominant representation for the trauma, it implied the sacral mystery, the "awe-fullness," of the transcendental tradition. *Holocaust* became part of contemporary language as an English symbol that stood for that thing that could not be named.[42] As David Roskies once wrote, "it was precisely the nonreferential quality of 'Holocaust' that made it so appealing" (quoted in Garber and Zuckerman 1989: 201).

This new linguistic identity allowed the mass killings of the Jews to become what might be called a bridge metaphor: It provided the symbolic extension so necessary if the trauma of the Jewish people were to become a trauma for all humankind. The other necessary ingredient, psychological identification, was not far behind. It depended on configuring this newly weighted symbolization of evil in a different narrative frame.

Suffering, Catharsis, and Identification. The darkness of this new postwar symbolization of evil cast a shadow over the progressive story that had thus far narrated its course. The story of redeeming Nazism's victims by creating a progressive and democratic world order could be called an ascending narrative, for it pointed to the future and suggested confidence that things would be better over time. Insofar as the mass killings were defined as a Holocaust, and insofar as it was the very emergence of this sacred-evil, not its eventual defeat, that threatened to become emblematic of "our time,"[43] the progressive narrative was blocked, and in some manner overwhelmed, by a sense of historical descent, by a falling away from the good. Recent Holocaust commentators have drawn this conclusion time and again. According to the progressive narrative, the Nazis' mass murder of the Jews would provide a lesson for all humankind, a decisive learning process on the way to a better world. Reflecting on the continuing fact of genocidal mass murders in the post-Holocaust world, Hartman revealingly suggests that "these developments raise questions about our species, our preconceptions that we are the human, the 'family of man.' Or less dramatically, we wonder about the veneer of progress, culture, and educability."

In dramaturgical terms, the issue concerns the position occupied by evil in the historical narrative. When Aristotle first defined tragedy in the *Poetics*, he linked what I have here called the weight of the representation of suffering to temporal location of an event in a plot:

> Tragedy is the representation of a complete, i.e., whole action *which has some magnitude* (for there can be a whole action without magnitude). A whole is that which has a beginning, a middle and a conclusion. A beginning is that which itself does not of necessity follow something else, but after which there naturally is, or comes into being, something else. A conclusion, conversely, is that which itself naturally follows something else, either of necessity or for the most part, but has nothing else after it. A middle is that which itself naturally follows something else, and has something else after it. Well-constructed plots, then, should neither begin from a random point nor conclude at a random point, but should use the elements we have mentioned. (Aristotle 1987: 3.2.1, italics added)

In the progressive narrative frame, the Jewish mass killings were not an end but a beginning. They were part of the massive trauma of the Second World War, but in the postwar period they and related incidents of Nazi horror were regarded as a birth trauma, a crossroads in a chronology that would eventually be set right. By contrast, the newly emerging world-historical status of the mass murders suggested that they represented an end point, not a new beginning, a death trauma rather than a trauma of birth, a cause for despair, not the beginning of hope. In place of the progressive story, then, there began to emerge the narrative of tragedy. The end point of a narrative defines its telos. In the new tragic understanding of the Jewish mass murder, suffering, not progress, became the telos toward which the narrative was aimed.

In this tragic narrative of sacred-evil, the Jewish mass killings become not an event in history but an archetype, an event out of time. As archetype, the evil evoked an experience of trauma greater than anything that could be defined by religion, race, class, region – indeed, by any conceivable sociological configuration or historical conjuncture. This transcendental status, this separation from the specifics of any particular time or space, provided the basis for psychological identification on an unprecedented scale. The contemporary audience cares little about the second and third installments of Sophocles' archetypal story of Oedipus, the tragic hero. What we are obsessed with is Oedipus' awful, unrecognized, and irredeemable mistake, how he finally comes to recognize his responsibility for it, and how he blinds himself from guilt when he understands its full meaning. Tragic narratives focus attention not on some future effort at reversal or amelioration – "progress," in the terms I have employed here – but on the nature of the crime, its immediate aftermath, and on the motives and relationships that led up to it.

A tragic narrative offers no redemption in the traditionally religious, Judeo-Christian sense.[44] There is no happy ending, no sense that something else could have been done, and no belief that the future could, or can, necessarily be changed. Indeed, protagonists are tragic precisely because they have failed to exert control over events. They are in the grip of forces larger than themselves – impersonal, even inhuman forces that often are not only beyond control but, during the tragic action itself, beyond comprehension. This sense of being overwhelmed by unjust force or fate explains the abjection and helplessness that permeate the genre of tragedy and the experience of pity it arouses.

Instead of redemption through progress, the tragic narrative offers what Nietzsche called the drama of the eternal return. As it now came to be understood, there was no "getting beyond" the story of the Holocaust. There was only the possibility of returning to it: not transcendence but catharsis. Hartman resists "the call for closure" on just these grounds. "Wherever we look, the events of 1933–45 cannot be relegated to the past. They are not over; anyone who comes in contact with them is gripped, and finds detachment difficult." Quoting from Lawrence Langer's *Admitting the Holocaust*, Hartman suggests that "those who study it must 'reverse history and progress and find a way of restoring to the imagination of coming generations the depth of the catastrophe'" (Hartman 1996: 2, 5).

As Aristotle explained, catharsis clarifies feeling and emotion. It does not do so by allowing the audience to separate itself from the story's characters; a separation, according to Frye, that defines the very essence of comedy (Frye 1971 [1957]). Rather, catharsis clarifies feeling and emotion by forcing the audience to identify with the story's characters, compelling them to experience their suffering with them, and to learn, as often they did not, the true causes of their death. That we survive and they do not, that we can get up and leave the theater while they remain forever prostrate – this allows the possibility of catharsis, that strange combination of cleansing and relief, that humbling feeling of having been exposed to the dark and sinister forces that lie just beneath the surface of human life and of having survived.[45] We seek catharsis because our identification with the tragic narrative compels us to experience dark and sinister forces that are also inside of ourselves, not only inside others. We "redeem" tragedy by experiencing it, but despite this redemption, we do not get over it. Rather, to achieve redemption we are compelled to dramatize and redramatize, experience and reexperience the archetypal trauma. We pity the victims of the trauma, identifying and sympathizing with their horrible fate. Aristotle argued that the tragic genre could be utilized only for the "sorts of occurrence [that] arouse dread, or compassion in us" (Aristotle 1987: 4.1.2). The blackness of tragedy can be achieved only if, "first and foremost, the [suffering] characters should be good," for "the plot should be constructed in such a way that, even without seeing it, someone who hears about the incidents will shudder and feel pity at the outcome, as someone may feel upon hearing the plot of the Oedipus" (4.2.1, 4.1.1.3). It is not only the fact of identification, however, but also its complexity that makes the experience of trauma as tragedy so central to the assumption of moral responsibility, for we identify not only with the victims but with the perpetrators as well. The creation of this cultural form allows the psychological activity of internalization rather than projection, acceptance rather than displacement.[46]

The Trauma-Drama of Eternal Return. In the tragic narration of the Holocaust, the primal event became a "trauma-drama" that the "audience" returned to time and time again. This became, paradoxically, the only way to ensure that such an event would happen "never again." This quality of compulsively returning to the trauma-drama gave the story of the Holocaust a mythical status that transformed it into the archetypical sacred-evil of our time. Insofar as it achieved this status as a dominant myth, the tragedy of the Holocaust challenged the ethical self-identification, the self-esteem, of modernity – indeed, the very self-confidence that such a thing as "modern progress" could continue to exist. For to return to the trauma-drama of the Holocaust, to identify over and over again with the suffering and helplessness of its victims, was in some sense to give that confidence-shattering event a continuing existence in contemporary life. It was, in effect, to acknowledge that it *could* happen again.

In this way, the tragic framing of the Holocaust fundamentally contributed to postmodern relativism and disquiet. Because the tragic replaced the progressive narrative of the Nazi mass murder, the ethical standards protecting good from evil seemed not nearly as powerful as modernity's confident pronouncements had promised they would be. When the progressive narrative had organized understanding, the Nazi crimes had been temporalized as "medieval," in order to contrast them with the supposedly civilizing standards of modernity. With the emergence of the more tragic perspective, the barbarism was lodged within the essential nature of modernity itself.[47] Rather than maintaining and perfecting modernity, as the postwar progressive narrative would have it, the path to a more just and peaceful society seemed now to lead to postmodern life (Bauman 1989).[48]

It would be wrong, however, to imagine that because a trauma-drama lies at the center of the Holocaust's tragic narration, with all the ambition of exciting pity and emotional catharsis that this implies, that this lachrymose narrative and symbol actually became disconnected from the ethical and the good.[49] While it is undeniable that the Jewish mass killings came to assume a dramaturgical form, their significance hardly became aestheticized – that is, turned into a free-floating, amoral symbol whose function was to entertain rather than to instruct.[50] The events of the Holocaust were not dramatized for the sake of drama itself but, rather, to provide what Martha Nussbaum once described as "the social benefits of pity" (Nussbaum 1992).[51] The project of renaming, dramatizing, reifying, and ritualizing the Holocaust contributed to a moral remaking of the (post) modern (Western) world. The Holocaust story has been told and retold in response not only to emotional need but also to moral ambition. Its characters, its plot, and its pitiable denouement have been transformed into a less nationally bound, less temporally specific, and more universal drama. This dramatic universalization has deepened contemporary sensitivity to social evil. The trauma-drama's message, like that of every tragedy, is that evil is inside all of us and in every society. If we are all the victims and all the perpetrators, then there is no audience that can legitimately distance itself from collective suffering, either from its victims or from its perpetrators.

This psychological identification with the Jewish mass killings and the symbolic extension of its moral implications beyond the immediate parties involved has stimulated an unprecedented universalization of political and moral responsibility. To have created this symbol of sacred-evil in contemporary time, then, is to have so enlarged the human imagination that it is capable, for the first time in human history, of identifying, understanding, and judging the kinds of genocidal mass killings in which national, ethnic, and ideological groupings continue to engage today.[52] This enlargement has made it possible to comprehend that heinous prejudice with the intent to commit mass murder is not something from an earlier, more "primitive" time or a different, "foreign" place, committed by people with values we do not share. The implication of the tragic narrative is not that progress has become impossible. It has had the salutary effect, rather, of demonstrating that progress is much more difficult to achieve than moderns once believed. If progress is to be made, morality must be universalized beyond any particular time and place.[53]

The New Social Processes

Most Western people today would readily agree with the proposition that the Holocaust was a tragic, devastating event in human history. Surely it was, and is. One implication of my discussion, however, is that this perception of its moral status is not a natural reflection of the event itself. The Jewish mass killings first had to be dramatized – as a tragedy. Some of the most eloquent and influential Holocaust survivors and interpreters have disagreed sharply, and moralistically, with this perspective, insisting that fictional representations must not be allowed to influence the perception of historical reality. In 1978, Elie Wiesel excoriated NBC for producing the *Holocaust* miniseries, complaining that "it transforms an ontological event into soap-opera" and that "it is all make-believe." Because "the Holocaust transcends history," Wiesel argued, "it cannot be explained nor can it be visualized" (Wiesel 1978: 1). In response to *Schindler's List*, Claude Lanzman said much the same thing. Writing that the Holocaust "is above all unique in that it erects a ring of fire around itself," he claimed that "fiction is a transgression" and that "there are some things that cannot and should not be represented" (quoted in Hartman 1996: 84).[54]

I take a very different perspective here. Thus far I have reconstructed the internal patterning of the culture structure that allowed the new, tragic dramatization to take place. I would like now to turn to the historically specific social processes, both symbolic and social

63

structural, that made this new patterning attractive and, eventually, compelling. While my reference here is primarily to the United States, I believe some version of this analysis also applies to those other Western societies that attempted to reconstruct liberal democracies after the Second World War.[55]

I have earlier shown how the struggle against anti-Semitism became one of the primary vehicles by which the progressive narrative redeemed those who had been sacrificed in the war against Nazi evil. Fighting anti-Semitism was not the only path to redemption, of course; for America and its victorious allies, there was a whole new world to make. At the same time, the struggle against anti-Semitism had a special importance. The understanding of Nazism as an absolute evil stemmed not only from its general commitment to anti-civil domination but also from its effort to legitimate such violence according to the principles of prejudice and primordiality. Because the Jewish people were by far the most conspicuous primordial target, symbolic logic dictated that to be anti-Nazi was to be anti-anti-Semitic.[56]

As I have also suggested, the rhetoric and policies of this anti-anti-Semitism did not require that non-Jewish Americans positively identify with Jews, any more than the role that the Holocaust played in the postwar progressive narrative depended on a sense of identification with the weary and bedraggled survivors in the concentration camps themselves. To narrate the Holocaust in a tragic manner, however, did depend on just such an identification being made. This identification was a long time in coming, and it depended on a number of factors unrelated to public opinion and cultural change.[57] Nonetheless, it certainly depended, in addition to such social structural factors, on the fact that the cultural idiom and the organizational apparatus of anti-Semitism had, indeed, been attacked and destroyed in the early "progressive" postwar years, and that, for the first time in American history, Jews seemed, to a majority of Christian Americans, not that much different from anybody else. As the tragic narrative crystallized, the Holocaust drama became, for an increasing number of Americans, and for significant proportions of Europeans as well, the most widely understood and emotionally compelling trauma of the twentieth century. These bathetic events, once experienced as traumatic only by Jewish victims, became generalized and universalized. Their representation no longer referred to events that took place at a particular time and place but to a trauma that had became emblematic, and iconic, of human suffering as such. The horrific trauma of the Jews became the trauma of all humankind.[58]

The Production of New Social Dramas

How was this more generalized and universalized status achieved? Social narratives are not composed by some hidden hand of history. Nor do they appear all at once. The new trauma-drama emerged in bits and pieces. It was a matter of this story and that, this scene and that scene from this movie and that book, this television episode, and that theater performance, this photographic capturing of a moment of torture and suffering. Each of these glimpses into what Meyer Levin had called, in April 1945, "the very crawling inside of the vicious heart" contributed some element to the construction of this new sensibility, which highlighted suffering, helplessness, and dark inevitability and which, taken together and over time, reformulated the mass killing of the Jews as the most tragic event in Western history. It is not the purpose of the following to provide anything approaching a thick description of this process of symbolic reconstruction but only to identify the signposts along this new route and the changing "countryside" that surrounded it.

Personalizing the Trauma and its Victims. In the course of constructing and broadcasting the tragic narrative of the Holocaust, there were a handful of actual dramatizations – in books, movies, plays, and television shows – that played critically important roles. Initially formulated for an American audience, they were distributed world wide, seen by tens and possibly hundreds of millions of persons, and talked incessantly about by high-, middle-, and lowbrow audiences alike. In the present context, what seems most important about these dramas is that they achieved their effect by personalizing the trauma and its characters. This personalization brought the trauma-drama "back home." Rather than depicting the events on a vast historical scale, rather than focusing on larger-than-life leaders, mass movements, organizations, crowds, and ideologies, these dramas portrayed the events in terms of small groups, families and friends, parents and children, brothers and sisters. In this way, the victims of trauma became everyman and everywoman, every child and every parent.

The prototype of this personalizing genre was Anne Frank's famous *Diary.* First published in Holland in 1947,[59] the edited journals appeared in English in 1952. They became the basis for a Pulitzer Prize-winning Broadway play in 1955 and in 1959 a highly acclaimed and equally popular but immensely more widely influential Hollywood movie. This collective representation began in Europe as the journal recorded by a young Dutch girl in hiding from the Nazis and evolved, via a phase of Americanization, into a universal symbol of suffering and transcendence. This transmogrification was possible, in the first place, precisely because Anne's daily jottings focused less on the external events of war and Holocaust – from which she was very much shut off – than on her inner psychological turmoil and the human relationships of those who shared her confinement. Anne's father, Otto Frank, the only family member surviving the camps, supervised the publications and dramatizations of his daughter's journals, and he perceived very clearly the relation between Anne's personal focus and the *Diary*'s potentially universalizing appeal. Writing to Meyer Levin, a potential dramatist who insisted, by contrast, on the specifically Jewish quality of the reminiscence, Otto Frank replied that

> as to the Jewish side you are right that I do not feel the same you do . . . I always said that Anne's book is not a war book. War is the background. It is not a Jewish book either, though [a] Jewish sphere, sentiment and surrounding is the background . . . It is read and understood more by gentiles than in Jewish circles. So do not make a Jewish play out of it. (Quoted in Doneson 1987: 152)[60]

When dramatists for the *Diary* were finally chosen – Francis Goodrich and Albert Hackett – Frank criticized their initial drafts on similar grounds.

> Having read thousands of reviews and hundreds of personal letters about Anne's book from different countries in the world, I know what creates the impression of it on people and their impressions ought to be conveyed by the play to the public. Young people identify themselves very frequently with Anne in their struggle during puberty and the problems of the relations [between] mother–daughter are existing all over the world. These and the love affair with Peter attract young people, whereas parents, teachers, and psychologists learn about the inner feelings of the young generation. When I talked to Mrs [Eleanor] Roosevelt about the book, she urged me to give permission for [the] play and film as only then we could reach the masses and influence them by the mission of the book which she saw in Anne's wish to work for mankind, to achieve something valuable still after her death, her horror against war and discrimination. (Quoted in Doneson 1987: 153)

This impulse to facilitate identification and moral extension prompted the dramatists to translate into English the *Diary*'s pivotal Hanukkah song, which was sung, and printed, in the original Hebrew in the earlier book version. They explained their reasoning in a letter to Frank. To have left the song in its original Hebrew, they wrote, would set the characters in the play apart from the people watching them ... for the majority of our audience is not Jewish. And the thing that we have striven for, toiled for, fought for throughout the whole play is to make the audience understand and identify themselves ... to make them one with them ... that will make them feel "that, but for the grace of God, might have been I". (Quoted in Doneson 1987: 154)

Frank agreed, affirming that it "was my point of view to try to bring Anne's message to as many people as possible even if there are some who think it a sacrilege" from a religious point of view (quoted in Doneson 1987: 154). Years later, after the unprecedented success of both the theatre and screen plays, the dramatists continued to justify their decision to abandon Hebrew in the dramaturgic terms of facilitating psychological identification and symbolic extension.

What we all of us hoped, and prayed for, and what we are devoutly thankful to have achieved, is an identification of the audience with the people in hiding. They are seen, not as some strange people, but persons like themselves, thrown into this horrible situation. With them they suffer the deprivations, the terrors, the moments of tenderness, of exaltation and courage beyond belief. (Quoted in Doneson 1987: 155)

In the course of the 1960s, Anne Frank's tragic story laid the basis for psychological identification and symbolic extension on a mass scale. In 1995, the director of Jewish Studies at Indiana University reported that

The Diary of a Young Girl is ... widely read in American schools, and American youngsters regularly see the stage and film versions as well. Their teachers encourage them to identify with Anne Frank and to write stories, essays, and poems about her. Some even see her as a kind of saint and pray to her. During their early adolescent years, many American girls view her story as their story, her fate as somehow bound up with their fate. (Rosenfeld 1995: 37)

The symbolic transformation effected by Anne Frank's Diary established the dramatic parameters and the stage for the rush of books, television shows, and movies that in the decades following crystallized the mass murder of the Jews as the central episode in a tragic rather than progressive social narrative. As this new genre became institutionalized, representation of Nazism and the Second World War focused less and less on the historical actors who had once been considered central. In 1953 the acclaimed Billy Wilder movie Stalag 17 had portrayed the grueling plight of US soldiers in a German prisoner-of-war camp. It never mentioned the Jews (Shapiro 1992: 4).

In the early 1960s, a widely popular evening television show, *Hogan's Heroes,* also portrayed American soldiers in a Nazi prison. It didn't mention "Jews," either. Indeed, the prison camp functioned as a site for comedy, lampooning the misadventures arising from the casual intermixing of Americans with Nazi camp guards and often portraying the latter as bemusing, well-intended buffoons. By the late 1960s, neither comedy nor romance was a genre that audiences felt comfortable applying to that earlier historical time. Nor was it possible to leave out of any dramatization what by then was acknowledged to be the period's central historical actor, the concentration-camp Jews.[61]

This transition was solidified in Western popular culture by the miniseries *Holocaust,* the stark family drama that unfolded over successive evenings to a massive American audience in April 1978. This four-part, nine-and-a-half-hour drama, watched by nearly 100 million Americans, personalized the grisly and famous landmarks of the Third Reich, following ten years in the lives of two fictional families, one of assimilated Jews and the other of a high-ranking SS official.

This extraordinary public attention was repeated, to even greater cathartic effect, when the bathetic drama was later broadcast to record-breaking television audiences in Germany.[62] German critics, commentators, and large sections of the public at large were transfixed by what German commentators described as "the most controversial series of all times" and as "the series that moved the world." During and after this German broadcast, which was preceded by careful public preparation and accompanied by extensive private and public discussion, German social scientists conducted polls and interviews to trace its remarkable effects. They discovered that the resulting shift in public opinion had put a stop to a burgeoning "Hitler revival" and quelled long-standing partisan demands for "balance" in the presentation of the Jewish mass murder. In the wake of the drama, neutralizing terms like "the Final Solution" gave way in German popular and academic discussion to the English term *Holocaust,* and the German Reichstag removed the statute of limitations on Nazis who had participated in what were now defined not as war crimes but as crimes against humanity. The trauma-drama thus continued to work its universalizing effects.[63]

Enlarging the Circle of Perpetrators. Corresponding to the personalization that expanded identification with the victims of the tragedy, a new understanding developed of the perpetrators of the Holocaust that removed them from their historically specific particularities and made them into universal figures with whom members of widely diverse groups felt capable not of sympathizing but of identifying. The critical event initiating this reconsideration was undoubtedly the 1961 trial of Adolf Eichmann in Jerusalem. Here was a personal and singular representation of the Nazis' murders brought back into the present from the abstract mists of historical time, compelled to "face the music" after being captured by Israeli security forces in a daring extralegal mission right out of a spy novel or science fiction book. The trial received extraordinary press coverage in the United States. That summer, Gallup conducted a series of in-depth interviews with five hundred randomly selected residents of Oakland, California, and found that 84 percent of those sampled met the minimum criterion for awareness of this faraway event, a striking statistic, given American indifference to foreign affairs (Lipstadt 1996: 212, n. 54). At least seven books were published about Eichmann and his trial in the following year (196).

The first legal confrontation with the Holocaust since Nuremburg, the trial was staged by Israel not to generalize away from the originating events but to get back to them. As Prime Minister Ben-Gurion put it, the trial would give "the generation that was born and educated after the Holocaust in Israel . . . an opportunity to get acquainted with the details of this tragedy about which they knew so little" (Braun 1994: 183). The lessons were to be drawn from, and directed to, particular places and particular peoples, to Germany, the Nazis, Israel, and the Jews – in Ben-Gurion's words, to "the dimensions of the tragedy which *our people* experienced" (Lipstadt 1996: 213, italics added). By the time it was over, however, the Eichmann trial paradoxically had initiated a massive universalization of Nazi evil, best captured by Hannah Arendt's enormously controversial insistence that the trial compelled recognition of the "banality of evil." This framing of Nazi guilt became highly influential, even as it was sharply and bitterly disputed by Jews and non-Jews alike. For as a banally evil person, Eichmann could be "everyman." Arendt herself had always wanted to make just such a point. In her earliest reaction to the Nazi murders, the philosopher had expressed horror and astonishment at the Nazis' absolute inhumanity. For this she was rebuked by her mentor and friend Karl Jaspers, who cautioned against making the Nazis into "monsters" and "supermen." To do so, Jaspers warned, would merely confirm the Nazis in their grandiose Nietzchean fantasies and relieve others of responsibility as well.[64] Because of Arendt's singular influence, the antagonists in the trauma began to seem not so different from anybody else.[65] The trial and its aftermath eventually became framed in a manner that narrowed the once great distance between postwar democratic audience and evil Nazis, connecting them rather than isolating them from one another. This connection between audience and antagonist intensified the trauma's tragic dramaturgy.

During this same period, other forces also had the effect of widening the circle of "perpetrators." Most spectacularly, there was Stanley Milgram's experiment demonstrating that ordinary, well-educated adult men would "just follow the orders" of professional authority, even to the point of gravely endangering the lives of innocent people. These findings raised profoundly troubling questions about the "good nature" of all human beings and the democratic capacity of any human society. Milgram appeared on the cover of *Time* magazine, and "the Milgram experiment" became part of the folklore of the 1960s. It generalized the capacity for radical evil, first demonstrated by the Nazis, to the American population at large, synergistically interacting with the symbolic reconstruction of perpetrators that Arendt on Eichmann had begun. In one interview Milgram conducted with a volunteer after he had revealed to him the true nature of the experiment, the volunteer remarked: "As my wife said: 'You can call yourself Eichmann'" (quoted in Novick 1999: 137).[66]

In the decades that followed, other powerful cultural reconstructions of the perpetrators followed in this wake. In 1992, Christopher Browning published a widely discussed historical ethnography called *Ordinary Men: Reserve Police Battalion 101 and the Final Solution in Poland* (Browning 1992), which focused on the everyday actions and motives of Germans who were neither members of the professional military nor particularly ideological but who nonetheless carried out systematic and murderous cleansings of the Jews. When four years later Daniel Goldhagen published *Hitler's Willing Executioners: Ordinary Germans and the Holocaust* (1996), his aim was to shift blame back to what he described as the unprecedented and particular kind of anti-Semitism, what he called "eliminationist," of the Germans themselves. Browning's critical response to Goldhagen was based on historical evidence, but it also decried the moral particularity that Goldhagen's argument seemed to entail. Indeed, Browning connected his empirical findings about the "ordinariness" of perpetrators to the necessity for universalizing the moral implications of Nazi crimes, and in doing so he pointed all the way back to Milgram's earlier findings.

What allowed the Nazis to mobilize and harness the rest of society to the mass murder of European Jewry? Here I think that we historians need to turn to the insights of social psychology – the study of psychological reactions to social situations ... We must ask, what really is a human being? We must give up the comforting and distancing notions that the perpetrators of the Holocaust were fundamentally a different kind of people because they were products of a radically different culture. (Browning, 1996: A72)[67]

In the realm of popular culture, Steven Spielberg's blockbuster movie *Schindler's List* must also be considered in this light. In a subtle but unmistakable manner, the movie departicularizes the perpetrators by showing the possibilities that "even Germans" could be good.[68]

Losing Control of the Means of Symbolic Production

It was in this context of tragic transformation – as personalization of the drama increased identification beyond the Jewish victims themselves, and as the sense of moral culpability became fundamentally widened beyond the Nazis themselves – that the United States government, and the nation's authoritative interlocutors, lost control over the telling of the Holocaust story. When the American government and its allies defeated Nazi Germany in 1945 and seized control of strategic evidence from the death camps, they had taken control of the representation process away from the Nazis and assured that the Jewish mass murder would be presented in an anti-Nazi way. In this telling of the story, naturally enough, the former Allies – America most powerfully but Britain and France as well – presented themselves as the moral protagonists, purifying themselves as heroic carriers of the good. As the 1960s unfolded, the Western democracies were forced to concede this dominant narrative position. This time around, however, control over the means of symbolic production changed hands as much for cultural reasons as by the force of arms.[69]

In the "critical years" from the mid-1960s to the end of the 1970s, the United States experienced a sharp decline in its political, military, and moral prestige. It was during this period that, in the eyes of tens of millions of Americans and others, the domestic and international opposition to America's prosecution of the Vietnam War transformed the nation, and especially its government and armed forces, into a symbol not of salvationary good but of apocalyptic evil. This transformation was intensified by other outcroppings of "the sixties," particularly the revolutionary impulses that emerged out of the student and black power movements inside the United States and guerilla movements outside it. These "real-world" problems allowed

71

the United States to be identified in terms that had, up until that time, been reserved exclusively for the Nazi perpetrators of the Holocaust. According to the progressive narrative, it could only be the Allies' Second World War enemy who represented radical evil. As America became "Amerika," however, napalm bombs were analogized with gas pellets and the flaming jungles of Vietnam with the gas chambers. The powerful American army that claimed to be prosecuting a "good war" against Vietnamese communists – in analogy with the lessons that Western democracies had learned in their earlier struggle against Nazism – came to be identified, by influential intellectuals and a wide swath of the educated Western public, as perpetrating genocide against the helpless and pathetic inhabits of Vietnam. Bertrand Russell and Jean-Paul Sartre established a kind of counter-"War Crimes Tribunal" to apply the logic of Nuremberg to the United States. Indefensible incidents of civilian killings, like the My Lai massacre of 1968, were represented not as anomalous incidents, but as typifications of this new American-made tragedy.[70]

This process of material deconstruction and symbolic inversion further contributed to the universalization of the Holocaust: It allowed the moral criteria generated by its earlier interpretation to be applied in a less nationally specific and thus less particularistic way. This inversion undermined still further the progressive narrative under which the mass killings of the Jews had earlier been framed. The ability to leave the trauma-drama behind, and to press ahead toward the future, depended on the material and symbolic existence of an unsullied protagonist who could provide salvation for survivors by leading them into the promised land. "Vietnam" and "the sixties" undercut the main agent of this progressive narrative. The result was a dramatic decline in the confidence that a new world order could be constructed in opposition to violence and coercion; if the United States itself committed war crimes, what chance could there be for modern and democratic societies ever to leave mass murder safely behind?

As a result of these material and symbolic events, the contemporary representatives of the historic enemies of Nazism lost control over the means of symbolic production. The power to present itself as the purified protagonist in the world-wide struggle against evil slipped out of the hands of the American government and patriotic representatives more generally, even as the framing of the drama's triggering trauma shifted from progress to tragedy. The ability to cast and produce the trauma-drama, to compel identification and channel catharsis, spread to other nations and to anti-government groups, and even to historic enemies of the Jewish people. The archetypical trauma-drama of the twentieth century became ever more generalized and more accessible, and the criteria for moral responsibility in social relations, once closely tied to American perspectives and interests, came to be defined in a more evenhanded, more egalitarian, more self-critical – in short, a more universalistic – way.

Perhaps the most visible and paradoxical effect of this loss of the American government's control over the means of symbolic production control was that the morality of American leadership in the Second World War came to be questioned in a manner that established polluting analogies with Nazism.[71] One issue that now became "troubling," for example, was the justification for the Allied firebombings of Dresden and Tokyo. The growing climate of relativism and reconfiguration threatened to undermine the coding, weighting, and narrating that once had provided a compelling rationale for those earlier events that were in themselves so massively destructive of civilian life. In a similar manner, but with much more significant repercussions, the symbolic implications of the atomic bombings of Hiroshima and Nagasaki began to be fundamentally reconfigured.

From being conceived as stages in the unfolding of the progressive narrative, influential groups of Westerners came to understand the atomic bombings as vast human tragedies. Younger generations of Americans, in fact, were increasingly responsive to the view of these events that had once been promoted exclusively by Japan, the fascist Axis power against which their elders had waged war. The interpretation of the suffering caused by the atomic bombings became separated from the historical specifics of time and place. With this generalization, the very events that had once appeared as high points of the progressive narrative came to be constructed as unjustifiable, as human tragedies, as slaughters of hundreds of thousands of innocent and pathetic human beings – in short, as typifications of a "Holocaust."[72]

Perhaps the most pointed example of what could happen after America lost control over the Holocaust story was the way in which its redemptive role in the narrative was challenged. Rather than being portrayed as the chief prosecutor of Nazi perpetrators – as chief prosecutor, the narrative's protagonist along with the victims themselves – the American and the British wartime governments were accused of having at least indirect responsibility for allowing the Nazis to carry out their brutal work. A steady stream of revisionist historical scholarship emerged, beginning in the 1970s, suggesting that the anti-Semitism of Roosevelt and Churchill and of American and British citizens had prevented them from acting to block the mass killings; for they had received authenticated information about German plans and activities as early as June 1942.[73]

For many, this analogical linkage between the Allies and the perpetrators quickly became accepted as historical fact. On September 27, 1979, when the President's Commission on the Victims of the Holocaust issued a report recommending the American establishment of a Holocaust Museum, it listed as one of its primary justifications that such a public construction would give the American nation an opportunity to compensate for its early, "disastrous" indifference to the plight of the Jews (quoted in Linenthal 1995: 37). When the museum itself was eventually constructed, it enshrined this inversion of the progressive narrative in the exhibitions themselves. The third floor of the museum is filled with powerfully negative images of the death camps, and is attached by an internal bridge to a tower whose rooms display actual artifacts from the camps. As visitors approach this bridge, in the midst of the iconic representations of evil, they confront a photomural of a US Air Force intelligence photograph of Auschwitz-Birkenau, taken on May 31, 1944. The text attached to the mural informs visitors: "Two freight trains with Hungarian Jews arrived in Birkenau that day; the large-scale gassing of these Jews was beginning. The four Birkenau crematoria are visible at the top of the photograph" (quoted in Linenthal 1995: 217). Placed next to the photomural is what the principal ethnographer of the museum project, Edward Linenthal, has called "an artifactual indictment of American indifference." It is a letter, dated August 14, 1944, from John J. McCloy, assistant secretary of war. According to the text, McCoy "rejected a request by the World Jewish Congress to bomb the Auschwitz concentration camp." This rejection is framed in the context not of physical impossibility, or in terms of the vicissitudes of a world war, but as the result of moral diminution. Visitors are informed that the US Air Force "could have bombed Auschwitz as early as May 1944," since US bombers had "struck Buna, a synthetic-rubber works relying on slave labor, located less than five miles east of Auschwitz-Birkenau." But despite this physical possibility, the text goes on to note, the death camp "remained untouched." The effective alignment of Allied armies with Nazi perpetrators is more than implicit: "Although bombing Auschwitz would have killed many prisoners, it would also have halted the operation of the gas chambers and, ultimately, saved the lives of many more" (quoted in Linenthal 1995: 217–18). This authoritative reconstruction is not a brute empirical fact, any more than the framework that had previous sway. In fact, within the discipline of American history, the issue of Allied indifference remains subject to intensive debate (Linenthal 1995: 219–24).[74] At every point in the construction of a public discourse, factual chronicles must be encased in symbolically coded and narrated frames.

Eventually, this revision of the progressive narrative about exclusively Nazi perpetrators extended, with perhaps even more profound consequences, to other Allied powers and to the neutrals in that earlier conflict as well. As the charismatic symbol of French resistance to German occupation, Charles de Gaulle had woven a narrative, during and after the war, that purified his nation by describing it as first the victim and later the courageous opponent of Nazi domination and the "foreign" collaborators in Vichy.[75] By the late 1970s and 1980s, however, a younger generation of French and non-French historians challenged this definition, seriously polluting the earlier Republican government, and even some of its postwar socialist successors, by documenting massive French collaboration with the anti-democratic, anti-Semitic regime.[76]

In the wake of these reversals, it seemed only a matter of time until the nations who had been "neutral" during the earlier conflict would also be forced to relinquish symbolic control over how their own stories were told, at least in the theater of Western opinion, if not on their own national stage. Austria, for example, had long depicted itself as a helpless victim of Nazi Germany. When Kurt Waldheim ascended to the position of secretary-general of the United Nations, however, his hidden association with the Hitler regime was revealed, and the symbolic status of the Austrian nation, which rallied behind their ex-president, began to be publicly polluted as a result.[77] Less than a decade later, Switzerland became subject to similar inversion of its symbolic fortunes. The tiny republic had prided itself on its long history of decentralized canton democracy and the benevolent, universalizing neutrality of its Red Cross. In the mid-nineties, journalists and historians documented that the wartime Swiss government had "purified" Nazi gold. In return for gold that had been plundered from the bodies of condemned and already dead Jews, Swiss bankers gave to Nazi authorities acceptable, unmarked currency that could much more readily be used to finance the war.

This discussion of how the non-Jewish agents of the progressive narrative were undercut by "real-world" developments would be incomplete without some mention of how the Israeli government, which represented the other principal agent of the early, progressive Holocaust story, also came to be threatened with symbolic

75

reconfiguration. The rise of Palestinian liberation movements inverted the Jewish nation's progressive myth of origin, for it suggested, at least to more liberally inclined groups, an equation between Nazi and Israeli treatment of subordinate ethnic and religious groups. The battle for cultural position was not, of course, given up without a fight. When Helmut Schmidt, chancellor of West Germany, spoke of Palestinian rights, Menachem Begin, prime minister of Israel, retorted that Schmidt, a Wehrmacht officer in the Second World War, had "remained faithful to Hitler until the last moment," insisting that the Palestine Liberation Organization was a "neo-Nazi organization" (quoted in Novick 1994: 161). This symbolic inversion *vis-à-vis* the newly generalized and reconfigured Holocaust symbol was deepened by the not-unrelated complicity of Israel in the massacres that followed the Lebanon invasion and by the documented reports of Palestinian torture and occasional death in Israeli prisons.

The Holocaust as Bridging Metaphor

Each of the cultural transformations and social processes I have described has had the effect of universalizing the moral questions provoked by the mass killings of the Jews, of detaching the issues surrounding the systematic exercise of violence against ethnic groups from any particular ethnicity, religion, nationality, time, or place. These processes of detachment and deepening emotional identification are thoroughly intertwined. If the Holocaust were not conceived as a tragedy, it would not attract such continuous, even obsessive attention; this attention would not be rewarded, in turn, if the Holocaust were not understood in a detached and universalizing way. Symbolic extension and emotional identification both are necessary if the audience for a trauma, and its social relevance, are to be dramatically enlarged. I will call the effects of this enlargement the "engorgement of evil."

Norms provide standards for moral judgment. What is defined as evil in any historical period provides the most transcendental content for such judgments. What Kant called radical evil, and what I have called here, drawing on Durkheim, sacred-evil, refers to something considered absolutely essential to defining the good "in our time." Insofar as the "Holocaust" came to define inhumanity in our time, then, it served a fundamental moral function. "Post-Holocaust morality"[78] could perform this role, however, only in a sociological way: it became a bridging metaphor that social groups of uneven power and legitimacy applied to parse ongoing events as good and evil in real historical time. What the "Holocaust" named as the most fundamental evil was the intentional, systematic, and organized employment of violence against members of a stigmatized collective group, whether defined in a primordial or an ideological way. Not only did this representation identify as radical evil the perpetrators and their actions but it polluted bystanders as well. According to the standards of post-Holocaust morality, one became normatively required to make an effort to intervene against any holocaust, regardless of personal consequences and cost. For as a crime against humanity, a "holocaust" is taken to be a threat to the continuing existence of humanity itself. It is impossible, in this sense, to imagine a sacrifice that would be too great when humanity itself is at stake.[79]

Despite the moral content of the Holocaust symbol, then, the primary, first-order effects of this sacred-evil do not work in a ratiocinative way. Radical evil is a philosophical term, and it suggests that evil's moral content can be defined and discussed rationally. Sacred-evil, by contrast, is a sociological term, and it suggests that defining radical evil, and applying it, involves motives and relationships, and institutions, that work more like those associated with religious institutions than with ethical doctrine. In order for a prohibited social action to be powerfully moralized, the symbol of this evil must become engorged. An engorged evil overflows with badness. Evil becomes labile and liquid; it drips and seeps, ruining everything it touches. Under the sign of the tragic narrative, the Holocaust did become engorged, and its seepage polluted everything with which it came into contact.

Metonymy

This contact pollution established the basis for what might be called metonymic guilt. Under the progressive narrative, guilt for the genocidal mass killings depended on being directly and narrowly responsible in the legal sense worked out and applied at the Nuremberg trials. It was not a matter simply of being "associated" with mass murders. In this legal framework, any notion of collective responsibility, the guilt of the Nazi party, the German government, much less the German nation, was ruled as unfair, as out of bounds. But as the Holocaust became engorged with evil, and as post-Holocaust morality developed, guilt could no longer be so narrowly confined. Guilt now came from simple propinquity, in semiotic terms from metonymic association.

To be guilty of sacred-evil did not mean, anymore, that one had committed a legal crime. It was about the imputation of a moral one. One cannot defend oneself against an imputed moral crime by pointing to exculpating circumstances or lack of direct involvement. The issue is one of pollution, guilt by actual association. The solution is not the rational demonstration of innocence but ritual cleansing: purification. In the face of metonymic association with evil, one must engage in performative actions, not only in ratiocinative, cognitive arguments. As the "moral conscience of Germany," the philosopher Jürgen Habermas, put it during the now famous *Historichstreich* among German historians during the 1980s, the point is to "attempt to expel shame," not to engage in "empty phrases" (quoted in Kampe 1987: 63). One must *do* justice and *be* righteousness. This performative purification is achieved by returning to the past, entering symbolically into the tragedy, and developing a new relation to the archetypal characters and crimes. Habermas wrote that it was "only after and through Auschwitz" that postwar Germany could once again attach itself "to the political culture of the West" (quoted in Kampe 1987: 63). Retrospection is an effective path toward purification because it provides for catharsis, although of course it doesn't guarantee it. The evidence for having achieved catharsis is confession. If there is neither the acknowledgment of guilt nor sincere apology, punishment in the legal sense may be prevented, but the symbolic and moral taint will always remain.

Once the trauma had been dramatized as a tragic event in human history, the engorgement of evil compelled contemporaries to return to the originating trauma-drama and to rejudge every individual or collective entity who was, or might have been, even remotely involved. Many individual reputations became sullied in this way. The list of once admired figures who were "outed" as apologists for, or participants in, the anti-Jewish mass murders stretched from such philosophers as Martin Heidegger to such literary figures as Paul de Man and such political leaders as Kurt Waldheim. In the defenses mounted by these tarnished figures or their supporters, the suggestion was never advanced that the Holocaust does not incarnate evil – an inhibition that implicitly reveals the trauma's engorged, sacred quality. The only possible defense was that the accused had, in fact, never been associated with the trauma in any way.

More than two decades ago, the US Justice Department established the Office of Special Investigation, the sole purpose of which was to track down and expel not only major but also minor figures who had been associated in some manner with Holocaust crimes. Since then, the bitter denunciations of deportation hearings have echoed throughout virtually every Western country. In such proceedings, the

emotional-cum-normative imperative is to assert the moral require-
ments for humanity. Media stories revolve around questions of the
"normal," as in how could somebody who seems like a human being,
who since the Second World War has been an upstanding member
of the (French, American, Argentinian) community, have ever been
involved in what now is universally regarded as an anti-human event?
Issues of legality are often overlooked, for the issue is purification of
the community through expulsion of a polluted object.[80] Frequently,
those who are so polluted give up without a fight. In the spate of
recent disclosures about Jewish art appropriated by Nazis and currently belonging to Western museums, directors have responded
simply by asking for time to catalogue the marked holdings to make
them available to be retrieved.

Analogy

The direct, metonymic association with Nazi crimes is the most overt
effect of the way evil seeps from the engorged Holocaust symbol,
but it is not the cultural process most often employed. The bridging metaphor works much more typically, and profoundly, through
the device of analogy. In the 1960s and 1970s, such analogical
bridging powerfully contributed to a fundamental revision in moral
understandings of the historical treatment of minorities inside the
United States. Critics of earlier American policy, and representatives
of minority groups themselves, began to suggest analogies between
various minority "victims" of white American expansion and the
Jewish victims of the Holocaust. This was particularly true of
Native Americans, who argued that genocide had been committed
against them, an idea that gained wide currency and that eventually
generated massive efforts at legal repair and monetary payments.[81]
Another striking example of this domestic inversion was the dramatic reconfiguration, in the 1970s and 1980s, of the American
government's internment of Japanese-American citizens during the
Second World War. Parallels between this action and Nazi prejudice and exclusion became widespread, and the internment camps
became reconfigured as concentration camps. What followed from
this symbolic transformation were not only formal governmental "apologies" to the Japanese-American people but also actual
monetary "reparations."

In the 1980s, the engorged, free-floating Holocaust symbol became
analogically associated with the movement against nuclear power and
nuclear testing and, more generally, with the ecological movements

that emerged during that time. Politicians and intellectuals gained influence in their campaigns against the testing and deployment of nuclear weapons by telling stories about the "nuclear holocaust" that would be unleashed if their own, democratic governments continued their nuclear policies. By invoking this Holocaust-inspired narrative, they were imagining a disaster that would have such generalized, supranational effects that the historical particularities of ideological rightness and wrongness, winners and losers, would no longer matter. In a similar manner, the activists' evocative depictions of the "nuclear winter" that would result from the nuclear holocaust gained striking support from the images of "Auschwitz," the iconic representations of which were rapidly becoming a universal medium for expressing demented violence, abject human suffering, and "meaningless" death. In the environmental movement, claims were advanced that the industrial societies were committing "ecological genocide" against species of plant and animal life and that there was a danger that Earth itself would be exterminated.

In the 1990s, the evil that seeped from the engorged metaphor provided the most compelling analogical framework for framing the Balkan events. While there certainly was dispute over which historical signifier of violence would provide the "correct" analogical reference – dictatorial purge, ethic rampage, civil war, ethnic cleansing, or genocide – it was the engorged Holocaust symbol that propelled first American diplomatic and then American–European military intervention against Serbian ethnic violence.[82] The part played by this symbolic analogy was demonstrated during the early US Senate debate in 1992. Citing "atrocities" attributed to Serbian forces, Senator Joseph Lieberman told reporters that "we hear echoes of conflicts in Europe little more than fifty years ago." During the same period, the Democratic presidential nominee, Bill Clinton, asserted that "history has shown us that you can't allow the mass extermination of people and just sit by and watch it happen." The candidate promised, if elected, to "begin with air power against the Serbs to try to restore the basic conditions of humanity," employing antipathy to distance himself from the polluting passivity that had retrospectively been attributed to the Allies during the initial trauma-drama itself (quoted in *Congressional Quarterly*, August 8, 1992: 2374). While President Clinton initially proved more reluctant than candidate Clinton to put this metaphorical linkage into material form – with the resulting deaths of tens of thousands of innocents – it was the threat of just such military deployment that eventually forced Serbia to sign the Dayton Accords and to stop what were widely represented, in the

American and European media, as its genocidal activities in Bosnia and Herzegovina.

When the Serbians threatened to enter Kosovo, the allied bombing campaign was initiated and justified by evoking the same symbolic analogies and antipathies. The military attacks were represented as responding to the widely experienced horror that the trauma-drama of the Holocaust was being reenacted "before our very eyes." Speaking to a veterans' group at the height of the bombing campaign, President Clinton engaged in analogical bridging to explain why the current Balkan confrontation should not be understood, and thus tolerated, as "the inevitable result . . . of centuries-old animosities." He insisted that these murderous events were unprecedented because they were a "systematic slaughter," carried out by "people with organized, political and military power," under the exclusive control of a ruthless dictator, Slobodan Milosevic. "You think the Germans would have perpetrated the Holocaust on their own without Hitler? Was there something in the history of the German race that made them do this? No. We've got to get straight about this. This is some-thing political leaders do" (*New York Times,* May 14, 1999: A 12).

The same day in Germany, Joschka Fischer, foreign minister in the coalition "Red–Green" government, appeared before a special congress of his Green Party to defend the allied air campaign. He, too, insisted that the uniqueness of Serbian evil made it possible to draw analogies with the Holocaust. Fischer's deputy foreign min-ister and party ally, Ludger Volmer, drew rousing applause when, in describing President Milosevic's systematic cleansing policy, he declared: "My friends, there is only one word for this, and that word is Fascism." A leading opponent of the military intervention tried to block the bridging process by symbolic antipathy. "We are against drawing comparisons between the murderous Milosevic regime and the Holocaust," he proclaimed, because "doing so would mean an unacceptable diminishment of the horror of Nazi Fascism and the genocide against European Jews." Arguing that the Kosovars were not the Jews and Milosevic not Hitler protected the sacred-evil of the Holocaust, but the attempted antipathy was ultimately unconvincing. About 60 percent of the Green Party delegates believed the analogies were valid and voted to support Fischer's position.[83]

Two weeks later, when the allied bombing campaign had not yet succeeded in bringing Milosevic to heel, President Clinton asked Elie Wiesel to make a three-day tour of the Kosovar Albanians' refugee camps. A spokesperson for the US embassy in Macedonia explained that "people have lost focus on why we are doing what we are doing" in the bombing campaign. The proper analogy, in other words, was not being consistently made. The solution was to create direct, metonymic association. "You need a person like Wiesel," the spokesperson continued, "to keep your moral philosophy on track." In the lead sentence of its report on the tour, the *New York Times* described Wiesel as "the Holocaust survivor and Nobel Peace Prize winner." Despite Wiesel's own assertion that "I don't believe in drawing analogies," after visiting the camps analogizing was precisely the rhetoric in which he engaged. Wiesel declared that "I've learned something from my experiences as a contemporary of so many events." What he had learned was to apply the post-Holocaust morality derived from the originating trauma-drama: "When evil shows its face, you don't wait, you don't let it gain strength. You must intervene" (Rohde 1999: 1).

During that tour of a camp in Macedonia, Elie Wiesel had insisted that "the world had changed fifty years after the Holocaust" and that "Washington's response in Kosovo was far better than the ambivalence it showed during the Holocaust." When, two weeks later, the air war, and the growing threat of a ground invasion, finally succeeded in expelling the Serbian forces from Kosovo, the *New York Times* "Week in Review" section reiterated the famous survivor's confidence that the Holocaust trauma had not been in vain, that the drama erected on its ashes had fundamentally changed the world, or at least the West. The Kosovo war had demonstrated that analogies were valid and that the lessons of post-Holocaust morality could be carried out in the most utterly practical way.

> It was a signal week for the West, no doubt about it. Fifty-four years after the Holocaust revelations, America and Europe had finally said "enough," and struck a blow against a revival of genocide. Serbian ethnic cleansers were now routed; ethnic Albanians would be spared further murders and rapes. Germany was exorcising a few of its Nazi ghosts. Human rights had been elevated to a military priority and a preeminent Western value. (Wines 1999: 1)

Twenty-two months later, after Western support had facilitated the electoral defeat of Milosevic and the accession to the Yugoslav presidency of the reformer Vojilslav Kostunica, the former Serbian president and accused war criminal was arrested and forcibly taken to jail. While President Kostunica did not personally subscribe to the authority of the war crimes tribunal in The Hague, there was little doubt that he had authorized Milosevic's imprisonment under intensive American pressure. Though initiated by the Congress rather than the US President, George W. Bush responded to the arrest by

Holocaust typification. He spoke of the "chilling images of terrified women and children herded into trains, emaciated prisoners interned behind barbed wire and mass graves unearthed by United Nations investigators," all traceable to Milosevic's "brutal dictatorship" (quoted in Perlez 2001: 6). Even among those Serbian intellectuals, like Aleksa Djilas, who criticized the Hague tribunal as essentially a political and thus particularistic court, there was recognition that the events took place within a symbolic framework that would inevitably universalize them and contribute to the possibility of a new moral order on a less particularist scale. "There will be a blessing in disguise through his trial," Djilas told a reporter on the day after Milosevic's arrest. "Some kind of new international order is being constructed, intentionally or not ... Something will crystallize: what kinds of nationalism are justified or not, what kinds of intervention are justified or not, how much are great powers entitled to respond, and how. It will not be a sterile exercise" (Erlanger 2001: 8).

In the 1940s, the mass murder of the Jews had been viewed as a typification of the Nazi war machine, an identification that had limited its moral implications. Fifty years later, the Holocaust itself had displaced its historical context. It had itself become the master symbol of evil in relation to which new instances of grievous mass injury would be typified.[84]

Legality

As the rhetoric of this triumphant declaration indicates, the generalization of the Holocaust trauma-drama has found expression in the new vocabulary of "universal human rights." In some part, this trope has simply degendered the Enlightenment commitment to "the universal rights of man" first formulated in the French Revolution. In some other part, it blurs the issue of genocide with social demands for health and basic economic subsistence. Yet from the beginning of its systematic employment in the postwar period, the phrase has also referred specifically to a new legal standard for international behavior that would simultaneously generalize and make more precise and binding what came to be regarded as the "lessons" of the Holocaust events. Representatives of various organizations, both governmental and nongovernmental, have made sporadic but persistent efforts to formulate specific, morally binding codes, and eventually international laws, to institutionalize the moral judgments triggered by metonymic and analogic association with the engorged symbol of evil. This possibility has inspired the noted legal theorist Martha

Minow to suggest an unorthodox answer to the familiar question: "Will the twentieth century be most remembered for its mass atrocities?" "A century marked by human slaughter and torture, sadly, is not a unique century in human history. Perhaps more unusual than the facts of genocides and regimes of torture marking this era is the invention of new and distinctive legal forms of response" (Minow 1998: 1).

This generalizing process began at Nuremberg in 1945, when the long-planned trial of Nazi war leaders was expanded to include the moral principle that certain heinous acts are "crimes against humanity" and must be recognized as such by everyone (Drinan 1987: 334). In its first report on those indictments, the *New York Times* insisted that while "the authority of this tribunal to inflict punishment is directly derived from victory in war," it derived "indirectly from an intangible but nevertheless very real factor which might be called the dawn of a world conscience" (October 9, 1945: 20). This universalizing process continued the following year, when the United Nations General Assembly adopted Resolution 95, committing the international body to "the principles of international law recognized by the charter of the Nuremberg Tribunal and the judgment of the Tribunal" (quoted in Drinan 1987: 334).[85] Two years later, the United Nations issued the Universal Declaration of Human Rights, whose opening preamble evoked the memory of "barbarous acts which have outraged the conscience of mankind."[86] In 1950, the International Law Commission of the United Nations adopted a statement spelling out the principles that the Declaration implied. "The core of these principles states that leaders and nations can be punished for their violations of international law and for their crimes against humanity. In addition, it is not a defense for a person to state that he or she was required to do what was done because of an order from a military or civilian superior" (quoted in Drinan 1987: 334).

In the years since, despite President Truman's recommendation that the United States draft a code of international criminal law around these principles, despite the "human rights" foreign policy of a later Democratic president, Jimmy Carter, and despite the nineteen UN treaties and covenants condemning genocide and exalting the new mandate for human rights, new international legal codes were never drafted (Drinan 1987: 334). Still, over the same period, an increasingly thick body of "customary law" was developed that militated *against* nonintervention in the affairs of sovereign states when they engage in systematic human rights violations.

The long-term historical significance of the rights revolution of the last fifty years is that it has begun to erode the sanctity of state sovereignty and to justify effective political and military intervention. Would there have been American intervention in Bosnia without nearly fifty years of accumulated international opinion to the effect that there are crimes against humanity and violations of human rights which must be punished wherever they arise? Would there be a safe haven for the Kurds in northern Iraq? Would we be in Kosovo? (Ignatieff 1999: 62)[87]

When the former Chilean dictator Augusto Pinochet was arrested in Britain and detained for more than a year in response to an extradition request by a judge in Spain, the reach of this customary law and its possible enforcement by national police first became crystallized in the global public sphere. It was at about the same time that the first internationally sanctioned War Crimes Tribunal since Nuremberg began meeting in The Hague to prosecute those who had violated human rights on any and all sides of the decade's Balkan wars.

The Dilemma of Uniqueness

As the engorged symbol bridging the distance between radical evil and what at some earlier point was considered normal or normally criminal behavior, the reconstructed Holocaust trauma became enmeshed in what might be called the dilemma of uniqueness. The trauma-drama could not function as a metaphor of archetypal tragedy unless it were regarded as radically different from any other evil act in modern times. Yet it was this very status – as a unique event – that eventually compelled it to become generalized and departicularized. For as a metaphor for radical evil, the Holocaust provided a standard of evaluation for judging the evility of other threatening acts. By providing such a standard for comparative judgment, the Holocaust became a norm, initiating a succession of metonymic, analogic, and legal evaluations that deprived it of "uniqueness" by establishing its degrees of likeness or unlikeness to other possible manifestations of evil.

In this regard, it is certainly ironic that this bridging process, so central to universalizing critical moral judgment in the post-Holocaust world, has time after time been attacked as depriving the Holocaust of its significance. Yet these very attacks have often revealed, despite themselves, the trauma-drama's new centrality in ordinary thought and action. One historically oriented critic, for example, mocked the new "Holocaust consciousness" in the United States, citing the fact that the Holocaust "is invoked as reference point in discussions of everything from AIDS to abortion" (Novick 1994: 159). A literature professor complained about the fact that "the language of 'Holocaust'" is now "regularly invoked by people who want to draw public attention to human-rights abuses, social inequalities suffered by racial and ethnic minorities and women, environmental disasters, AIDS, and a whole host of other things" (Rosenfeld 1995: 35). Another scholar decried the fact that "any evil that befalls anyone anywhere becomes a Holocaust" (quoted in Rosenfeld 1995: 35).[88]

While no doubt well-intentioned in a moral sense, such complaints miss the sociological complexities that underlie the kind of cultural-moral process I am exploring here. Evoking the Holocaust to measure the evil of a non-Holocaust event is nothing more, and nothing less, than to employ a powerful bridging metaphor to make sense of social life. The effort to qualify as the referent of this metaphor is bound to entail sharp social conflict, and in this sense social relativization, for successful metaphorical embodiment brings legitimacy and resources. The premise of these relativizing social conflicts is that the Holocaust provides an absolute and nonrelative measure of evil. But the effects of the conflict are to relativize the application of this standard to any particular social event. The Holocaust is unique and not unique at the same time. This insoluble dilemma marks the life history of the Holocaust, once it had become a tragic archetype and a central component of moral judgment in our time.[89] Inga Clendinnen has described this dilemma in a particularly acute way, and her observations exemplify the metaphorical bridging process I have tried to describe here.

There have been too many recent horrors, in Rwanda, in Burundi, in one-time Yugoslavia, with victims equally innocent, killers and torturers equally devoted, to ascribe uniqueness to any one set of atrocities on the grounds of their exemplary cruelty. I find the near-random terror practiced by the Argentinean military, especially their penchant for torturing children before their parents, to be as horrible, as "unimaginable," as the horrible and unimaginable things done by Germans to their Jewish compatriots. Certainly the scale is different – but how much does scale matter to the individual perpetrator or the individual victim?

Again, the willful obliteration of long-enduring communities is surely a vast offence, but for three years we watched the carpet-bombings of Cambodia, when the bombs fell on villagers who could not have had the least understanding of the nature of their offence. *When we think of innocence afflicted, we see those unforgettable children of the Holocaust staring wide-eyed into the camera of their killers, but we also see the image of the little Vietnamese girl, naked, screaming, running down a dusty road, her back aflame with American napalm.* If we grant that "holocaust," the total consumption of offerings by fire, is sinisterly appropriate for the murder of those millions who found their only graves in the air, it is equally appropriate for the victims of Hiroshima, Nagasaki and Dresden [and for] Picasso's horses and humans screaming [in *Guernica*] under attack from untouchable murderers in the sky. (Clendinnen 1999: 14, italics added)

Forgetting or Remembering?

Routinization and Institutionalization

As the sense that the Holocaust was a unique event in human history crystallized and its moral implications became paradoxically generalized, the tragic trauma-drama became increasingly subject to memorialization. Special research centers were funded to investigate its most minute details and to sponsor debates about its wider applications. College courses were devoted to it, and everything, from university chairs to streets and parks, was named for it. Monuments were constructed to honor the tragedy's victims. Major urban centers in the United States, and many outside it as well, constructed vastly expensive, and vastly expansive, museums to make permanent its moral lessons. The US military distributed instructions for conducting "Days of Remembrance," and commemorative ceremonies were held annually in the Capitol Rotunda.

Because of the dilemma of uniqueness, all of these generalizing processes were controversial; they suggested to many observers that the Holocaust was being instrumentalized and commodified, that its morality and affect were being displaced by specialists in profit-making on the one hand and by specialists in merely cognitive expertise on the other. In recent years, indeed, the idea has grown that the charisma of the original trauma-drama is being routinized in a regrettably, but predictably, Weberian way.[90]

The moral learning process that I have described in the preceding pages does not necessarily deny the possibility that instrumentalization develops *after* a trauma-drama has been created and *after* its moral lessons have been externalized and internalized. In American history, for example, even the most sacred of the founding national traumas, the Revolution and the Civil War, have faded as objects of communal affect and collective remembering, and the dramas associated with them have become commodified as well. Still, the implications of what I have presented here suggest that such routinization, even when it takes a monetized and commodified form, does not necessarily indicate meaninglessness. Metaphorical bridging shifts symbolic significance, and audience attention, from the originating trauma to the traumas that follow in a sequence of analogical associations. But it does not, for that, inevitably erase or invert the meanings associated with the trauma that was first in the associational line. Nor does the effort to concretize the cultural meanings of the trauma in monumental forms have this effect. The American Revolution and the Civil War both remain resources for triumphant and tragic narration, in popular and high culture venues. It is only very infrequently, and very controversially, that these trauma-dramas are subjected to the kind of comic framing that would invert their still sacred place in American collective identity. As I have mentioned earlier, it is not commodification, but "comedization" – a change in the cultural framing, not a change in economic status – that indicates trivialization and forgetting.

Memorials and Museums: Crystallizing Collective Sentiment

A less Weberian, more Durkheimian understanding of routinization is needed. When they are first created, sacred-good and sacred-evil are labile and liquid. Objectification can point to the sturdier embodiment of these moral values, and even of the experiences they imply. Currently, the intensifying momentum to memorialize the Holocaust indicates a deepening institutionalization of its moral lessons and the continued recalling of its dramatic experiences rather than their routinization and forgetting. When, after years of conflict, the German parliament approved a plan for erecting a vast memorial of two thousand stone pillars to the victims of the Holocaust in the heart of Berlin, a leading politician proclaimed: "We are not building this monument solely for the Jews. We are building it for ourselves. It will help us confront a chapter in our history" (Cohen 1999: 3).

In the Holocaust museums that are sprouting up throughout the Western world, the design is not to distance the viewer from the object in a dry, deracinated, or "purely factual" way. To the contrary, as a European researcher into this phenomenon has remarked, "Holocaust museums favor strategies designed to arouse strong emotions and particular immersion of the visitor into the past" (Baer 1999).[91] The informational brochure to the Simon Wiesenthal Museum of Tolerance in Los Angeles, which houses the West Coast's largest Holocaust exhibition, promotes itself as a "high tech, hands-on experiential museum that focuses on . . . themes through interactive exhibits" (Baer 1999).

From its very inception in 1979, the Holocaust Museum in Washington, DC, was metonymically connected to the engorged symbolism of evil. According to the official report submitted to President Jimmy Carter by the President's Commission on the Victims of the Holocaust, the purpose of the museum was to "protect against future evil" (quoted in Linenthal 1995: 37). The goal was to create a building through which visitors would reexperience the original tragedy, to find "a means," as some central staff members had once put it, "to convey both dramatically and soberly the enormity of the human tragedy in the death camps" (quoted in Linenthal 1995: 212).[92] Rather than instrumentalizing or commodifying, in other words, the construction was conceived as a critical means for deepening psychological identification and broadening symbolic extension. According to the ethnographer of the fifteen-year planning and construction process, the design team insisted that the museum's interior mood should be so "visceral" that, as the ethnographer of the construction put it, museum visitors "would gain no respite from the narrative."

> The feel and rhythm of space and the setting of mood were important. [The designers] identified different qualities of space that helped to mediate the narrative: constructive space on the third floor, for example, where as visitors enter the world of the death camps, the space becomes tight and mean, with a feeling of heavy darkness. Indeed, walls were not painted, pipes were left exposed, and, except for fire exits and hidden elevators on the fourth and third floors for people who, for one reason or another, had to leave, there is no escape (quoted in Linenthal 1995: 169)

According to the Museum's head designer,

> the exhibition was intended to take visitors on a journey . . . We followed those people under all that pressure as they moved from their normal lives into ghettos, out of ghettos onto trains, from trains to camps, within the pathways of the camps, until finally to the end . . . If visitors could take that same journey, they would understand the story because they will have experienced the story. (Quoted in Linenthal 1995: 174)[93]

The dramatization of the tragic journey is in many respects quite literal, and this fosters identification. The visitor receives a photo passport/identity card representing a victim of the Holocaust, and the museum's permanent exhibition is divided into chronological sections. The fourth floor is "The Assault: 1933–9," the third floor "The

Holocaust: 1940–4," and the second floor "Bearing Witness: 1945." At the end of each floor, visitors are asked to insert their passports to find out what happened to their identity-card "alter egos" during that particular phase of the Holocaust tragedy. By the time visitors have passed through the entire exhibit, they will know whether or not the person with whom they have been symbolically identified survived the horror or perished (Linenthal 1995: 169).

The identification process is deepened by the dramatic technique of personalization. The key, in the words of the project director, was connecting museum visitors to the "real faces of real people" (Linenthal, 1995: 181).[94]

> Faces of Holocaust victims in the exhibition are shattering in their power . . . Polish school teachers, moments before their execution, look at visitors in agony, sullen anger, and despair . . . Two brothers, dressed alike in matching coats and caps, fear etched on their faces, gaze at the camera, into the eyes of the visitors . . . The Faces . . . assault, challenge, accuse, and profoundly sadden visitors throughout the exhibition. (174)[95]

At every point, design decisions about dramatization were made with the narrative of tragedy firmly in mind. Exhibit designers carefully avoided displaying any of the camp prisoners' "passive resistance," for fear it would trigger progressive narratives of heroism and romance. As an historian associated with such decisions remarked, the fear was that such displays might contribute to an "epic" Holocaust narrative in which resistance would gain "equal time" with the narrative of destruction (Linenthal 1995: 192). This dark dramatization, however, could not descend into a mere series of grossly displayed horrors, for this would undermine the identification on which the very communication of the tragic lessons of the Holocaust would depend.

> The design team faced a difficult decision regarding the presentation of horror. Why put so much effort into constructing an exhibition that was so horrible that people would not visit? They worried about word-of-mouth evaluation after opening, and feared that the first visitors would tell family and friends, "Don't go, it's too horrible." . . . The museum's mission was to teach people about the Holocaust and bring about civic transformation; yet . . . the public had to desire to visit. (198)

It seems evident that such memorializations aim to create structures that dramatize the tragedy of the Holocaust and provide opportunities for contemporaries, now so far removed from the original scene, powerfully to reexperience it. In these efforts, personalization remains an immensely important dramatic vehicle, and it continues to provide the opportunity for identification so crucial to the project of universalization. In each Holocaust museum, the fate of the Jews functions as a metaphorical bridge to the treatment of other ethnic, religious, and racial minorities.[96] The aim is manifestly not to "promote" the Holocaust as an important event in earlier historical time, but to contribute to the possibilities of pluralism and justice in the world of today.

From Liberators to Survivors: Witness Testimonies

Routinization of charisma is certainly an inevitable fact of social life, and memorialization a much-preferred way to understand that it can institutionalize, and not only undermine, the labile collective sentiments that once circulated in a liquid form. It is important also not to view the outcome of such processes in a naturalistic, noncultural way. It is not "meaning" that is crystallized but particular meanings. In terms of Holocaust memorialization and routinization, it is the objectification of a narrative about tragedy that has been memorialized, not a narrative about progress.

The postwar memorials to the Second World War were, and are, about heroism and liberation. They centered on American GIs and the victims they helped. If the Holocaust had continued to be narrated within the progressive framework of the anti-Nazi war, it would no doubt have been memorialized in much the same way. Of course, the very effect of the progressive narrative was to make the Holocaust less visible and central, with the result that, as long as representations of contemporary history remained within the progressive framework, few efforts to memorialize the Holocaust were made. For that very reason, the few that were attempted are highly revealing. In Liberty State Park, in New Jersey, within visual sight of the proud and patriotic Statue of Liberty, there stands a statue called *Liberation*. The metal sculpture portrays two figures. The larger, a solemn American GI, walks deliberately forward, his eyes on the ground. He cradles a smaller figure, a concentration camp victim, whose skeletal chest, shredded prison garb, outstretched arms, and vacantly staring eyes exemplify his helplessness (Young 1993: 320–32). Commissioned not only by the State of New Jersey but also by a coalition of American Legion and other veterans' organizations, the monument was dedicated only in 1985. During the ceremony, the state's governor made a speech seeking to reconnect the progressive narrative still embodied by the "last good war" to the growing centrality of the Holocaust narrative, whose symbolic and moral importance had by then already begun to far outstrip it. The defensive and patriotic tone of the speech indicates that, via this symbolic linkage, the state official sought to resist the skepticism about America's place in the world, the very critical attitude that had helped frame the Holocaust in a narrative of tragedy.

> To me, this monument is an affirmation of my American heritage. It causes me to feel deep pride in my American values. The monument says that we, as a collective people, stand for freedom. We, as Americans, are not oppressors, and we, as Americans, do not engage in military conflict for the purpose of conquest. Our role in the world is to preserve and promote that precious, precious thing that we consider to be a free democracy. Today we will remember those who gave their lives for freedom. (321)

The *Liberation* monument, and the particularist and progressive sentiments it crystallized, could not be further removed from the memorial processes that have crystallized in the years since. Propelled by the tragic transformation of the Jewish mass murder, in these memorials the actions and beliefs of Americans are often implicitly analogized with those of the perpetrators, and the US Army's liberation of the camps plays only a minimal role, if any. In these more universalized settings, the focus is on the broader, world-historical causes and moral implications of the tragic event, on creating symbolic extension by providing opportunities for contemporaries to experience emotional identification with the suffering of the victims.

It was in the context of this transformation that there emerged a new genre of Holocaust writing and memorializing, one that focuses on a new kind of historical evidence, direct "testimony," and a new kind of historical actor, the "survivor." Defined as persons who lived through the camp experiences, survivors provide a tactile link with the tragic event. As their social and personal role was defined, they began to write books, give speeches to local and national communities, and record their memories of camp experiences on tape and video. These testimonies have become sacralized repositories of the core tragic experience, with all the moral implications that this suffering has come to entail. They have been the object of two amply funded recording enterprises. One, organized by the Yale University Video Archive of the Holocaust, was already begun in 1981. The other, the Shoah Visual History Foundation, was organized by the film director Steven Spielberg in 1994, in the wake of the world-wide effects of his movie *Schindler's List*.

Despite the publicity these enterprises have aroused and the celebrity that has accrued to the new survivor identity, it is important to see that this new genre of memorialization has inverted the language of liberation that was so fundamental to the earlier, progressive form. It has created not heroes but anti-heroes. Indeed, those who have created and shaped this new genre are decidedly critical of what they see as the "style of revisionism that crept into Holocaust writing after the liberation of the camps." They describe this style as a "natural but misguided impulse to romanticize staying alive and to interpret painful endurance as a form of defiance or resistance" (Langer, 2000: xiv). Arguing that survivor testimony reveals tragedy, not triumph, they suggest that it demands the rejection of any progressive frame.

> No one speaks of having survived through bravery or courage. These are hard assessments for us to accept. We want to believe in a universe that rewards good character and exemplary behavior. We want to believe in the power of the human spirit to overcome adversity. It is difficult to live with the thought that human nature may not be noble or heroic and that under extreme conditions we, too, might turn brutal, selfish, "too inhuman." (Greene and Kumar, 2000: xxv–xxvi)

In reacting against the heroic, progressive frame some of these commentators go so far as to insist on the inherent "meaninglessness" of the Holocaust, suggesting that the testimonies reveal "uncompensated and unredeemable suffering" (Langer 2000: xv). Yet it seems clear that the very effort to create survivor testimony is an effort to maintain the vitality of the experience by objectifying and, in effect, depersonalizing it. As such, it helps to sustain the tragic trauma-drama, which allows an ever-wider audience redemption through suffering. It does so by suggesting the survival not of a few scattered and particular victims but of humanity as such.

> The power of testimony is that it requires little commentary, for witnesses are the experts and they tell their own stories in their own words. The perpetrators work diligently to silence their victims by taking away their names, homes, families, friends, possessions, and lives. The intent was to deny their victims any sense of humanness, to erase their individuality and rob them of all personal voice. Testimony reestablishes the individuality of the victims who survived – and in some instances of those who were killed – and demonstrates the power of their voices. (Greene and Kumar, 2000: xxiv)

Those involved directly in this memorializing process see their own work in exactly the same way. Geoffrey Hartman, the director of the Yale Video Archive, speaks about a new "narrative that emerges through the alliance of witness and interviewer" (Hartman 1996: 153), a narrative based on the reconstruction of a human community.

> However many times the interviewer may have heard similar accounts, they are received as though for the first time. This is possible because, while the facts are known, while historians have labored – and are still laboring – to establish every detail, each of these histories is animated by something in addition to historical knowledge: there is a quest to recover or reconstruct a recipient, an "affective community" . . . and [thus] the renewal of compassionate feelings. (153–4)

However "grim its contents," Hartman insists, testimony does not represent an "impersonal historical digest" but, rather, "that most natural and flexible of human communications, a story – a story, moreover, that, even if it describes a universe of death, is communicated by a living person who answers, recalls, thinks, cries, carries on" (Hartman 1996: 154). The president of the Survivors of the Shoah Visual History Foundation, Michael Berenbaum, suggesting that the goal of the Spielberg group is "to catalogue and to disseminate the testimonies to as many remote sites as technology and budget will permit, [a]ll in the service of education," ties the contemporary moral meaning of the historical events to the opportunity for immediate emotional identification that testimonies provide: "In classrooms throughout the world, the encounter between survivors and children [has] become electrifying, the transmission of memory, a discussion of values, a warning against prejudice, anti-semitism, racism, and indifference" (Berenbaum, 1998: xi).

Is the Holocaust Western?

While the rhetoric of Holocaust generalization refers to its *Weltgeschichte* relevance – its world-historical relevance – throughout this chapter I have tried to be careful in noting that this universalization has primarily been confined to the West. Universalization, as I have described it, depends on symbolically generated, emotionally vicarious participation in the trauma-drama of the mass murder of the Jews. The degree to which this participation is differentially distributed throughout the West is itself a question that further research will have to pursue. This "remembering" is much more pronounced in Western Europe and North America than in Latin America. Mexicans, preoccupied with their national traumas dating back to the European conquest, are much less attached to the "Holocaust" than their northern neighbors – against whose very mythologies Mexicans often define themselves. The result may be that Mexican political culture is informed to a significantly lesser degree by "post-Holocaust morality." On the other hand, it is also possible that Mexicans translate certain aspects of post-Holocaust morality into local terms – for example, into the willingness to limit claims to national sovereignty in the face of demands by indigenous groups legitimating themselves in terms of broadly human rights.

Such variation is that much more intense when we expand our assessment to non-Western areas. What are the degrees of attachment to, vicarious participation in, and lessons drawn from the Holocaust trauma in non-Western civilizations? In Hindu, Buddhist, Confucian, Islamic, African, and still-communist regions and regimes, reference to the Holocaust, when made at all, is by literary and intellectual elites with markedly atypical levels of participation in a global discourse that remains dominated by the United States and Western Europe. Of course, non-Western regions and nations have their own identity-defining trauma-dramas (see Chapter 4, below). What is unclear is the degree to which the cultural work that constructs these traumas, and responds to them, reaches beyond issues of national identity and sovereignty to the universalizing, supranational ethical imperatives increasingly associated with the "lessons of post-Holocaust morality" in the West.

The authorized spokespersons for Japan, for example, have rarely acknowledged the empirical reality of the horrific mass murder their soldiers inflicted on native Chinese in Nanjing, China, during the runup to the Second World War – the "Rape of Nanjing." Much less have they apologized for it, or made efforts to share in the suffering of the Chinese people in a manner that would point to a universalizing ethic by which members of different Asian national and ethnic groupings could be commonly judged. Instead, the atomic bombings of Hiroshima have become an originating trauma for postwar Japanese identity. While producing an extraordinary commitment to pacifism, the dramatization of this trauma, which was inflicted on Japan by its wartime enemy, the United States, has had the effect of confirming rather than dislodging Japan in its role as narrative agent (Hashimoto 2011). The trauma has functioned, in other words, to block any effort to widen the circle of perpetrators, making it less likely that the national history of Japan will be submitted to some kind of supranational standard of judgment.

Such submission is very difficult, of course, in any strongly national context, in the West as well as in the East. Nonetheless, the analysis presented here compels us to ask this question: Can countries or civilizations that do not acknowledge the Holocaust develop universalistic political moralities? Obviously, non-Western nations cannot "remember" the Holocaust, but in the context of cultural globalization they certainly have become gradually aware of its symbolic meaning and social significance. It might also be the case that non-Western nations can develop trauma-dramas that are functional equivalents to the Holocaust (see Chapter 5 below: The Partition chapter). It has been the thesis of this chapter that moral universalism rests on social processes that construct and channel cultural trauma. If this is indeed the case, then globalization will have to involve a very different kind of social process than the ones that students of this supranational development have talked about so far: East and West, North and South must learn to share the experiences of one another's traumas and to take vicarious responsibility for the other's afflictions (see Chapter 6, below).

Geoffrey Hartman has recently likened the pervasive status of the Holocaust in contemporary society to a barely articulated but nonetheless powerful and pervasive legend. "In Greek tragedy . . . with its moments of highly condensed dialogue, the framing legend is so well known that it does not have to be emphasized. A powerful abstraction, or simplification, takes over. In this sense, and in this sense only, the Holocaust is on the way to becoming a legendary event" (Hartman 2000: 16).

Human beings are storytelling animals. We tell stories about our triumphs. We tell stories about tragedies. We like to believe in the verisimilitude of our accounts, but it is the moral frameworks themselves that are real and constant, not the factual material that we employ them to describe. In the history of human societies, it has often been the case that narrative accounts of the same event compete with one another, and that they eventually displace one another over historical time. In the case of the Nazis' mass murder of the Jews, what was once described as a prelude and incitement to moral and social progress has come to be reconstructed as a decisive demonstration that not even the most "modern" improvements in the condition of humanity can ensure advancement in anything other than a purely technical sense. It is paradoxical that a decided increase in moral and social justice may eventually be the unintended result.

HOLOCAUST AND TRAUMA: MORAL RESTRICTION IN ISRAEL

(with Shai M. Dromi)

"Yad Vashem Fires Employee Who Compared Holocaust to Nakba"
Yad Vashem has fired an instructor who compared the trauma of
Jewish Holocaust survivors with the trauma experienced by the
Palestinian people in Israel's War of Independence. Itamar Shapira,
29, of Jerusalem, was fired before Passover from his job as a docent at
the Holocaust Martyrs' and Heroes' Remembrance Authority, after a
teacher with a group of yeshiva students from Efrat made a complaint.
Shapira had worked at Yad Vashem for three and a half years . . .
 Shapira confirmed, in a telephone conversation with Haaretz, that
he had spoken to visitors about the 1948 massacre at Deir Yassin. He
said he did so because the ruins of the Arab village, today a part of
Jerusalem's Givat Shaul neighborhood, can be seen as one leaves Yad
Vashem. "Yad Vashem talks about the Holocaust survivors' arrival
in Israel and about creating a refuge here for the world's Jews. I said
there are people who lived on this land and mentioned that there are
other traumas that provide other nations with motivation," Shapira
said. "The Holocaust moved us to establish a Jewish state and the
Palestinian nation's trauma is moving it to seek self-determination,
identity, land and dignity, just as Zionism sought these things," he said.
The institution's position is that the Holocaust cannot be compared to
any other event and that every visitor can draw his own political conclusions . . . "Yad Vashem would have acted unprofessionally had Itamar
Shapira continued his educational work for the institute," [Yad Vashem
spokeswoman Iris] Rosenberg said. Yad Vashem employs workers and
volunteers from the entire political and social spectrum, who know how
to separate their personal position from their work, she said.
 Shapira said Vad Yashem chooses to examine only some of the events
that took place in the War of Independence. "It is being hypocritical. I
only tried to expose the visitors to the facts, not to political conclusions.
If Yad Vashem chooses to ignore the facts, for example the massacre at

Deir Yassin, or the Nakba ["The Catastrophe," the Palestinians' term for what happened to them after 1948], it means that it's afraid of something and that its historical approach is flawed," Shapira said.

Haaretz, April 23, 2009

"Gaza: Cleric Denounces Possible Holocaust Education"
A Hamas spiritual leader said Monday that teaching Palestinian children about the Nazis' murder of six million Jews would be a "war crime." The leader, Yunis al-Astal, lashed out after hearing that the United Nations Relief and Works Agency was considering the introduction of Holocaust lessons in some of the 221 schools the United Nations [runs] in Gaza. Adding the Holocaust to the curriculum would amount to "marketing a lie and spreading it," Dr. Asatal wrote in a statement. An Israeli government spokesman, Mark Regev, said the comments were "obscene." A United Nations official said no decision had been made on Holocaust education in Gaza.

New York Times, September 1, 2009

These disheartening reports, appearing in two of the world's most sophisticated, liberal, and democratic newspapers, illustrate the idea at the core of this book. References to trauma, and representations about it, are not just individual but social and collective. Who was responsible for a collective trauma, who were its victims, and what was the trauma's moral lessons for our own time? These are not simply theoretical or empirical issues for professional social scientists. They are fundamental concerns of everyday life, matters for reporting in daily newspapers and web sites, and they powerfully affect contemporary conflicts at the individual, institutional, national, and global levels.[1]

As these reports also demonstrate, however, the manner in which collective traumas are presented in everyday life is naturalistic, to the point of being intellectually naive. Traumas are spoken about as if they are simply historical facts, as things that happened, clearly understood events, empirical things that can either be recognized or ignored. How we choose to react to the facts of trauma is presented as if it were simply a matter of personal, individual reflection.

According to the cultural sociological approach, however, neither of these latter suppositions is correct. Collective traumas are not found; they are made. Something awful usually did occur, but how it is represented remains an open question, subject to whirling spirals of signification, fierce power contests, simplifying binaries, subtle stories, fickle audiences, and counter-narrations. Individuals do not respond to traumas but to trauma constructions. How they come to reflect upon them is certainly a matter for individual conscience, but it is also a massively collective thing. Individuals experience the pain and suffering of defeat, and the hopes for future emancipation, in terms of collective stories that engulf and instruct them, sometimes in positive, sometimes in frightening, ways.

In the preceding chapter on the Nazi murder of six million Jews, I explored how the representation of this horrendous event shifted, in the half-century after it transpired, from "war crime" to "Holocaust." As a heinous event associated with Nazism, the mass murder was initially contextualized inside the culture structures that had framed the Second World War, a civilization-versus-barbarism binary, on the one hand, and a progressive narrative of modern amelioration, on the other. For two decades afterward, this binary and narrative frame allowed Western nations to keep the mass murder of the Jews, even as it remained ferociously stigmatized, as an event very much relegated to the past. In the postwar period, people looked to the future and engaged in reconstruction. They saw themselves as building a new, modern, and civilized society, one in which Nazi genocide would never be allowed to happen again. These efforts at civil repair were not illusory. Democracies were reconstructed from dictatorships, and millennia-long anti-Semitic barriers were overcome. Nevertheless, in the course of the 1960s, this grand narrative of postwar progress, which had sequestered racial, religious, and ethnic mass murder in a distant past began, began to be vulnerable and to change.

Collective traumas are complex symbolic-cum-emotional constructions that have significant autonomy from, and power over, social structure and interests in the more material sense. At the same time, however, trauma constructions are affected by the kinds of social groups that promote them, by the distribution of resources to broadcast them, and by the institutional structure of the social arenas in which their construction takes place. With the rise of anti-Western, anti-colonial movements abroad, and the emergence of anti-war movements and racial and ethnic movements of liberation at home, the postwar protagonists of the progressive narrative were profoundly challenged. Their purity became polluted by association with their own ethnic, racial, and religious massacres, and their ability to maintain the civilization-barbarism binary destroyed. Rather than being seen as carriers of universalism, they were accused of being primordial and particularistic themselves. It was as these new understandings developed that the shift from "war crime" to "Holocaust" emerged. Rather than being relegated to the past, the dangers of massive racial, ethnic, and religious domination, and

99

even mass murder, moved forward into the present. They became part of modernity. For contemporaries, the Holocaust shifted from a progressive to a tragic narrative. It became a story about hubris and punishment, a trauma-drama that evoked sorrow and pity; its victims became objects of universal identification, and its perpetrators were now constructed as representing humanity rather than any particular national group. Its bathetic denouement provided a drama of eternal return which contemporaries felt compelled to revisit over and over again. The Holocaust came to be seen as the singular representation of the darkness of the twentieth century, the humbling lesson on which was erected postmodern doubt. Yet, this humbling and tragic lesson also opened up the possibility for judging present and future humankind by a new, more universal moral standard.

I conducted the research for Chapter 2 in the late 1990s. That was a time of cautious optimism. The American and European intervention in Kosovo seemed to provide singular evidence for the universalizing power of the Holocaust effect. Dictatorships were still being turned into democracies, and there was a bubbling effervescence about the emergence of global civil society. It was a time to focus on the emergence of global narratives about the possibility of justice, among which there was no more surprising and inspiring story than the transvaluation of the Jewish mass murder from an historically situated war crime into a tragic trauma-drama whose moral lessons had become central to all modernity. In the words of Bernhard Giesen, this transvaluation process provided "a new transnational paradigm of collective identity" (Giesen 2009: 114), according to which the Holocaust became the "global icon of evil."

We live now in a darker time, more divided, more violent, more tense. We have become much more cautious about the possibilities for a global civil society, more sensitive to the continuing festering of local wounds and their often explosive and debilitating world-wide effects. This is the time to explore the relationship between cultural trauma and collective identity in a different way, elaborating the theory so that it can explain not only more universalizing but also more particularistic and deleterious results. In the present chapter, we return to the historical genealogy of the Holocaust, but connect it with the emergence of a radically different carrier group, a drastically divergent social setting, and spirals of signification that depart sharply in their symbolic meanings and moral implications. We connect Holocaust symbolization not to pluralist Western democracies but to a democracy bent on securing the foundations of a single religion, not to a postwar national context but to a nation founded in war, facing challenges to its very existence for decades, right up until today. For this Jewish nation, despite its progressive aspirations, the memory of the Jewish mass murder connoted tragedy from the outset, and the catharsis produced by iterations of the trauma-drama sustained moral strictures of more particularistic and primordial than universal and civil kinds.

Tragic Dramas, Divergent Effects

Tragic narratives compel members of a collectivity to narrate and symbolically re-experience the suffering of a trauma's victims. If these victims are represented narrowly – as simply the story tellers themselves – the tragic trauma-drama is unlikely to generate sympathy for those on the other side. It creates not identification with extended others but with the story tellers' own ancestors, those who share the same primordial identity as the victims' themselves. The tragic trauma-drama produces catharsis, but it is not the enlightening pity that Aristotle once described. It is more self-pity, a sentiment that blocks identification and undermines the expansion of moral feeling that such contemporary neo-Aristotelians as Martha Nussbaum have prescribed. Rather than a universalizing love for the other, what emerges from such trauma work is a more restrictive self-love, a feeling that cuts imaginative experience short, encouraging emotional splitting and moral scapegoating.

In this emplotment, the moral implications of the drama of eternal return are inverted. Not being able to get beyond the originating trauma, feeling compelled again and again to return to it, reinforces rather than mitigates the particularistic hatreds that inspired the aggression and murder of that earlier time. Narrowing rather than universalizing in morality and affect, earlier hatreds are reproduced, not overcome. Rather than expanded human sympathy for the other, we have Hitler revenging the defeated German people, Serbia's ethnic cleansing, and India and Pakistan's bloody-minded struggles against Islamic and Hindu "intruders" today.[2] We also have the *Nakba*, the construction of the catastrophe that Israeli's founding is believed to have created for the Palestinian people, a trauma that inspires the violently anti-Jewish and anti-Israeli struggles by Palestinian people and Arab states against Zionism and the Israeli state. These polarizing, trauma-inspired struggles have fuelled the tragic-cum-primordial narratives that prevent peace between Arabs and Jews in the Middle East today.

An Israeli Patriot's Lament

In the middle of 2007, David Remnick, the editor of the *New Yorker* magazine, published a controversial "Letter from Jerusalem." It was a conversation with Avraham Burg, once Speaker of the Israel Knesset and former chair both of the World Zionist Organization and the Israeli Jewish Agency. Remnick's conversation with the now embittered Israeli leader points directly to the social processes we wish to illuminate here. "As of this moment," Burg observes, "Israel is a state of trauma in nearly every one of its dimensions." Insisting that this is "not just a theoretical question," he asks, "would our ability to cope with Iran not be much better if we renewed in Israel the ability to trust the world?" It is because Israelis identify the Holocaust with their betrayal by Christian Europe, Burg reasons, that they do not possess the necessary reserve of trust that could propel a process of peace. "We say we do not trust the world, they will abandon us," Burg explains. Seeing "Chamberlain returning from Munich with the black umbrella," Israelis draw the conclusion "we will bomb them alone" (Remnick 2007). It is because of this trauma construction, Burg believes, that so many Israelis feel they must go it alone. He finds this path deeply self-defeating. "Would it not be more right," he asks, "if we didn't deal with the problem on our own but, rather, as part of a world alignment beginning with the Christian churches, going on to the governments and finally the armies?"

In its early "optimistic years," Burg tells Remnick, Israel was different. Paradoxically, "the farther we got from the camps and the gas chambers, the more pessimistic we became and the more untrusting we became toward the world." As Burg sees it, this narrative shift has produced chauvinism and selfishness. Today, the Holocaust trauma fragments and divides, allowing conservative Israelis to justify oppressing Palestinians. It is because of their Holocaust consciousness, Burg insists, that his contemporaries are not "sensitive enough to what happens to others and in many ways are too indifferent to the suffering of others. We confiscated, we monopolized, world suffering. We did not allow anybody else to call whatever suffering they have 'holocaust' or 'genocide,' be it Armenians, be it Kosovo, be it Darfur." The Holocaust trauma is remembered in a manner that makes a significant swath of Israeli society impervious to criticism: "'Occupation? You call this occupation? This is nothing compared to the absolute evil of the Holocaust!' And if it is nothing compared to the Holocaust then you can continue. And since nothing, thank God, is comparable to the ultimate trauma, it legitimizes many things."

102

Jewish Dreams of Post-Tragedy

It might have seemed, from a more naturalistic perspective, that the Holocaust would be written directly on the body of Israel and its Jews, whether via first-hand experience or by primordial identification. From a cultural sociological perspective, however, meaning-work is contingent. For Israel and its Jewish people, the meaning and message of the Holocaust has been up for grabs, crystallized in strikingly divergent ways. "The memory of the Holocaust and its victims," Yechiam Weitz observes, "was accompanied by unending political strife"; these debates "were always ... bitter, full of tension and emotional," and occasionally "violent and even deadly" (Weitz 1995: 130).[3]

The millennia-long sufferings of the Jewish people created an historical memory of persecution. These tragic iterations were ritualized in Jewish religious ceremonies, constituting a cultural legacy that seemed to demand not progress but eternal return. While the post-Enlightenment European emancipation of ghettoized Jews triggered a more progressive narrative, the backlash against Jewish incorporation that exploded in the last decades of the nineteenth century, and accelerated during the early twentieth, pushed European Jewry to look backward again. Zionism emerged in response to this stinging disappointment. It fought against not only anti-Semitism but the fatalism and pessimism that so often had marked the Jewish tradition itself. It promised that, if a homeland were regained, the Jewish people would be landed and citied, and their history rewound. The story of the Jewish people could start over again in a healthy and "normal" way.[4]

Zionist Struggles, Holocaust Memories

This historic dream came to earth in a land peopled mostly by others. Israel's founding did instantiate the progressive narrative of Zionism, but in a decidedly triumphalist and militarized manner. From the late nineteenth and early twentieth centuries, growing Zionist settlement faced increasingly embittered antagonists, not only indigenous Palestinians but other, better organized Arab Muslim populations.[5] The troubles escalated during the 1920s, reaching their first peak in the 1929 Palestine riots, which killed approximately 250 people and presaged the decades of wrenching conflicts that lay ahead (Gavish 2005).

Could the Zionists have understood their potential opponents in anything other than an antagonistic way? In fact, different sorts of relations were possible, and some were tried. Of course, the options narrowed substantially after the murder of six million. The heinous event gave an extraordinary urgency to the Jewish exodus from Europe, both inside and outside the Jewish community itself. The British folded up their Mandate and the United Nations declared a fragile, and almost universally unpopular, two-state solution. Even then, however, there was more than one path to take. Despite their territorial ambitions, the more left-wing, socialist, and democratic Israeli fighters conducted their struggles in less violent and pugnacious, more civilly regulated ways. Right-wing Zionists, epitomized by the notorious Stern Gang, were more aggressively violent, demonstrating much less concern for non-Jewish life, whether British, Arab, Palestinian, Muslim or Christian.[6]

Amid the chaotic conditions and competing ambitions of this postwar struggle, Israel declared its independence, the Arab states and Palestinians declared and acted upon their opposition, and the historical options narrowed further still. Zionist forces engaged in pitched battles against local Palestinian fighters and invading Arab armies. Jewish soldiers individually, and the emerging Jewish nation collectively, experienced this birth struggle as a matter of life or death. "We, the Jewish Israelis," the psychiatrist Dan Bar-On recalled, "saw ourselves as surrounded by enemies and having to struggle, physically and mentally, for our lives and survival" (Bar-On 1997: 90). Feelings of compassion for displaced Palestinians – who were equally endangered, and most directly by Israel's own army – were cast aside. Whether or not Israeli individuals and the nation collectively made an explicit analogy with the Holocaust – and we argue here that, by and large, they did not – there seems little doubt the only recently terminated and extraordinarily searing experience of racially motivated mass murder contributed to the emerging Jewish nation's sense of itself as uniquely a victim.

Trauma and Primordiality

The Israeli state, established on the blood sacrifice of its courageous but also often dangerously aggressive army, honored its soldier-martyrs and inscribed in historical memory the trauma-inspired lesson that only military strength could prevent Jewish defilement and murder from ever happening again.[7] For the new nation's first two decades, the historical record shows, the school textbooks of Israeli children were filled with deeply polluting descriptions of Arabs as savage, sly, cheaters, thieves, robbers, provocateurs, and terrorists. As one Israeli historian has suggested, during these early decades the national narrative hewed closely to the "tradition of depicting Jewish history as an uninterrupted record of anti-Semitism and persecution" (Podeh 2000: 75–6). The continuing Arab military campaign against Israel was represented inside this frame. Palestinian violence was analogized with pre-Independence "pogroms" against Jews, and Palestinian and Arab leaders were depicted as only the most recent in "a long line of 'oppressors' of Jews during the course of their history" (ibid.).[8]

Insofar as this trauma-construction conceived Israeli's origin as an iteration of the Jewish Holocaust experience, an aggressive and military response to the "Palestinian problem" became the only conceivable "solution" to the subjective fears of Israelis and the objective dangers that a series of Arab attacks posed to their nation. And, indeed, so long as military power seemed a viable method of wiping the historical slate clean, even the progressive narrative of democratic Zionism was deeply compromised, linking bereavement and triumph in an inward-turning, particularistic way (Ben-Amos and Bet-El 1999: 267).[9] When Holocaust Day was officially declared in 1951, it was not considered a major event, its tragic narration sitting uncomfortably alongside Zionism's future-oriented founding myth. One effort at metonymic resolution placed Holocaust Day one week before the Memorial and Independence Day sequence, in the period that followed upon the Passover celebration of Jewish enslavement and emancipation.[10] The Holocaust holiday, in other words, pointed backward and forward at the same time and, in both directions, remained resolutely particularistic. In its tragic mode, it mourned "the modern attempt to annihilate the Jewish people"; in its progressive mode, it celebrated the Warsaw Ghetto uprising as "the heroic spark" that had reignited Israel's birth (Ben-Amos and Bet-El 1999: 272).

In fact, constructing parallels between the Holocaust and Israeli wars was more than a metonymic matter. Strong metaphorical resemblances were established between the holidays marking them as well. On the eve of both holidays, businesses, coffee shops and cinemas close early. Radio stations replace their regular broadcasting schedules with melancholic Israeli songs, and television channels feature documentaries about the Holocaust and the Israeli wars. Schools devote these holy days to commemoration and hold compulsory memorial ceremonies. Although these ceremonies are planned and conducted by representatives of the student body, they closely resemble one another, drawing from the same limited, iconic cultural corpus. Many of the same poems are recited; many of the same songs are sung; similar imagery is projected, and parallel dress codes are required. A state ceremony is broadcast live through most public TV and radio stations on both days (Handelman and Katz 1990: 192–5). Another feature the holidays share is the sirens that provide temporal and moral demarcation. "On the appointed minute, and for one minute's duration, siren blasts shriek in every village, town and city in the land. Human life stands still, people stop in their tracks, vehicles stop in mid-intersection . . . All is silent" (ibid.: 193). These sirens, which in other contexts and with different modulation serve as an air-raid warning, not only enforce the short period of shared commemoration but also emphasize the incorporation of the victims of the Holocaust into the Jewish-Israeli collectivity.[11] However, while creating an analogy between those who perished in Europe and those who died defending Israel, it also creates a clear hierarchy between them. While the former, the Holocaust victims, are commemorated by one siren blast on the morning of the Holocaust Memorial Day, the latter, the fallen soldiers, are commemorated by two blasts, one on the eve of Memorial Day and the other the following morning.

At the heart of the Independence Day ritual is a binary that contrasts the "passive Diaspora Jewry" of the pre-Holocaust period, "sheep to the slaughter," with the "active Zionism" of post-Holocaust Israel, "which had fought successfully for statehood." For its part, Holocaust Day ceremonies are often accompanied by a similar pairing. Such phrases as "from Holocaust to heroism" and "from Holocaust to revival/establishment"[12] signify a Zionist chronology that leads from Holocaust in the Diaspora to Jewish revival via the establishment of modern Israel. These binaries inspire a progressive narrative according to which "resistance fighters . . . and soldiers in the War of Independence became the protagonists of the ceremony." It was via such a political-cum-cultural process that youthful Israel, in Bar-On's words, "crossed the fragile distinction from being morally right as a persecuted people" – for whom "persecution became imbedded in our internal representations throughout the ages of the Diaspora" – to being a dominant and aggressive military power, one which did not "attempt to include the relevant 'other' but rather to ignore or disgorge him" (Shamir, Yitzhaki-Verner and Bar-On 1996: 195).

This construction of a causal relationship between the Holocaust and Israeli war was dramatized in a closely watched and influential television series. *Pillar of Fire* first aired in 1981 on what was then the nation's only television channel, the government-run Channel 1. This series narrates the history of the Jewish people in the first half of the twentieth century from a distinctively Zionist perspective, encapsulating what later came to be criticized as the hegemonic Israeli narrative (Shejter 2007). *Pillars of Fire* led the viewer from the tragedy of the Final Solution to the heroic Warsaw Ghetto uprising; from there to the Jewish Brigades, which volunteered to serve in the British army and assist the Allied forces in their war against Germany; then onward toward the struggle of the Zionist leadership against the British forces who prevented Jews from immigrating to Palestine; and it concludes with Israel's declaration of independence and the ensuing war with the Arab nations.

This historical account rests on a self-justifying, narrowly particularistic, and deeply primordial reconstruction of the Holocaust trauma, one that continues to exert great influence up to this day. The Jewish fighters are cast as protagonists. Arrayed against them is the long list of their historical antagonists: the Germans and their accomplices; the British, who stood between Jewish refugees and the soon-to-be Israelis; the Allied Forces, who intervened too late and failed to save European Jews from the Final Solution; Arab-Palestinians and the surrounding nations, who opposed the establishment of the Jewish State; and Europeans, who resented the Jewish survivors and greeted their return to their original residences with several postwar *pogroms*. The binary of Jew and Gentile, a defining characteristic of most Jewish communities since biblical times, is thus reformulated inside the Zionist narrative. Instead of leading, as it did in earlier times, to social seclusion, on the one hand, and moral calls for a more just and universal order, on the other, the new Jewish-Israeli narrative reinforces the militaristic and exclusionary aspects of Zionism. Foreign nations have proven to be untrustworthy. Israel can rely only on the resources of the Jewish people and its own military strength to defend itself.

Shifting Constructions, New Sympathies

Only later, as Israel became more embattled and militarized Zionism stymied and wounded, did this ambiguous and narrow reconstruction of the Jewish nation's founding began to falter. It is revealing that Holocaust Day became more culturally significant as the trauma-drama framing it became more insistently pessimistic. A series of symbolic developments contributed to this darkening before the social arena for the performance of militarized Zionism actually changed. For example, the trial of Adolf Eichmann, a Nazi official publicly tried for war crimes in 1961, exposed the Israeli public to a multitude of testimonies which brought to light the horrendous war experiences of Holocaust survivors. After more than a decade in which the personal stories were belittled in favor of the collective progressive narrative, these relived testimonies set in motion a new, more privatizing Holocaust memory. Not only a national disaster brought on by the passiveness of Diasporic Jewry, the Holocaust now became a collection of personal tragedies, to be sympathized with and commemorated, and also avenged.[13]

This turn toward tragedy deepened after the Yom Kippur War in 1973, when Israel barely escaped a catastrophic military defeat. With this event, the social arena for the performance of collective trauma was changed. The war experience allowed the particularistic approach to the identities at stake to be challenged in a subtle but powerful way. A newly experienced "feeling of dread," according to a contemporary Israeli observer, meant "diminished importance of the fighter as a Zionist role model" and the corresponding reconstruction of the Holocaust drama in a manner, complementary to the post-Eichmann privatization, that "placed a bolder emphasis on the suffering of the victims and focused greater attention on daily life in the ghettoes and camps." As a consequence, "a different type of bravery was now given prominence – one that was non-military, but involved survival under oppressive conditions" (Ben-Amos and Bet-El 1999: 270).[14] For many Israelis, the published photographs of Israeli prisoners during the 1973 war triggered familiar possibilities of Jewish destruction and defeat. Moshe Dayan, who was Minister of Defense at that time, spoke about his anxieties as evoking nothing short of the "collapse of the 'Third Temple'" (Karsh 2000: ix). Dayan iterates here the Jewish memory of the worst catastrophe of biblical times: foreign conquest of Jerusalem and expulsion of Israelites from their land. Until the Yom Kippur War, only the Holocaust was comparable to this founding trauma of "Rabbinic Judaism." Dayan's poignant metaphor draws on the power of these two traumas, equating military defeat in 1973 with the worst historical disasters in the Jewish historical imagination.

From this point onward, the enduring conflict between more particularizing and more universalizing constructions of the Jewish trauma-drama became crystallized inside Israeli society. Of course, a sense of victimhood continued to permeate political discourse in Israel's third decade. The Six-Day War of 1967, the 1967–70 War of Attrition, the Munich Massacre of 1972, the Entebbe Operation of 1976, and the punctuating acts of terrorism undertaken by the Palestine Liberation Organization left deep marks on Israeli society, becoming frequent trauma-recalling and trauma-inducing features of public discourse. Conservative Prime Minister Menachem Begin made prominent use of Holocaust imagery in his political speeches, warning time and again against the "return of Auschwitz" in reference to threats from the Palestinians and Arab nations. Begin was indeed one of the key figures in the politization of the Holocaust in the political discourse of Israel. His vision of an anti-Semitic world against which Israel stands alone was a dominant theme in his speeches and writings.

> No one came to save us – neither from the East nor from the West. For this reason, we have sworn a vow, we, the generation of extermination and rebirth: Never again will we put our nation in danger, never again will we put our women and children and those whom we have a duty to defend – if necessary at the cost of our lives – in range of the enemy's deadly fire. (Cited in Segev 1993: 398)

But the conflation of Holocaust and Israeli enemies was not confined to the right-wing "Likud" side. Leading Labor politician Abba Eban famously compared the option of a return to the pre-1967 borders of Israel with a return to the borders of Auschwitz.[15] When speaking of the Arab–Israeli conflict, soldiers and politicians frequently expressed concerns about a Holocaust-like disaster looming over their heads.[16] Such narrative inscriptions of Holocaust tragedy inside the long history of Jewish suffering provided further justification for violent resistance against those were perceived as purely external threats.

The new post-1973 context, however, also allowed the tragic construction of the Holocaust trauma to provide a different kind of script, one that could connect Jewish Israelis with Palestinian suffering. An Israeli peace movement emerged that put land for peace on the table, and a new generation of critical historians righteously exposed Israeli complicity in Palestinian expulsion. Leftist intellectuals introduced such new critical concepts as "cognitive militarism."[17] More moderate observers spoke about the decline of "collective commemoration" and the growth of a more individual centered, rights-based political culture (Bilu and Witztum 2000: 25).

Such "devaluation of the myth of heroism" (ibid.: 23) intensified after the 1982 Lebanon War, whose military frustrations produced feelings of futility and whose massacres at Sabra and Shatila ignited

109

feelings of humiliation. In their initial response to the massacres, conservative Likud government officials lashed out against accusations of Israeli complicity. They described them as "a blood libel against the Jewish state and its Government," framing them in terms of historical anti-Semitism against the Jewish people. In response to this defensive and narrowly primordial construction, hundreds of thousands of Israelis organized a massive protest in Tel Aviv.[18] This unprecedented expression of criticism and anti-war feeling triggered the creation of a Commission of Inquiry. Chaired by former Supreme Court Justice Yitzhak Kahan, the investigation produced sharply critical findings and made significant recommendations for reform. While it was Lebanese Phalangists who had carried out the massacre against Palestinians, the Kahan Commission found that the Jewish government had indirect responsibility and declared Ariel Sharon, then Minister of Defense, directly responsible for not preventing the massacre (Kahan Commission 1983). The events surrounding the Lebanon invasion and the self-critical reaction to it not only created more universalizing trauma constructions inside Israel but also triggered a global reaction that, according to one French observer, allowed the normative symbolization of Holocaust "to be turned against those to whom it hitherto protected." For the first time, "large swathes of international public opinion distanced themselves from the policy of Israel" (Wieviorka 2007: 57). Two decades later, the Israeli feminist critic Ronit Lentin (2000) asserted that this new spiral of signification had made an expanded solidarity possible.

Only after Lebanon did the suffering of others, particularly of Palestinian children, not Jewish suffering, become a principal subject of Israeli literary and poetic discourses. For the first time, the death of Palestinians was described using *Shoah* images. Palestinian fate was equated with the fate of the Jews, as Israeli poets and playwrights reflected and compelled Jewish understanding of the suffering of the Palestinians (Lentin 2000: 145).[19] This new understanding went hand in hand with a weariness of Prime Minster Begin's Holocaust-driven militarism and criticism of the Holocaust's role in Israeli politics. In an open letter to the prime minister, Israeli writer Amos Oz remarked:

> Often I, like many Jews, find at the bottom of my soul a dull sense of pain because I did not kill Hitler with my own hands . . . Tens of thousands of dead Arabs will not heal that wound . . . Again and again, Mr Begin, you reveal to the public eye a strange urge to resuscitate Hitler in order to kill him every day anew in the guise of terrorists. (Cited in Segev 1993: 400)

Palestinian Counter-Narrative of Trauma

Throughout this period of symbolic reconstruction, the emergent Palestinian national movement played a significant role, creating new "realities on the ground" that provided a new dramatic field of performative possibilities. Its energetic and aggressive ideology, and often murderous tactics, presented undeniable evidence of a previously "invisible" nation and people, making it more difficult, though not of course impossible, to narrate a progressive story of emancipation on the Israeli side. Yet, the PLO's terrorism severely restricted its dramatic appeal. In the late 1970s, the world's best-known Palestinian intellectual, Edward Said, declared that, while "we have gained the support of all the peoples of the Third World," the "remarkable national resurgence" of the "Palestinian *idea*" had not yet succeeded, for "we have been unable to interest the West very much in the justice of our cause" (Said 1979: xi–x, italics in source). While acknowledging how much he resented "the ways in which the whole grisly matter is stripped of all its resonances and its often morally confusing detail, and compressed simply, comfortably, inevitably under the rubric of 'Palestinian terror'," Said declared himself "horrified at the hijacking of planes, the suicidal missions, the assassinations, the bombing of schools and hotels."

Said believed that this performative failure would have to be redressed. To attract a Western audience, the trauma-drama of Palestinian suffering would have to be told in a different way. For there to be "some sense of the larger Palestinian story from which all these things came," Said explained, there must be a new and more compelling focus on "the reality of a collective national trauma [that is] contained for every Palestinian in the question of Palestine" (ibid.: xii). A new progressive counter-trauma narrative was projected, describing Palestinian suffering, Western/Israeli domination, and an heroic anti-colonial movement for liberation. It provided a new symbolic protagonist with whom a widening circle of Western citizens, and the developing group of self-critical Israelis, could identify, or at least support ambivalently. This possibility deepened among many Israelis in the wake of the first Intifada, the relatively nonviolent Palestinian uprising that began in 1987. It was this expanding structure of solidary feeling that became powerfully institutionalized in the treaties and ceremonies marking the Oslo peace process in 1993.

111

Right-Wing Backlash

What has been described as the emergence of "post-Zionism" was constrained, though not entirely cut short, by the assassination of Prime Minister Yitzhak Rabin in 1995 (Cohen 1995). Rabin's cruelly calculated murder managed to short-circuit processes of civil repair that had, in no small part, been fuelled by the manner in which the Holocaust trauma specifically, and Jewish suffering more generally, was being symbolically and morally recast. This murderous short-circuiting demonstrated the ambiguous and contradictory trauma constructions that emerged in response to Israeli's post-1967 history. While the earlier, more particularistic trauma-drama had been challenged, much of its narrowly primordial power had certainly remained. Indeed, even as the Yom Kippur War and the difficulties that unfolded in its aftermath allowed the creation of a more universalizing tragic narrative, they also energized a much more particularistic kind of tragic story, one that was distinctively more anti-civil than the Israeli nation's ambiguously progressive founding myth. And even as the emerging Palestinian movement provided opportunities for cross-national solidarity, it had an equal and opposite effect. Alongside and competing with the Palestinian protagonist with whom the left could identify, Palestinian actions offered the growing backlash movement a more sharply defined, polluted antagonist against whom to carry on Israel's long-standing primordial fight.

In 1977, the right-wing Likud party took power on a platform demanding continued occupation and usurpation of the "holy lands," its leaders and supporters fervently opposed to any Palestinian accord. During the course of this backlash movement there also emerged *Gush Emunim* (literally "Block of the Faithful"), whose supporters began a decades-long, highly successful campaign to take Jewish possession of occupied Palestinian lands. The religious Zionist ideology initially inspiring *Gush Emunim* was not militarist. Emerging in response to the seemingly "miraculous" 1967 war, it narrated the military acquisition of Judea, Samaria, and Sinai, which had taken just six days, as a millennial sign of the Jewish people's imminent salvation. In opposition to the traditional views of Orthodox Judaism, *Gush Emunim* viewed building, settling and developing – whether in prewar Israel or in the Occupied Territories – as a positively sanctioned commandment. The movement's activity's soon generated intense opposition nonetheless. Illegal settlements were forcibly removed time and again, only to be reinstated by *Gush Emunim*. Public opinion remained largely unsupportive, the expected salvation did not arrive, and the

Egyptian–Israeli peace accord forced withdrawal from Sinai and the first massive settlement removal in 1982. Its messianic aspirations thwarted, *Gush Emunim* turned from messianic to militaristic narrations of expanded settlement.[20]

In the years that followed, "settler" became as ubiquitous a trope in conservative Israeli society as "survivor." Indeed, the former collective representation drew its symbolic strength from the latter. For the dominant factions of the Israeli right, Jews needed desperately to annex every inch of Palestinian land that surrounded them, for every non-Jewish person was a potential enemy.[21] They had learned this deeply anti-civil lesson from their tragic, and primordial, reconstruction of the Holocaust trauma. Because they experienced the Jewish victimhood of those terrible days as never having gone away, they could glean no bridging metaphors from their re-experience of trauma. Instead, they felt compelled to frame every conflict with outsiders in a boundary-making way.[22]

When the Likud Minister of Education delivered her Holocaust Day speech in 2001, she proclaimed complete identification with the protagonists in the original trauma. "We shouldn't suppose," she insisted, "that we differ from our grandfathers and grandparents who went to the gas chambers." Rejecting a progressive narrative that would dramatize the distance between the situation of Jews then and now, she insisted "what separates us from them is not that we are some sort of new Jew." What has changed is not the opposition between Jew and Gentile but its asymmetry. The Jewish side can now be armed. The Minister explained, "The main difference is external: we have a state, a flag and army." During the historical Holocaust, by contrast, the Jews had been "caught in their tragedy, [for] they lacked all three" (cited in Feldman 2002: 1). The trauma-drama points toward an ineluctable solution: Only power and violence that can save contemporary Jews from suffering their ancestors' fate.

Caught up inside this narrowly constructed trauma-drama, the majority of the Israeli right has identified the peace process with Jewish annihilation. In the months before Yitzhak Rabin's assassination, ultra-orthodox and right-wing magazines attacked the general-turned-peacemaker as a "traitor" and "madman," suggesting he was "anti-religious" and even "non-Jewish." He and his Foreign Minister, Shimon Peres, were depicted as members of the *Judenrat* and *Kapos*, the infamous Nazi-appointed Jewish leaders who had collaborated in the administration of the death camps. At the anti-government demonstrations that grew increasingly aggressive in the months and weeks before his murder, Rabin was portrayed in posters wearing an S.S. uniform and cap (Lentin 2000: 148). These disturbing images point to the construction of a trauma-drama that is increasingly radical and particularist. Mainstream Zionism casts Israeli-Jews as protagonists and Arabs as antagonists. The new conception marks Israeli settlers as victims, and any political or military party that attempts to evict them as Nazis. This trauma rhetoric framed resistance to the first large-scale eviction of Israeli settlers from the Sinai, which was mandated by the peace agreement with Egypt in 1982. In the final clash between the settlers and Israeli military forces who forcibly removed them, the settlers placed yellow stars on their chests, echoing the emblems that European Jews had been forced to wear under Nazi occupation.

Since 1982, the settlement movement has grown considerably not only in size but also in influence. In the 2005 Disengagement, Israeli forces withdrew unilaterally from the Gaza Strip and Northern Samaria, and 25 settlements were dismantled. These powerful challenges to the anti-Palestinian land movement triggered more intense invocations of the Holocaust trauma in response. Soldiers sent to forcibly evict settlements were met with sobbing children wearing yellow stars, asking with raised hands, "Have you come to take us to the gas chamber?" Settlers prepared Auschwitz-like uniforms to be worn on eviction day. Pro-settlement activists broadly referred to soldiers and Israeli leaders as *Judenrat*, which drew censure from Holocaust survivors and anti-settlement political activists alike (Maariv 2004, 2005; Yediot Aharonot 2005). The mainstream Zionist invocation of the Holocaust trauma-drama justified anti-Arab and anti-Palestinian violence in the name of creating and defending Israel. The right-wing pro-settlement variation on this theme understands such violence differently, as an act of defiance. As the Nazis obliterated Jewish communities in Europe, so were Israeli leaders destroying the Jewish communities in the Occupied Territories.

Left-Wing Inhibition

Faced with such powerfully reactionary trauma constructions, the response of the left would seem clear. Drawing on the relatively autonomous cultural power of Holocaust symbolism, it could challenge the social instantiations on which right-wing deployments of the narrative rest. Building on the earlier peace movement, it could broaden solidarity by identifying the Palestinians as the victims of a Holocaust-like disaster themselves. That such counter-narratives only rarely appear in the highly polarized political conflicts that mark contemporary Israel, even among fierce opponents of the settlement movement, is not only a politically debilitating but an empirically perplexing fact.

Western critics of Israel's occupation policy, whether Jewish or not, do not share this difficulty. In the 2008 animated pseudo-documentary *Waltz with Bashir,* Israeli journalist Ron Ben-Yshay recounts his arrival at Sabra and Shatila at the massacre's end. "Do you remember the photo from the Warsaw Ghetto? The one with the kid raising his hands?" he asks his interviewer. The next shot shows a group of Palestinian women and children raising their hands while being led by gun-bearing Phalangists to their certain deaths. The following shot is a close-up of one of this group of victims, a solemn child of approximately the same age as the Jewish child from the Warsaw Ghetto. This potently inverted analogy strongly appeals to critical audiences outside of Israel. *Waltz with Bashir* was nominated for an Academy Award. Such inversion, however, rarely surfaces inside Jewish-Israeli discourse itself.

Post-Zionist scholars have certainly deconstructed the once widely accepted causal relationship between the Holocaust and the establishment of Israel. They have challenged the Zionist founders' claim that the establishment of Israel was the only possible response to the Holocaust and the only feasible solution to the anti-Semitism of the Diaspora and have voiced criticisms of its political and militaristic appropriation (e.g., Zertal 2005). While these radical arguments have not been universally accepted among critical Israelis, they reveal the persisting identification of certain Israeli left-wing circles with the suffering of the Palestinians.

Yet, when speaking out publicly against the occupation, critical Israelis today rarely evoke rhetorical solidarity with Palestinians. When Holocaust imagery is employed, it is directed inward, toward Jewish-Israeli leaders and institutions, identifying them as anti-Palestinian "perpetrators." Philosopher Yeshayahu Leibowitz publicly called Israeli military units "Judeo-Nazis" (*New York Times* 1994). Historian Moshe Zimmerman asserted that his ability to study extremist settlers was limited because the Jewish children of occupied Hebron resemble Hitler Youth. The Leibowitz interview became notorious. Zimmerman was sued for libel (Nudel 1995; Zimmermann v. Yedioth Communication 2005). In a similar incident, scandal erupted and legal proceedings ensued over a letter addressed to a settler in "KZ Kiryat Arba," widely understood as "Concentration Camp Kiryat Arba," an identification that clearly equated Jewish settlement with Nazi Holocaust crimes. While acknowledging that "doubtlessly,

115

the defendant intended to claim that the plaintiff is an evil man," the presiding judge in the case adamantly maintained that, no matter how evil the settler seemed, the defendant could not have intended to link him with Nazism: "He did not mean to say that the plaintiff is, God forbid, a Nazi." The judge's reasoning underscores the difficulty of universalizing the Holocaust trauma in Israel today. "As a Jew," he explained, "the plaintiff cannot be anything but a victim of the Nazis" (Haetzni v. Tomarkin 1986).

There are several reasons for this discursive inhibition. One undoubtedly is that Israel's inability to come to terms with the Palestinian question has produced increasing radicalism, violence, and anti-Israeli, often anti-Semitic stereotypes among a significant part of the Palestinian resistance. Another, less noted reason has to do with the centrality of the army in Israeli society. Most Israeli-Jews, both men and women, have compulsory military duty of two to three years starting at the age of eighteen. Many voluntarily extend their service to gain benefits and professional development, and most men remain in reserve duty until the age of forty. To severely criticize the military by comparing it to the bitterest antagonist in modern Jewish history is to pollute not only the military *per se* but also, indirectly, the whole of Israeli society. Institutional setting plays a vital role in trauma construction, filtering and tilting the spiral of signification.

Whatever the causes, the result of this constraint on the signification process has been to deprive Israeli critics of a potent political weapon. Because post-Zionists criticize the intertwining of Holocaust and national founding narrative as a forced marriage, they are compelled generally to avoid evoking the trauma-drama in a political context. This allows the meaning of the Holocaust to be monopolized by nationalist and conservative forces.

Is there Hope?

Recently, however, there have been moves to appropriate the Holocaust in ways that allow parallels to be made. In 2009, after a mosque was burned down in a Palestinian village, most likely by Jewish settlers, the Chief Rabbi of Israel Yona Metzger paid a visit to the village elders and offered his condolences and support. "We, the people of Israel," Rabbi Metzger told them, "have a trauma from 70 years ago when the greatest destruction we have ever known, the Holocaust, started with the burning of synagogues on Kristallnacht" (Yediot Aharonot 2009). What is striking about this statement is that

116

it came not come from the extreme left, but from the religious center, from one of the highest ranking religious authorities in the country. By polluting the arsonists and the group from which they were supposed to have emerged – the extreme factions of the settlers – as being anti-democratic or even anti-Jewish, Rabbi Metzger is creating a long-overdue bridge between Palestinian and Jewish suffering. Such new metaphoric associations, this recent event suggests, do not only originate in liberal democratic groups but can also derive from an identification between religions. Several days after the arson, a delegation of rabbis and religious representatives from the Jewish settlement of Tekoa presented a new Koran to the Palestinian village's elder to replace the one burned. "We want to create new conditions between Jews and Arabs," said a member of the delegation. "Jewish law also forbids damaging a holy place" (Haaretz 2009).

Critical and even moderate Israelis have been increasingly concerned by the Holocaust's role in collective memory and contemporary policies alike. According to the Israeli right, to recognize the rights of Palestinians is to become an enemy of the Jewish people. Solidarity cannot extend beyond the boundaries of one's own group. It must be primordial, not civil. So reconstructed, the trauma-drama of the Holocaust is a recipe for conflict without end. If this view should prevail, it would not only be severely destabilizing in geopolitical terms. It would assault the universalizing moral principles that the memory of the Holocaust calls upon us to sustain. Changing this symbolic constriction is a prerequisite if peaceful coexistence is ever to reign. A recent issue of the well established journal *Israel Studies* is entitled "Israelis and the Holocaust: Scars Cry Out for Healing."[23] We agree.

— 4 —

MASS MURDER AND TRAUMA: NANJING AND THE SILENCE OF MAOISM

(with Rui Gao)

Events are one thing, their interpretation another. We know this in our individual lives: How, after we experience something, we often need to think further about what it means. On the collective level, it is the same, only more so. Things happen, but their representation is up in the air. What determines the collective representation of a social event? One important element is the established understandings that precede it. These set a kind of base line, a broad language that supplies basic intuitions about what things mean. But pre-existing understandings are general; they must be interpreted *vis-à-vis* any specific event. There are always new and specific interpretations offered for every social event. They are proposed by individuals, but most often by institutions and carrier groups: parties, ethnic, class, gender, and racial groups; national representatives; and states. Via the symbolic media of communication, "claims" are proposed about what has just happened and what it means. If an event becomes significant, there is a struggle over representation, and in the course of this struggle, meanings can be changed, sometimes in drastic ways.

What affects this outcome? One factor is how effectively such symbolic claims are made. In 1847, two relatively unknown social philosophers, Karl Marx and Fredrich Engels, were engaged by a small group of German émigré workers in London to make a claim on their behalf. Against the background of early industrial capitalism, Marx and Engels cast a complaint so broad and so big – and they wrote it so skillfully – that their claim resounded for more than a century and eventually changed the world. *The Communist Manifesto* defined a trauma (capitalist exploitation), identified victims (the industrial proletariat) and perpetrators (the bourgeoisie), and set forth a solution

(Communist revolution) that became fateful for Western and Eastern peoples alike.

These challenges are faced by every trauma claim, if it is to be generalized as a wound to the broader collectivity. Claims may be made on behalf of this or that group, but they must then be convincingly projected to a broader collectivity. This cultural work is a complex process. It begins with defining, symbolizing, and dramatizing what "happened." In the course of this narration, the identity of the victims must be established, and so must the identity of the perpetrators, tasks which are related to defining the trauma but have independence from it as well. Finally, a solution appropriate to these three "facts" must be proposed. The stakes are obviously high, and cultural struggle ensues over each phase of this trauma-creating process. Social resources such as power, status, and money vitally affect, but do not by themselves determine, the outcome. If a trauma-interpretation succeeds, it can put the carrier group into power, and its members have the chance to institutionalize their interpretation of past events in powerful ways.[1]

The Nanjing Massacre and its Initial Constructions

In Nanjing, China, in December 1937, an event transpired that, sixty years later, a young Chinese American author would characterize as "the forgotten Holocaust" (Chang 1997).[2] After a six-month struggle against Chiang Kai-shek's armies in the Yangtze Valley, Japanese military forces invaded the bustling coastal city of Nanjing and engaged in a premeditated, systematic campaign of mass murder. Using such primitive techniques as cannons, pistols, fire, and swords, the soldiers created a horrendous massacre in which blood literally flowed through the streets. Seven weeks later, more than one-quarter million Chinese lay dead.[3]

Certainly, what came to be known, in the West, as the "Rape of Nanjing" was immensely traumatic for the individuals who lived in that tragically desiccated city. The cultural sociological question is why this event did not become traumatic on a more collective level as well. Why did it not became a major point of reference for China as a nation, searing itself into the collective memory, defining institutions, and demanding reform – as the nuclear bombings of Hiroshima and Nagasaki did for the Japanese people, the Jewish genocide for the Germans, and the enslavement of Africans for many groups in the West?[4]

119

The Japanese massacre in Nanjing did not escape notice. For many contemporaries, inside China and outside, it was the subject of great consternation, despair, and dispute. Western observers were in and around Nanjing, as diplomats, missionaries, and journalists. They broadcast alarmed and urgent representations of the event, and reports appeared in large black letters in newspapers and newsreels around the world. The horror was clear, the victims observed, and the perpetrators clearly seen as Japanese.

This initial construction of the mass murder does not, at first glance, seem cultural at all. The contemporary accounts, and retrospective histories such as Chang's, are angry descriptions that present themselves in an entirely naturalistic manner, as simply narrating a series of actually existing facts. If we step back from these accounts, however, we can see that the initial reports of alarm and outrage were deeply informed by the existing cultural structures of their time. We do not have to deny the brutal facts of the massacre, for example, to see that the reports were made in the context of the binary coding of "West" versus "East." The Second World War had not yet been declared, so that even representatives of the German Nazi government could criticize the massacre from within this centuries-long symbolic binary, and they did.[5] The barbarians from the East were at it again, acting in an unchristian way. For these Western observers, then, the massacre was seen against the backdrop of Japan's polluted rising sun; the shocking birth of an industrial Japan; its early victories over China and Russia; its occupation of Manchuria and Korea; and its militarization from the 1920s onward – all of which were constructed as an unprecedented, and unjustified, Eastern challenge to the West.

This "cultural stuff" mediated the feeling and perception of the mass murder at Nanjing for the Western audience; it was not only empathy for the Chinese victims or ethical outrage as such. As the cultural-historical framework changed, the Nanjing Massacre faded from view. When Americans themselves became the object of "Japanese perfidy," at Pearl Harbor on December 7, 1941, it became, in the words of President Franklin Roosevelt, "a day of infamy" that would live "forever," and the trauma was consecrated by the American people for the next fifty years. Yet, while the death of many hundreds of Americans on that sunny and peaceful morning in Hawaii truly was a human tragedy, it represented a mere asterisk in the history of human perfidy, a blip compared to the truly horrendous massacres in Nanjing that had occurred only slightly more than four years before.

It is collective identity that matters in the construction of trauma, and the scope of this identity depends on identifying with a putative trauma's victims. It was Americans who had died at Japanese hands in Hawaii, and their deaths had been claimed as a national wound by no less than the president of the United States. Constructed as further evidence of the barbaric "East," the event immediately became a national American trauma. Its solution was the Pacific War and the achievement of Japan's unconditional surrender, and it "required" inflicting revenge on hundreds of thousands of Japanese.

This shift from Western concern to Western silence about the massacre in Nanjing makes cultural sense, then, even if it was unjustifiable from an ethical point of view and inexplicable from a purely rational, naturalistic perspective. What seems more difficult to perceive is why this trauma also disappeared from the consciousness of the Chinese.

The Disappearance of the Nanjing Massacre

Contemporary awareness of the massacre, and extraordinary concern about it, had also initially extended to the Chinese. On December 20, 1937, on the front page of *Jiu Guo Shi Bao* (*Saving the Country Times*), a newspaper produced by Chinese Communist Party (CCP) members in Paris, there is a brief report on the retreat of the Kuomintang (Nationalist) army from Nanjing, the capital city. While most of this article reports on the action and strategy of the army, a short paragraph records eyewitness testimony that three hundred Kuomintang POWs had been shot by the Japanese invaders and that their mutilated bodies had been piled high in the city's streets. Fuller reports on the atrocity appeared in a later issue. In an article, entitled "The Killing and Raping by the Japanese Enemy Are Inhuman Atrocities"(*Jiu Guo Shi Bao*, 1/31/1938: 1),[6] a writer listed dozens of horrendous atrocities, including the "killing competitions," drawing mainly from published reports of foreign witnesses. At the end of the article, the writer cried out that such outrageous brutality must be revenged – that "those who do not want their own people to be wantonly murdered, who do not want their own sisters to be raped," they must take action. To fight "until the last trench" would "be not only to defeat the enemy of China but also to wipe out evils against all of humanity!" (*Jiu Guo Shi Bao*, 1/31/1938: 1). Similarly heightened rhetoric can be found in a short commentary in *Qun Zhong* (*The Masses*), a CCP weekly journal published in Hankou city, on January 1, 1938. Under the title "Enemy Atrocities Despised by Humanity" (*Qun Zhong*, Vol. 1, 1938: 56),[7] the massacre in Nanjing is depicted as the most "unprecedented bloody brutality that human history ever recorded," as a declaration of war against not only the Chinese nation but also the human race. The last short piece on the massacre appears in the January 29, 1938 issue of *Qun Zhong* and briefly mentions the infamous "killing competition."

These representations of the massacre were crowded into the time immediately following the incident, the short period of active attention that usually characterizes the span of media coverage for important news happenings. After this brief window, the record goes virtually silent. Indeed, with the scant exceptions we will note below, there is virtually no reference to the Nanjing Massacre, in the literature produced by the CCP, either before or after the 1949 revolution, for almost half a century. It can fairly be said that the infamous incident, widely publicized and remembered at the time, vanished from the Chinese nation's tightly controlled mediascape after its intense, but very brief, initial coverage.

In what follows, we are primarily concerned with the Communist reaction to the Nanjing Massacre, for it was on this left side of China's twentieth-century civil war that control of the national collective identity came to be settled. The CCP's "nationalist" opponents did, in fact, give to the massacre more significant attention. In the International Military Tribunal of the Far East, in 1945, legal claims about the Nanjing events were made by the anti-Communist Kuomintang (KMT) that had fought the CCP for decades and had represented the government of China both during the War of Resistance and afterward until 1949. Kuomintang media also offered fervent representations of the massacre on its tenth anniversary, in 1947. The first of these claims, however, were confined largely to the international legal-institutional sphere, and they were quickly dropped from Kuomintang's priority as the government shifted its postwar energies back to the fight against the CCP. As for the second group of the KMT representations – those that emerged around the massacre's tenth anniversary – they were contextualized in a manner that relativized their significance, as we shall later see.[8]

When the Communists took power in 1949, the silence about Nanjing continued. For at least two decades after the revolution, the massacre went thoroughly unmentioned in the new China's elementary and junior middle school history texts.[9] For instance, in the 1950 edition of the history textbook for the final year of elementary school, when the text came to the temporal point of the incident, there is simply this plain, brief, and passive voice sentence: "Nanjing was lost on December 13."[10] Similarly, in the 1956 edition of a junior middle school history manual, the Nanjing tragedy did not make it into the narrative devoted to historical occurrences in 1937; instead, the text seemed keen on exposing the hopeless and breathless retreats of Kuomintang forces in the face of the invading Japanese army: "At the end of 1937, Kuomintang forces that were originally stationed in north central China had retreated to regions close to the banks of Yellow River. In central and south central China, Shanghai was lost in November 1937, and then Nanjing in December. By October the next year, the Japanese forces had occupied Guangzhou and then Wuhan. Thus, Kuomintang had thrown away half of China and fled all the way to Chongqing, Sichuan."[11] The silence on Nanjing even applied to some of the reference books that were made available to teachers.[12] It was not until 1979, forty years after the event, that a brief documentation of the massacre first appeared, in a history text for junior middle schools, and not until 1992 that the massacre entered into the required reading for elementary schools in post-Maoist China.[13]

This absence of representation in the identity-forming texts of young Chinese was matched by silence about the massacre in the public rhetoric broadcast to their parents. An examination of *People's Daily* articles between 1946 and 1982 finds only fifteen articles in which the key words "Nanjing Massacre" ever appeared. Even these articles were mostly not *about* the massacre, but, rather, arose in response to international conflicts, with reference to the massacre being made in the course of reporting about them. These articles do not refer to the massacre in their titles, and they take neither the event of the massacre nor its memorization as a main theme.[14]

In the years after the massacre, there may have been carrier groups inside Nanjing making claims about the terrible events of 1937, and perhaps elsewhere in China as well. There can be no doubt that hundreds of thousands of persons had to make individual sense of their calamitous losses. Whether some more collective efforts did emerge during these times is a topic for future research. We would have some reason to doubt, however, even if such efforts did occur, that they were able to push the trauma construction process very far. When Nanjing was controlled by the Japanese occupier, the trauma creation process was subject to control by the very groups who had perpetrated the crime. Evidence of the massacre was destroyed, observers silenced, and counternarratives disseminated throughout the occupied territories. Certainly, foreigners were not allowed to visit, and dissemblance was the order of the day.[15] All this recalls German Nazis and the Holocaust. The concentration and death camps were located on Nazi-occupied soil. It was impossible for these events to be consecrated and convincingly represented as evil as long as the perpetrators controlled the means of symbolic communication and the sites where the representation of genocide would have to be made.

This did not mean, however, that representations about trauma could not have been made from Chinese groups and areas outside Japanese control during the war period, and it certainly does not explain why the trauma process did not emerge after China's liberation from the Japanese in 1945, much less after the creation of a stable and more powerful Chinese state in 1949. What fascinates our historical and sociological imagination is that it did not. The reason is that the Chinese had other fish to fry. The potential carrier groups did not carry.

The Nationalists (KMT) and the Communists each had significant control over the means of symbolic production.[16] They not only had mass followings but also local, national, and world-wide audiences. If either had decided to make the Nanjing Massacre an issue – if either leadership had chosen to represent the Nanjing murders as a central trauma, projecting trauma narratives aimed at generating sympathy and interest – they would surely have been able to do so. What the effects of such representation might have been belong to the world of counterfactuals, but they are still worthy of speculation. If either of these carrier groups had been successful in projecting the Nanjing trauma experience, the massacre might well have become inscribed in the collective memories of "China," in one or another of its national guises, and, as a result, the massacre would be much more widely known in the world today. What might the results of such familiarity have been? The dissemination of a "Nanjing Massacre" trauma-drama might have compelled Japan's postwar leadership to confront not only its own war-related traumas, but its neighbors' as well, triggering an expansion of Japanese empathy and solidarity that would have had far-reaching consequences in contemporary Asia. A more widespread understanding of this trauma-drama might also have provided another, importantly different lesson about ethnic cleansing and genocide from which the putative "world community" would have searched for lessons.

But these are counterfactuals. The historical reality was different. The mass murder in Nanjing was not narrated as a collective trauma, and the opportunities to extend psychological identification and moral universalism were not taken up.[17] Again, the sociological question is why.

Concentrating on Other Traumas: The Paradoxes of Solidarity

The answer has to do with the paradoxes of solidarity, boundary-making, and collective identity. Traumas are constructed not only as threats to already existing collective identity, but also as symbolic vehicles that allow future collective identities to be formed. Neither for the Kuomintang nor for the Communists did the Nanjing Massacre fit with who they thought they were, and even less with who they wanted to become. Before, during, and after the Nanjing events, these two groups were engaged primarily with one another, in a massive, continent-wide civil war. Despite the Japanese invasion, and the eight long years of what came to be known as the "War of Resistance against Japan," neither side felt it was able to offer primary symbolic space to a powerful, massacring antagonist from the Japanese side. The KMT had nominally controlled Southern China in 1937, during the time and in the place the massacre had occurred. If they were to consecrate the massacre, they would have had to portray themselves as weak and ineffective victims; such imagery would not have sustained their all out war with the CCP. For the Communists, it would have been different; but collectivizing and commemorating the trauma would have symbolically unified the Chinese nation and defined as evil another nation, the Japanese. This would have contradicted the culture structures that motivated the revolutionary movement and that were already in place.

The system of cultural representations, against which the CCP perceived the events of those days, was sharply bifurcated. The CCP could not be itself without imagining a frightening and polluted antagonist on the other side. Mao Tse-Tung (1967: 7) famously made this a cardinal principle: "Who are our friends, and who are our enemies? This is a question of the first importance for the revolution." Marxist philosophy gave Mao a format for concretizing this cultural necessity in terms of the social contradictions – the signifieds – of that day. In his theoretical essay "On Contradictions," Mao (1962) was flexible about how this binary logic could be applied. There were, he suggested, major and minor contradictions, and the relationship between them changed continuously over historical time.[18] The sacred was always the proletariat, represented by the identity and behavior of the Party. But alliances could be made with other parties, too, and the profane Other could shift and change. Generally, the CCP's enemies included all those who opposed Communism and revolution; during the Japanese occupation, however, the Party formed a pragmatic alliance with the Kuomintang, allowing Japanese imperialists to become the main antagonist for the nation as a whole. But this marked only a temporary reconfiguring of the major contradiction. The main story line was different – publicly for many years before the occupation, privately inside the Party during the years of occupation, and publicly after the occupation and for decades after that.

Revolution as a Response to Trauma Construction

China had indeed suffered great traumas, but these were represented as injuries to the Communist collectivity itself and to the Chinese people insofar as they were signified symbolically through the Party's texts. According to official CCP histories, there had been a series of systematic persecutions and mass murders for more than twenty years, from 1927 to 1949. These had been perpetrated by the Kuomintang regime. In each and every single edition of required history textbooks, an independent section was devoted to vivid depictions of "the Anti-Revolutionary Incident of April 12th," widely known as the "April 12th Massacre,"[19] that portrayed, in gruesome and emotional language, how bodies of revolutionary people were piled up into huge mounds and "the entire streets were turned into ocean of blood!"[20] According to these school history texts, this "massacre" was perpetrated by the arch-traitor of revolution, Chiang Kai-shek, and together with the "July 15th Anti-Revolutionary Incident," [21] it commenced a series of dark historical moments known as "White Terror," during which vast numbers of CCP members and some enormous part of the revolutionary masses – "the most distinguished daughters and sons of the Chinese nation"[22] – were arrested, tortured, and "brutally massacred by Kuomintang regime."[23] Indeed, according to one text, during the period "from 1928 to 1930" alone, "the revolutionary martyrs that died under the butcher knife of Kuomintang amounted to 730,000."[24] Such merciless mass killing, moreover, was not halted when the KMT and the CCP were officially allied in the Second United Front during the War of Resistance. Lamented in all editions of required history texts[25] is the fact that, in 1941, just when the nation was in dire need of resistance forces, elite CCP fighters were subjected to a shameless ambush launched by a Kuomintang force, during which in a "bloody massacre," approximately 8000 of the CCP's "heroic revolutionary fighters" were "slaughtered" and "disastrous losses" incurred to CCP's fighting units (Lin 1965: 17).[26]

To have focused on the 1937 massacre of Nanjing's Chinese population – that included members of all classes, and a large dose of Kuomintang militia as well – would have defined the victims in the wrong way. Such a definition of victim groups was culturally prohibited.[27] For narrative purposes, the oppressed and traumatized had to be not just national compatriots but forces of progress. To have made the Japanese the principal perpetrators of this trauma would, from the perspective of the CCP, been equally wrongheaded in a symbolic sense. The perpetrators, like the victims, had to be part of the major contradiction, the core binary that identified pollution in terms of Marxian class analysis. Only if this binary and narrative were in place would the trauma story demand a resolution in the form of social revolution. In the alternative construction of massacre-induced trauma, by contrast, the story could have resolved itself in the defeat of the imperial Japanese army and international peace.

These underlying cultural forces were made visible immediately after the War of Resistance ended. The rapid return and powerful illumination of the chief enemy were made strikingly conspicuous by the contents of the *People's Daily* on August 15 and September 3, 1946, the dates, respectively, of the memorial day for the defeat of Japan and victory in the Second World War. One might have imagined that on these early anniversaries of such a devastating, almost decade-long war, the CCP would have paid homage to the memory of those who died in the struggle, denouncing the Japanese as perpetrators of unspeakable war crimes. It is striking that this was not the case. Forty-two articles appeared in the *Daily* on those two days. Thirteen were devoted to fierce condemnation of the Kuomintang Party and its US master for their evil-doings against the Chinese people. One article, for example, was headlined "Kuomintang Army Committed Looting, Raping and Killing Everywhere They Went!"[28] Another was entitled "The Kuomintang Government Insisted on Waging Civil War and the Economy Pushed to the Verge of Collapse."[29] Trauma-making and trauma-defining were clear themes, but the perpetrators were the Kuomintang civil enemy, not the foreigners, the Japanese. It was not the "rape of Nanjing" that was targeted, but the "raping" and "killing" that were "everywhere," which had been committed by other Chinese. The trauma was also economic; it involved poverty and exploitation, not only death and physical destruction. The antidote for these traumas was clear. Only the Communist Party could save the Chinese people. Indeed, the majority of the forty-two stories appearing in these anniversary issues were devoted to extolling how the Party had been saving "the people" from their misery.

To "liberate" the nation from trauma and to mobilize as many people and resources as possible for the revolution, there could only be one big devil, one single target toward which hatred and bitterness could be aimed. So attention shifted quickly away from bitterness against Japan to the urgent struggle against international and domestic class enemies. In this battle to overcome the great trauma, even the old devil could be recruited for help. Mao's Marxist narrative suggested that the Japanese "people" could be split off from Japan's ruling oligarchy and aligned with the progressive forces on the Chinese side. Two articles from the war-ending memorial issues did, in fact, deal with Japan. One suggested that "under the manipulation of the US Army, the Yoshida Government of Japan became more reactionary and there was a demonstration [against it] by more than 12,000 Japanese people in Tokyo." The second recorded that, "refusing to be utilized by the Kuomintang reactionaries, seven Japanese soldiers escaped to our army." Faced with the true trauma of capitalist domination, the Japanese masses were joining the "world people" in their struggle for socialism and democracy. Such culturally induced splitting of "Japanese" into polluted ruling class and purified proletariat had already been visible in the immediate aftermath of the Nanjing Massacre itself. On February 12, 1938, a long essay in *Qun Zhong* was entitled "Unite with the Anti-War People in the Enemy Country."[30] Two weeks later, in the same journal, another article was headlined "7500 Anti-War Youths Were Arrested in the Enemy Country." Indeed, on the second anniversary of the massacre, December 18, 1939, while not a single word about the earlier mass murder appeared in *New China News*, a lengthy article entitled "The Anti-War Voice of the Japanese People"[31] occupied a conspicuous position on page 2.

Under the sign of this Marxist binary, moreover, it made cultural sense that, as the Japanese perpetrators were demoted as antagonists, the weighting of evil would increasingly fall on the American side. In the civil war, the Americans had given tacit and often explicit support to the Kuomintang. In cultural if not historical terms, it made sense to align the Americans with the KMT as perpetrators of China's national trauma and to allow any reference to the former Japanese enemies to fall away. Throughout the post-1945 Civil War period, and extending well into the Korean War, CCP mass media highlighted how "US fascists" conspired with the Kuomintang Party in exploiting and killing the Chinese people, suppressing progressive causes all over the world, including the righteous struggle of the Japanese proletariat.[32]

Chinese Communist Party representations of the Kuomintang evolved in a parallel manner, from "robbers," "thieves," "bandits," and "pirates" to "traitors," "tyrants," and "fascists," and a series of heinous atrocities were attributed to them. Between 1946 and 1949, the *People's Daily* reported that it was Kuomintang airplanes that "bombarded Yanan and murdered innocent civilians" (8/15/1946: 1); that it was their "spiteful" spies who "came to sabotage the liberated areas" (9/3/1946: 2); that it was their corruption that "causes the masses of people to languish in the despair of starvation and poverty"(12/13/1946: 1; 9/13/1947: 1); that their callous apathy had "risked millions of people's lives by digging out the bank of the Daqing river" (9/3/1947: 1); that their stupidity had "harmed the interests of the nation in their negotiation with Japan" (8/15/1947: 1); and that their government had "corrupted the country and sold the country out to please its US master" (8/15/1946: 1; 9/31947: 1).

As our discussion suggests, the trauma-history constructed by the postwar CCP was generated less by "true events" of the time than by their emplacement inside a freestanding, already existing binary code and revolutionary narrative.[33]

This interpretation is supported by the fact that this postwar construction fit neatly inside two broader, more general, and pre-existing trauma stories, whose cultural structure it continued and helped complete. The first was the story the CCP told about itself from its founding in 1921 to the 1949 revolution, almost thirty years later. This history provided a familiar narration of traumatic collective experiences, with the Party and the people represented as victims and the Kuomintang Party as perpetrator. A series of famous phrases – speech genres, in Bakhtin's sense (1986) – condensed this cultural message. For example, *xue yu xing feng*, which translates as "bloody rain and gory wind," was coined by the CCP to evoke the incessant and heartless hounding and slaughter of revolutionaries by the KMT. The years immediately following this first chapter of CCP history, the "Great Revolution Period" of 1924–7, was concluded by a bloody massacre of CCP members by the Kuomintang "traitors" in 1927. This was followed by another "Great Revolution Period," from 1927 to 1937, known also as the Land Reform War time, memorialized by the epic Long March, the horrendously difficult thousand-mile march during which more than half the CCP army perished. During the ensuing period of Japanese occupation, when the Communist army "inspired the people to join the national united front to resist Japanese aggression" and to "battle courageously against the savage onslaughts of the Japanese invaders," the Kuomintang regime was represented not only as having failed to resist the invading army, but also as having repeatedly turned its guns toward its own people and the patriotic CCP members, sabotaging resistance, and "blockading the liberated areas in attempts to starve and exhaust us [i.e., the CCP]."[34] Perhaps nothing could be more concise and illustrative of the grisly picture of trauma as constructed by CCP narratives than the following quotation from the *The East Is Red*, a song and dance epic of the Chinese revolution. It reads: "From the beachhead of the Huangpu River, to the levees of the Pearl River, from the banks of Xiang River, to the head and tail of the Yellow River, from the inner plain of the Great Wall to the wildness out there, the entire nation was reddened by the blood of CCP members and revolutionaries."[35]

This second trauma story, which recounted the CCP's tragedy and triumph, was itself adumbrated inside the authorized history of the entire century-long period of China's encounter with Western modernity. *Sang quan ru guo* – literally, "losing the sovereignty and mortifying the nation" – communicates the collective trauma induced by the series of unequal treaties that China was forced to sign under the threat of more violent aggression. *Shui shen huo re* and *min bu liao sheng* – respectively, "in deep water and burning fire" and "there was no way for people to make a living" – figuratively evoked the inexpressible pain suffered by ordinary people under the stifling oppression of the "Three Big Mountains" – imperialism, feudalism, and bureaucratic capitalism – suggesting that the people were "constantly drowned in the depth of the water, and burned in heat of fire." Describing how the nation had sunk into a spiral of a dark abyss of despair, the CCP narration spoke about *duo zai duo nan*, which translates as "being plagued with manifold disasters," and *qian chuang bai kong*, "thousands of ulcers and hundreds of holes," which describes the traumatic effects in a metaphorically wrenching physical way. Performances of *The East Is Red* were inaugurated with an opening explication that reconstructs, in dramatic and expressive language, the abyss into which China had fallen since the mid-nineteenth century: "Gloom and darkness shrouded the earth and sky. The people groaned in misery ... The night was unending and the journey seemed endless. Dawn came slow [*sic*] to the Crimson Land!"[36]

Memorializing the Revolution:
Communism as the Trauma-Drama's Resolution

From definitions of trauma – the reconstruction of injury, victims, and perpetrators – visions of ameliorating and transcending action arise. In 1949, the triumphant new national anthem proclaimed that "from each one" of China's earlier traumas "the urgent call for action comes forth." By asserting the dreadfulness of its enemies and the awfulness of its wounds, the Party could highlight the heroic sacrifices it endured and the Herculean feats it had achieved, strengthening its savior status among the Chinese people. It was the Party and Chairman Mao who had come to the rescue of the dying nation and salvaged the masses from their miserable fate. The days of the "old society" were tragic and dark. The revolution brought light into this gloomy China sky. As one of the most widely circulating songs of that era proclaimed, "The East is red and the sun has risen; there came a Mao Tse-Tung from China who is the great savior of the people."

After the revolution, the trauma stories of these tragic but eventually triumphant struggles were disseminated via the media of mass communication in newspapers, magazines, radio, movies, plays, and novels, all of which promoted the vicarious experience of suffering and symbolic identification with the victims.[37] Memorial Day rituals and museums allowed these sentiments of trauma to be crystallized in more concrete, long-lasting ways. The most frequently visited and conspicuous was the sculpture standing in the center of *Tian'an men* Square that was inscribed in this way: "Long live the people's heroes who have died in the various struggles since 1840 for the cause of resisting enemies inside and outside China and the independence of the nation and the freedom and happiness of the people!" Memorial museums were erected to preserve and display the torture chambers and prisons where Communist traumas had taken place. They became popular sites of pilgrimage. One of the most widely known, in Sichuan province, came to be regarded as a sacred shrine that every Party member felt compelled to visit.[38]

Hong Ri (*The Red Sun*) was one of the most famous of the "revolutionary novels" to appear in the 1950s.[39] Widely read and beloved by young people of that time, it remains today part of the CCP's officially endorsed "Red Canon Series" recommended for people of all walks and ages. The story is about the civil war and is based, with small alterations, on a true story. Its major antagonist is Zhang Lingfu, a general in the Kuomintang "reactionary army," an archetypically evil figure who is depicted as cruel, rash, and stupid, and who has stubbornly persisted on the road to self-destruction in the fight against his own people. The Kuomintang army was predictably defeated, and Zhang Lingfu was killed in battle by the heroic protagonists of the People's Liberation Army. In the last pages of the novel, Lingfu's well-deserved sinful ending is portrayed without the slightest sense of mercy: "Lying on the ground was a huge body . . . of a purplish skin[,] the fat head was immersed in a pool of blood . . . Zhang

Lingfu, this sly, barbaric, and vile brute who used to lord it over the people, was killed by the bullets of PLA soldiers! In this tiny cave on the back of Men Liang Gu Mountain, he found his own grave" (Wu [1957] 2004: 534).

The evil figure of Zhang was so vividly delineated that he became one of the most widely known historical figures for generations of Chinese after 1949. Recently, however, there has circulated a "rumor" on the Chinese Internet that this polluted historical figure, Zhang Lingfu, actually was a great hero in the War of Resistance, who led the Kuomintang army in some of its toughest victories against Japan's invading army. According to historical accounts on the Kuomintang side, this "rumor" is historical fact. In the biography of Zhang published in Taiwan, Zhang was depicted as a distinguished military talent who had indeed achieved significant military feats in some major battles launched by Kuomintang forces against Japan that include the Changsha and Changde battles. It is also recorded in these biographies that, before Nanjing fell in 1937, Zhang had been fighting bravely in its vicinity, refusing to leave the battlefield even when his arm was severely wounded (see Huo 2008: 111–14, 126–31). The photograph of Zhang on the cover of one of these books shows a good-looking young man in uniform, a picture that makes the ugly "fat" body depicted at the end of *Hong Ri* barely imaginable. Whether this alternative historical account is historical fact or not, it serves to illustrate the distance between cultural representations of trauma and their "history." In terms of cultural logic, if not in historical fact, it is possible for brave soldiers who fought against the perpetrators of the "Rape of Nanjing" to become known by the victims of this atrocity as perpetrators themselves.[40] It is no wonder that a memorial museum for the massacre at Nanjing was not built until 1985, and that this dark day of human history has remained relatively unmarked up to the present day.

After Communism:
Writing "Nanjing" into China's Trauma-Drama

This does not mean, however, that CCP representations, *vis-à-vis* the Nanjing Massacre, have not changed. As we mentioned briefly earlier in this chapter, in 1982 there was a sudden eruption of articles about the massacre in *People's Daily*, and articles and reports concerning the incident have increasingly appeared. They have reported on such activities as the building of the 1985 memorial, the publication in 1987 of an historical book on the massacre, and on subsequent conferences and discussion panels about its history.

These articles have continued to operate within the binary Japanese people/Japanese elite. The former putatively share the innocent and righteous status of victims of the war with the Chinese people, while the latter are constructed as remnants who have somehow inherited the prewar imperialist ideology and who are responsible for all its evil-doings. According to this binary logic, for every article accusing the Japanese government of irresponsible behavior, there must be a counteracting article demonstrating how the ordinary Japanese people have shown sincere repentance and are now the true friends of the Chinese people. [41] Such symbolic opposition between the majority "people," who must be sacred according to Communist ideology, and the minority "rulers," who remain the source of all evils, continues one strand of the cultural logic that has regulated the representation of the massacre ever since 1937. It also reminds us that in China such mass media representations continue to be controlled by the Party state.

Yet, while the construction of this new attention remains entwined with earlier frames, the return to "Nanjing" marks a response to deeper concerns about collective identity.[42] The debacle of the Cultural Revolution, the death of Mao, the repudiation of revolutionary activism, and the clear, if resigned, acceptance of capitalist relations in production – these intertwined events have severely, if gradually, eroded the Chinese nation's cultural foundations. The response has been the current, highly fraught process of negotiating and constructing a new collective Chinese identity. It was at such an intersection of history that the massacre began to draw attention.

The old narrative of collective trauma has gradually lost its persuasiveness. Perhaps the story of the massacre harbors the potential for constructing a new traumatic history for the Chinese nation, whereby a post-Communist and more nationalist collective identity is coming into being.

Appendix I: The Yasukuni Shrine in Tokyo

Exhibition Hall 10: The "China Incident"

The Tokyo Shinto Memorial Shrine is dedicated to the souls of the Japanese who have died in national wars. In the 1980s, a private veterans' association funded an ambitious reconstruction project there.

The result is an elaborate multiroom museum that narrates Japan's foreign policy from a conservative perspective thoroughly justifying Japan's military campaigns from the Meiji Restoration onward, campaigns directed against Russia, Korea, China, Europe, and the United States. In Exhibition Hall 10, entitled the "China Incident," half the display is devoted to chronological description of the "China Incident 1937–8." This display includes seven different illustrative panels, each of which is accompanied by both Japanese and English descriptions. The fourth of these seven concerns the Nanjing "Incident." It is preceded by panels concerning the "China Incident" and the "Nanjing Operation." The narrative depicts the Chinese as the aggressors, and Japan as reluctantly responding on the grounds of self-defense. The Japanese invaders of Nanjing are constructed as civil and concerned with limiting violence. Rather than innocent victims of mass murder, the dead are constructed as "heavy casualties" that resulted from a two-sided military contest in which Chinese soldiers were vulnerable because their generals had either deserted or surrendered, even while ordering them to fight to the death. According to the narrative denouement, "the Chinese were soundly defeated" and "inside the city, the residents were once again able to live their lives in peace."

Below is a transcription of the relevant displays. We are grateful to Ms Haruna Yamakawa, an undergraduate student at Sophia University, for fact-checking this account and providing us with these transcriptions. (See also http://www.yasukuni.or.jp.)

支那事変
日中関係は、10年〔昭和——1935年〕8月の中国共産党の八・一宣言以来テロが続発し再び悪化した。翌11年12月の西安事件で、反共の蒋介石が共産　党との提携に踏み切ると反日行動は一層激しくなった。盧溝橋の小さな事件が、中国正規軍による日本軍への不法攻撃、そして日本軍の反撃で、北支那全域を戦　場とする北支事変となった。背景には、日中和平を拒否する中国側の意志があった。戦場を上海・南京へと拡大し、広大な国土全体を戦場として、日本軍を疲弊　させる道を選んだ蒋介石は、大東亜戦争終戦までの8年間を戦い、戦勝国側の一員となった。

China Incident

Sino–Japanese relations improved with the conclusion of the Tangau Agreement in 1933, but worsened again when Chinese terrorist acts followed the CCP Declaration of August 1935. The Xian Incident (December 1936) convinced Chiang to join the Communists in a united front against Japan, and hostilities escalated thereafter. In extending the hostilities to Shanghai and Nanjing, Chiang hoped to sap the strength of Japanese troops by turning all of China into a battlefield. Chiang fought fiercely for eight years, until the end of the Second World War, when he joined the ranks of the victors.

南京攻略作戦
中国の戦争意思を挫折させる目的で首都南京を包囲攻略した作戦。日本軍の開城勧告を拒否した防衛司令官唐生智が部隊に固守を命じて自らは逃走したため、戦闘が始まると指揮官を失った将兵は潰走または投降して壊滅。南京城は12月13日に陥落した。

Nanjing Operation

The purpose of the Nanjing Operation was to surround the capital, thus discouraging the Chinese from waging war against the Japanese. Tang Shengzhi, commander-in-chief of the Nanjing Defense Corps, ignored the Japanese warning to open the gates of the city. He ordered his troops to defend Nanjing to the death and then escaped. Therefore, when the leaderless Chinese troops either deserted or surrendered, Nanjing fell on December 13.

南京事件
昭和12年12月、南京を包囲した松井司令官は、隷下部隊に外国権益や難民区を朱書した要図を配布して「厳正な軍規、不法行為の絶無」を示達した。敗れた中国軍将兵は退路の下関に殺到して懺滅された。市内では私服に着替えて便衣服となった敗残兵の摘発が行われたが、南京城市内では、一般市民の生活に平和がよみがえった。

Nanjing Incident

After the Japanese surrounded Nanjing in December 1937, General Matsui Iwane distributed maps to his men with foreign settlements with the safety zone marked in red ink. Matsui told them that they were to observe military rules to the letter and that anyone committing unlawful acts would be severely punished. He also warned Chinese troops to surrender, but Commander-in-Chief Tang Shengzhi ignored the warning. Instead, he ordered his men to defend Nanjing to the death and abandoned them. The Chinese were soundly defeated, suffering heavy casualties. Inside the city, residents were once again able to live their lives in peace.

─── 5 ───

PARTITION AND TRAUMA: REPAIRING INDIA AND PAKISTAN

In this chapter,[1] I connect a model of collective trauma process, one that stresses its open-ended, cultural capacity for identity reconstruction, with a dynamic understanding of civil society, one that describes its contradictions and tensions as interlarded with its utopian possibilities. My broad interest is the possibility of global civil society, and how the national and colonial projects have challenged it in fundamental ways. My particular interest is postcoloniality, particularly in South Asia but also with reference to the Middle East.

The Promise of Civil Society

The return to civil society theorizing in recent decades represents a real advance in the conceptual capacity of social science, putting the culture and institutions of democracy back on the table after decades in which right-wing and left-wing theories of convergence minimized the difference between democratic and nondemocratic modernity. The challenge to this theoretical revival has been to make civil society more relevant to the complex, differentiated, and fragmented societies of the present day. In my own efforts, I have tried to move this discussion away from employing the concept of democracy to distinguish between types of society and toward employing it to distinguish between spheres inside of the same society. I have analyzed the cultural structures that are central to the civil sphere, and its central institutions as well (Alexander 2006), suggesting they are decidedly different from the discourses and institutions in such other, noncivil spheres as religion, economy, state, or family. The discourse that culturally constructs the civil sphere is composed of binary sets of positive and negative qualities, with such civil/democratic qualities as cooperation, solidarity, and rationality on the one side, and such anti-civil/non-democratic qualities as aggression, faction, and irrationality on the other. To the degree that there is a distinctive civil sphere that gains some traction and autonomy from noncivil spheres, the actions and motivations of groups, classes, and power holders are constructed in terms of this binary set, such that the placement of a subject to one side or the other confers civil legitimacy and allows inclusion, or creates anti-civil pollution and promotes exclusion. These discursive constructions are not entirely free-floating; they are made within institutional contexts. The civil sphere is organized by communicative institutions (media, polls, associations) and regulative institutions (law, voting, parties, office).

This new civil sphere theory allows us to look at exclusion and inclusion not simply as reflections of other processes – class, political, religious, or ethnic ones – or of developmental processes such as modernization, education, secularization. Theorizing the civil sphere is not a way of differentiating societies that have formal democracies from those that do not. It allows us to look at the more and less democratic tendencies and conflicts within a formally democratic society itself, mapping the relations between civil and noncivil spheres, examining the dynamics of social life in these terms.

When democracy is viewed in the earlier manner of civil society – as an all or nothing proposition rather than in terms of continuous conflicts between civil and noncivil spheres – it easily falls prey to ideological distortion. Recently, for example, it has seemed as if every social movement, and every nation building effort, proclaims its ambition to establish civil society, and once it has achieved its goals it has rarely hesitated in proclaiming that a civil society has, in fact, been achieved. These claims, however, are actually quite misleading. They elide the traumatic history of civil society, the experiences of exclusion, conflict, and repression that mark the continuous tension between civil and noncivil spheres. Indeed, celebrating the arrival of civil society has often made it more difficult to repair the particularistic, anti-civil streams of culture and institutional life that remain.[2]

From the time that nation-states were founded in the early modern period, strong claims were made, not only by politicians but also by social theorists, that a civil society had finally been established. There would no longer be violence but civility; no longer coercion but persuasion; no longer hatred and aggression but trust, tolerance, and cooperation; no longer exclusion but inclusion; no more religious

137

primordialism but mutual respect and recognition. These normative ambitions, however, were just that – ideal goals.

The centuries-long efforts to sustain an independent and powerfully regulative civil sphere were crisscrossed with destructive compromises, sometimes hidden in private domestic life, more often flaunted in public and justified by the binary discourse of civil society itself. The histories of national civil societies can be seen as efforts to defend or expand anti-civil instantiations, on the one side, and to narrow or obliterate them, on the other. There have been traumatic and horrific confrontations, and infamous acts of repression. At the same time – and often in their wake – a more independent and solidary civil sphere has often emerged. There have been successful efforts at religious disestablishment, anti-slavery movements, anti-racist amendments to constitutions, the inclusion of immigrants, women's emancipation, Jewish inclusion, the expansion of the franchise, social and sexual citizenship – in some times and places. Without celebrating a modernist mythology of progress, it seems clear that, after centuries of horrendous suffering, in many national settings the promises of civil society have become more substantive and less formal, not in a secular or evolutionary manner but episodically, with the working through of social traumas and the chaotic passage of time.

Yet the forces of war, colonialism, and postcolonialism remain. In the following, I understand these forces as challenges to the expansion of the civil sphere, as forces that undermine the effort to build an inclusive and solidaristic community not only inside but between national states. In considering the effects and after-effects of war and colonialism, I bring to bear a theory of cultural trauma. When collectivities are subjected to disruptive forces, they are challenged not only objectively but subjectively, with sharp and persistent questions arising about their constructions of collective identities. In the midst of intense social disruption, groups struggle with one another over prospective solutions. They offer competing constructions of the social trauma, identify victims and perpetrators differently, and offer distinctive resolutions. It is in the context of this trauma struggle that possibilities for the future emerge, that new boundaries for civil society can be made.

International Blockages to Civil Society (1): War

The nation-state has formed an outside boundary within which conflicts over inclusion and exclusion are waged on the domestic scene.

At its best, this national envelope has promoted civil "repair" in the name of enlightened patriotism. Yet, no matter how successful these repair projects have been – no matter how universal and inclusive on the inside – the outside of this national envelope has remained rooted in a troubling and paradoxical particularity. Outside the carefully circumscribed boundaries of the national envelope, the anti-civil contradictions of modernity have been flagrantly expressed, and there has been little effective reform. Wrapped inside the envelopes of their respective national states, civil spheres have often acted aggressively toward each other, embracing violence in a Hobbesian rather than Lockean way. That, after all, is the meaning of *realpolitik*.

In principle, the internal project of national civil societies is pacific and non-violent, a normative commitment made institutionally possible by a complex web of communicative and regulative institutions, and underwritten by the monopoly of violence secured by the democratic state. The external arc of national civil societies has been dramatically different. Throughout the history of modernity, national civil societies have been continually engaged in wars. Napoleon began his ruthless military expansion even as Kant sat in his study inscribing the obligations of civil morality. Napoleon legitimated his military campaign in a republican way, as a fight for universalism, one that would preserve and expand the Revolution's achievements and ideals. But the General fought also for the glory and power of France as a nation, and for his person and family. Victorious, the new Emperor created forms of pseudo-aristocratic military dictatorship that adumbrated the horrors of the century to come.

The frequency and barbarity of modern warfare has never become central to the narrative of modern social theory. This omission, so extraordinary in itself, has also made invisible the global civil repair efforts that have struggled to control the violent paroxysms of national civil states. For the most destructive of these national confrontations have, in fact, triggered trauma processes. In response to national humiliation, massive suffering, and political fragmentation, collective identities have been questioned and changed, and new understandings of nationalist and ethnic pathologies have emerged. The first far-reaching institutional effort to create a supra-national civil order emerged after the First World War, with the League of Nations; after the Second World War and the Holocaust, the United Nations appeared; after the Cold War, discourses about globalization circulated world wide. None of these projects succeeded; they must be understood, rather, as continuing the contradictory history of the civil society project itself.[3] It has certainly been as a result of such efforts that the idea of a global civil society has permanently entered into human history. Such an ideal has powerful normative force, and it is by no means completely without institutional form. Nonetheless, after post-Cold War genocides and ethnic cleansings, and post-millennium terrorism and imperialism, it is hard to take seriously claims that there is a new world order, or that society has entered a new post-ideological and post-national stage (see Chapter 6, below). "Today's myths of global cooperation" do indeed rest upon "sham and hypocrisy," as Partha Chatterjee (1993) claims.[4]

This international restriction of the civil society project is the elephant in the room (Zerubavel 2006). Because democratic consciousness and practice has generally been directed infra-nationally, the elephant has been conceptually invisible, either naturalized or simply wished away. Despite this silence, the elephant remains. The modern legitimation of war – the violent domination and destruction of one nation by another – has constituted an extraordinary roadblock to institutionalizing civil society in a global way.

International Blockages to Civil Society (2): Colonialism

Colonialism has been the other anti-civil outcropping of the international system, and it, too, remained "invisible" for a very long time. For centuries, the binary structure of democratic discourse celebrated the colonial project, as energizing a vast civilizing project that would convert pre-modern "barbarians" on a world-wide scale (Spurr 1993). In *Tristes Tropiques*, Lévi-Strauss remarks that the destruction of the world's aboriginal peoples is a genocide at the heart of civilization. From their beginnings in early modern times, Europe's new national Leviathans subdued, not only native peoples outside Europe, but also those who peopled highly developed civilizations outside the West, all in the name of civil salvation, both secular and sacred (Spur 1993; Todorov 1984).[5] Until the early twentieth century, colonialism was not a matter of left or right, but of modernity itself, a quest for expanding civil regulation over the culture of primitive anti-reason and the allegedly despotic nature of its institutions. The notion that non-Western societies suffered under "oriental despotism" constituted one of the core tropes that legitimated colonialism as a project of civil society. Even Marxism, while deploring the excesses of colonialism, viewed it as a necessary stage of evolution, confident that, in spreading modern capitalism, it would transform primitive barbarism and bring closer its socialist version of civil universalism.

140

Eventually, this extraordinarily aggressive Western intrusion was brought to heel, or at least subject to certain controls. Anti-colonial cultural and social movements emerged, constituting one of the principal forces for civil repair in the twentieth century. The triumphs of anti-colonial movements coincided with the great revival of postwar civil-feeling that marked the mid-twentieth century. Political leaders and intellectuals celebrated new levels of independence and self-government throughout the world, East and West, North and South. The demolition of colonialism, which unfolded over two decades following the Second World War, was indeed a great victory, eliminating a blatant and egregious violation of civil solidarity world-wide.

In those heady postwar years, it appeared that civil repair on a global scale was on the way. But the celebrations were premature, ignoring, once again, the contradictory character of civil society in its national form. While defeating colonialism meant liberation from direct European control, it also allowed the previously existing, or newly emergent, envelopes of region, religion, civilization, and especially nation to be restored. In the post-imperial moment that followed the First World War, the American President Woodrow Wilson had made a similar mistake of equating national self-determination with democratic emancipation. He had overlooked the anti-civil restrictions of the national form, and that false dawn contributed to a new round of world war. Forty years later the structural situation was not all that different. The emancipation from colonialism created newly independent nations, but the new nations themselves did not succeed. They were committed to civil repair, but they were bound and restricted by the envelope of the national state, and often by the boundaries of region, religion, and ethnicity as well.

Defeating Colonialism: Triumphant Postcoloniality

The problem was not only with the organizational forms that succeeded the colonial, but with the process of getting there. Victory over colonialism was not easy or automatic. It demanded great sacrifice, imposing staggering losses of treasure and life. The endgames – the actual moments of transition – were often particularly tumultuous and wrenching. The victorious leaders of new nations acknowledged these traumas. Yet, while they were not obliterated from postcolonial memory, such traumas of transition were culturally downplayed. The manner of remembrance polluted the colonial enemy, and sometimes regional opponents, but it did not leave any smudges on the faces of the leaders or the masses of the new postcolonial states.[6]

Postcolonial societies aimed to replicate, if in a new and better form, the modernity that the West had earlier achieved. Maoism, African and Arab socialism, India's third way, Asia's tigers – they would become modern but different. The leaders, intellectuals, and in no small part the masses of these new nations were very much at the center of the modernist project. They framed their collective identities inside the narrative of progress that had become extraordinarily powerful in that mid-century time. Looking to the future, not the past, the traumas of transition would be, as one recent observer has remarked, "overshadowed and redeemed by the new state" (Greenberg 2005: 91).

> Revolutionary historical events and leaders cast new citizens in pioneering roles in the forging of a nation. Nationalist feelings and identifications become paramount, enabling . . . even those who endured horrific suffering . . . to turn away from the traumatic past toward a brighter future and patriotic identity. (Greenberg 2005: 94)

According to these new founding myths, for example, while Indian leaders had lost Pakistan and compelled their followers to undergo the tumult of transition, a proud new nation had been created. For their part, Pakistani leaders proclaimed that, if Muslims suffered terribly during the transition, the state emerging from the trauma was well worth the fight, offering an historically unprecedented chance for Islam to regain a political form. The Partition was not to be regretted, secular and religious leaders declared; it had merely cut off a limb that had already been badly diseased. The leader of the struggle for Pakistani independence, Mohammed Ali Jinnah, likened Partition to "a surgical operation." The Indian leader Jawaharlal Nehru declared that by "cutting off the head we will get rid of the headache" (in Greenberg 2005: 92).

During these same postwar years, Israeli-Jews experienced a short and brutal War of Independence, on their way to creating their own postcolonial state. At first it triggered anxious fears of another mass extermination, but after the war was victorious it became hallowed because the "promised land" had been regained.

Even communities who lost out in the postcolonial transitions constructed their sufferings in an heroic and forward-looking way. For Palestinian Arabs, "1948" was *al-Nakba*, the Catastrophe, and *Nakba* Day an occasion of sorrow and lament. Yet, as one Palestinian intellectual has suggested, "the Palestinians have incorporated this and other failures into their national narrative as a case of heroic per-severance against impossible odds." Within this mythical structure, he observes, "repeated, crushing failure has been surmounted and . . . incorporated into the narrative of identity as triumph" (Khalidi 1997, in Greenberg 2005: 98).

Failed New States: Tragic Postcoloniality

A generation later there was vast disappointment. While some new nations did thrive, most floundered. New forms of suffering emerged – violence, domination, racial, religious, and ethnic upheaval, and anti-civil depredations of every conceivable kind. In the last decade of his life, Edward Said (2001: 208) became increasingly outspoken about how a "vast militarization overtook every society almost without exception in the Arab world" and lashed out at the "fright-ening consolidation of patriotism, assertions of cultural superiority, [and] mechanisms of control" that, in his view, had distorted postco-lonial Arab culture (Said 1988: 65). As the realities of postcolonial society sank in, the progressive narratives of founding were chal-lenged, and sometimes undermined. They were displaced by more tragic accounts, by stories that looked, not to the future, but back to the past. The leaders of the anti-colonial movements were now portrayed not as heroic, but, like the figures of classical tragedy, as deeply flawed. They were accused of hubris, and it was suggested that their seemingly heroic actions had created thoroughly unheroic, if not downright evil, results. The nations they founded were not democratic and modern but deeply compromised structures, as pri-mordial as they were universalistic. They had planted poisoned seeds, which had grown, in the postcolonial decades, into dangerous weeds that were fast destroying the promised land.[7] The South African sociologist Ari Sitas (2006; cf. Sitas forthcoming) articulates these frustrations, speaking both as observer and participant in the travails of postcolonial African nations. Citing "the untold forms of suffering by the classes that were supposed to be liberated," he explains that "the first generation after the Second World War still believed in the 'goodness' of the nation" and "in sacrifice and altruism, the necessary qualities for creating a future for the unborn."

> The state was the nation's avant-garde and the concentrate of force nec-essary for development. It accepted the paternalism of its rulers . . . The military, at least on the African continent, were seen in a rather positive

light after Independence. They constituted in their senior ranks an educated, modernist, and national stratum of people who could, people
believed, rise above ethnicity and patronage to save the nation from
itself and avoid collapse or secession. Instead the military ranks became
an effective means to state power and resources [which has] led to new
forms of exterminism, massacres, starvation and meaninglessness even
for idealistic combatants ... There were the coups and dictatorships,
their strong men and their entourages punting the national interest.
There were modalities of rule in Africa, provocatively described by
Achille Mbembe as "monstrous," "vulgar" and "grotesque." There
were also "classicides" and "ethnocides". (Ibid.)

In these new circumstances, it became a lot more difficult to overlook
the sufferings of postcolonial birth. Intellectuals and artists, political
activists and subalterns began to revisit and re-experience it. If suffering could not be redeemed via the modern state, the postcolonies
would have to go back behind it – by recalling, and reworking, the
painful stories and feelings of the earlier, postcolonial transition.
"With all the political, historical, and polemical argument that has
been waged on these issues," Paul Brass (2003: 74) observes, "it is
a very puzzling and extremely regrettable matter that there has been
so little significant, accurate, detailed reporting and accounting of ...
the feelings, attitudes, and consequences for the sufferers." If these
experiences were critically re-appropriated, perhaps those who had
been wounded could be imaginatively reclaimed. Memory would
come flooding back, solidarity expanded, and national identity
reconstructed. All this might finally allow civil repair in postcolonial
time. The "revulsion in our hearts and minds," Brass (2003: 89) suggests, "may contribute to the advancement of the cause of human
rights."

This decentering process was led by younger intellectuals and
artists, who accused their founding fathers of having failed the cause
of justice. A founder and leader of the widely influential Indian
journal *Subaltern Studies*, Rarajit Guha, condemns the "utopian
dreams" and the "hollow promises" of the revolutionary "elders,"
who had "failed to deliver the future" (Guha 1997: xii–xiii). In
a similar manner, in his revisionist biography of Mohammed Ali
Jinnah, the historian Ayesha Jalal demands, "How did a Pakistan
come about which fitted the interests of Muslims so poorly?" (Jalal
1985: 103). Guha evokes Salman Rushdie to describe "the disillusionment of the Midnight's Children (a generation so named in a
brilliant stroke of apt self-description by one of its most innovative
children)" (Guha 1997: xii).

Born to citizenship in a sovereign republic, they had their nationhood with all its promise already constituted for them. It was a promise that relied on the nation-state for its fulfillment. Once that failed to material-ize even two decades after Britain's retreat from South Asia, the despair that seized the younger generation in the 1970s could truly be ascribed to a disillusionment of hope. (Guha 1997: xii)

Responding to "the shameful violence that has become endemic in India in the matter of political relations between religious or linguistic communities," Partha Chatterjee, a leading feminist scholar of the subaltern, suggests "what is crucial . . . is for us to be able to show the many risky moments in this narrative of anti-colonial national-ism, the alternative sequences that were suppressed, the marks of resistance that we sought to be erased" (Chatterjee 1993: 156).

Much intellectual work of dissent in postcolonial countries is today per-forming precisely this task. It is arguing that the history of the transition from colonial to postcolonial regimes is highly problematical, that the promise of national emancipation was fulfilled, if not fraudulently, then certainly by the forcible marginalization of many who were supposed to have shared in the fruits of liberation. (Chatterjee 1993: 156)

A generation younger, Dipesh Chakrabarty looks back at the political-cum-scholarly project of postcolonial project in much the same way.

Subaltern Studies . . . was, in principle, opposed to nationalist histo-ries that portrayed nationalist leaders as ushering India and its people into some kind of precapitalist stage and into a world-historical phase of "bourgeois modernity", properly fitted out with the artifacts of democracy: the rights of citizenship, a market economy, freedom of the press, and the rule of law. There is no doubt that the Indian political elite internalized and used this language of political modernity, but this democratic tendency existed alongside and interlarded with undemo-cratic relationships of domination and subordination. (Chakrabarty 2002: 14)

These complaints about the contemporary condition of postcolonial societies are nested within accusations that the violent and primordial aspects of the transitions from colonialism have been covered up. Gyanbendra Pandey indignantly exclaims that the official, or "nation-alist," histories of the Indian state had virtually ignored the traumas of Partition (Pandey 1997: 4). Swarna Aiyar acknowledges that "partition and independence have played a major part in studies . . . devoted to the end-of-empire," and that "political, socio-economic, cultural, financial and communal explanations for the partition have been provided," yet he caustically inquires why "the actual massacres" – the "catastrophic events" themselves – have "remained seriously neglected" (Aiyar 1994: 14).[8] Seriously to consider these "exceptionally savage massacres," Aiyar suggests, is to discover that the discourse of Otherness was hardly confined to colonialism. It was employed by the postcolonial leaders themselves (Aiyar 1994: 14). They accused India's enemies of primordialism in order to escape from their own civil responsibility. Jill Dardur criticizes postcolonial Partition fiction for presenting collective actors as unthinking herds, and of using "madness" as a means of excusing the nationalist masses from responsibility (Dardur 2006: 20). According to Pandey (1997: 20), the communalism and violence that so strongly marked the colonial transition has inserted itself into the origins of modern Indian identity. It cannot, therefore, be relegated to "minor and irrelevant byways." Nor can it be blamed on the anti-civil qualities of non-Indians, most notably the Pakistanis. Postcolonial intellectuals and leaders, he charges, encouraged "the belief that the victims are real or potential monsters who have done all this and worse to 'us'."

The New Cultural Project: The Traumatic Rewinding of Postcoloniality

In focusing on the traumatic experiences of transition, these new "subaltern" intellectuals – historians, artists, literary analysts, and anthropologists – told the story in a new way. They stripped origin myths of projections and displacements. Accusing the founders, not others, of anti-civil behavior, they urged their fellow nationals to take responsibility back onto themselves. Rewinding the history of postcoloniality, they insisted that the outrageous behaviors and massive sufferings of transition had been central, not peripheral, to the origins of new states. Paul Brass contests the understanding of Partition as a "disastrous . . . disjuncture," a "regrettable but necessary catastrophe," a kind of "terrible accident that cannot be fit into the perceptions of the people of India and Pakistan concerning their past and future" (Brass 2003: 98). Pandey, referring to the peoples of northern India, Pakistan, and Bangladesh, proclaims that Partition was "*the* event of the twentieth century, equivalent in terms of trauma to World War I (the 'Great War') for Britain or World War II for France and Japan" (Pandey 1997: 6: original italics).

This trauma work is deeply connected to demands for civil repair in postcolonial societies in the present day. Condemning the "pathological socio-political system" that exists between, and within, contemporary India and Pakistan, Ishtiaq Ahmed describes a postcolonial situation that rests on narrow and particularistic solidarities, where "individuals not only prefer people of their own ethnic stock, culture, religion, language, nationality and so on, but dislike and despise those belonging to other groups" (Ahmed 2002: 10). When there is such "pathological politics, the 'enemy' becomes a faceless, indiscriminate lump of individuals, an ethnic mass, a target requiring and justifying punitive pre-emptive action" (Ahmed 2002: 11). Instead of cooperation and mutual identification, there is the radical division between friend and enemy; instead of the individual, the mass; instead of cooperation, aggression.

Guha envisions the link between the new revisionist history and contemporary demands for greater democracy in a Gramscian way. "The critiques addressed to the rulers of the day," he writes, extend "far beyond them to all incumbents of authority within the civil society" (Guha 1997: xiii). It is because of the "unresolved problems of its negotiation with civil society," he explains, that there has been the "growth and intensification of communal, castist, regionialist, and other particularist interests" in the present day (Guha 1997: xx). The Palestinian critic Rashid Khalidi similarly links his criticisms of contemporary Palestine to a revisionist account of the *Nakba*. Blame for the catastrophe cannot be placed on Israel alone. Arguing that responsibility rests also on the Palestinian side, Khalidi accuses Arab leadership of having suppressed an independent civil sphere. The Arab Higher Committee, and other Arab leaders during the Mandate period, "helped stifle the growth of national political parties like the Istiqlal, and independent grass-roots scouting, union, and religious organizations." The dearth of "representative institutions" that resulted from this suppression, he writes, "weakened the stature and credibility of the Palestinian leadership" (Khalidi 1997, quoted in Greenberg 2005: 107).

Israeli revisionism similarly challenged the founding mythology of the new Jewish state. According to the progressive narrative, Israeli's state builders had sought peace and cooperation, not a greater Israel, and they had been victims, not aggressors, during the 1948 war. The historian Benny Morris claimed, to the contrary, that ambitions for a greater Israel had been deep and wide, and had only temporarily been put aside. The nascent Israeli Army actually had cooperated with the invading armies of Arab states, which had shared Israeli's wish to prevent Palestinian Arabs from achieving statehood. Morris accuses Israeli leaders of having initiated ethnic cleansing, mass

147

expulsions, and atrocities in a cold-blooded, strategic, and calculating way, and he describes the cover-up by national and official historians that followed as deeply corrupt – "deceitful" and "misleading" (Morris 1994: 3). In his own controversial account of the Palestinian murders committed by the Yiftah Brigades at Lydda, in July, 1948, Morris pollutes not only the founders of the Jewish nation but their latter-day ideologists, accusing both of acting in a deeply anti-democratic manner: "Israeli historians called the affaire a 'rebellion' in order to justify the slaughter and the subsequent expulsion" (Morris 1994: 1).

The Traumatic Projection of New Civil Responsibilities

At the core of such postcolonial arguments is the homology between anti-democratic actions in the present and past. The aim of this trauma work is to re-construct the nature of transition events. Were they peaceful and well intentioned, or were they violent and aggressive? Through their texts, both fictional and factual, postcolonial intellectuals project the claim that the nation's origin was traumatic, that it polarized rather than united, sowing the seeds for the divisions that would ripen and molder in the present day. The issues surrounding the origins of the nation are shifted from the civil and heroic to the anti-civil and tragic side.

To reconsider the nature of the founding event, and to deconstruct its mythological chronology, is also to reconsider the relation of the contending parties. What motivated their actions toward one another? Who was to blame, and what were the consequences?

If the nature of this event is changed, the plot restructured, and the protagonists and antagonists switched sides, there is, inevitably, a transformed sense of current responsibilities. Those deemed once to be Others are now described as victims, not perpetrators. If the founding elite itself instigated the trauma, then it is they who must now be stigmatized. Long-standing enemies are purified. They deserve our sympathy, not our condemnation, and their suffering compels our identification. A broader solidarity becomes possible. If solidarity is expanded, the wounds of the past can be healed, and there can be civil repair. Chakrabarty says as much in his interpretation of the first-person narratives of Hindu Bengali refugees.

> If memory is to be that of trauma, it must place the event, the cause of trauma – in this case, the violence accompanying Partition – within a

148

past that gives force to the victim's claim. This past must be shared by narrator and audience. (Chakrabarty 2002: 33)

Like every civil sphere, the solidarity that can sustain a fuller and more vibrant postcolonial democracy has collective and individual sides, emphasizing obligations to the whole but also the agency and autonomy of constituent parts, whether individual or group. The subaltern historians may have been Marxist, but there is also a civil-democratic reason for their turn toward the masses and away from elite.[9] The explanatory struggle over political versus social history, in other words, also has normative aims. "The recent subaltern intervention," Jalal maintains, "deems the pain and violence that attended the lives of ordinary people to be far more important than the political fact of partition" (Jalal 1996: 681). But these subaltern intellectuals are careful also to insist that the masses are not dependent, or mass-like. They have a voice, and exercised it, for better or for worse, throughout the traumatic events that marked the birth of the nation. In the first issue of *Subaltern Studies*, Guha criticized both British and Indian historians for ignoring "the contributions made by people on their own, that is, independent of the elite, to the making and development of this nationalism" (Guha 1982, quoted in Chakrabarty 2002: 7). Twenty years later, Chakrbarty puts the same issue in a more explicitly liberal-democratic way. Emphasizing that "the task is to think of forms . . . that will contribute to struggles that aim to make the very process of achieving these outcomes as democratic as possible," he asks the same question: "How do we make the subalterns genuinely the subjects of their history?" (Chakrabarty 2002: 33)

The Birth Trauma as Anti-Civil Violence

It is inside these broad parameters that the democratizing project of the postcolonial trauma process rests. It unfolds as a series of homologies between past and present, between earlier and contemporary anti-civil violations. The dominant trope is "violence," the signifieds for this master signifier shifting with the specifics of nation and situation. In characterizing Partition violence in the Punjab, for example, Brass resists speaking only in terms of historical specificity, and demands that it be put onto a more generic plane.

Rather than attempt to define and label these great killings precisely, it is more helpful to think of forms of collective violence as placed along a continuum of overlapping categories that range from riots to pogroms,

149

massacres to genocides. Not only do these categories overlap, but they masquerade for each other, hide behind each other. (Brass 2003: 72)

While Aiyar presented his reassessment of the Sikh murder of Islams in the Punjab as a more objective history – it appeared in a special issue of *South Asia: Journal of South Asian Studies* – it is nested inside a series of civil-versus-anti-civil moral evaluations. Aiyar stresses how the mass migrations of the Partition were hardly voluntary, that they were, in fact, "conducted against a backdrop of immense brutality and violence and in an atmosphere inflamed with passions" (Aiyar 1994: 14). Describing the train massacres in Punjab, he recounts the "exceedingly brutal and gruesome nature of the violence." Rather than being an unintended consequence of Partition, he insists, it was strategic and intentional.

The methodical and systematic manner in which all these train attacks took place point to a high degree of planning and organization. Sikhs on railway platforms would observe Muslims entraining, and enter the same carriages. After the train's departure, they would single out the Muslims and push them out of the carriages or throw them out of the windows, at predecided spots, like railside telegraph poles that were marked with a white flag. There gangs of killers waited to complete the killing. Often the gangs conducting this operation had their couriers on trains who pulled the communication cord between stations, and the killer gangs then operated throughout the train (Aiyar 1994: 27, 37).

In concluding this account, Aiyar connects Partition violence to the Holocaust, the anti-civil event whose mythological narration has cast a dark shadow over modern times.

A British army officer touring Punjab at this time captured the ordeal of train travel for the hapless refugees when he wrote:

> Some of the events such as murder, brutality, looting, ill treatment of women and small children in evacuee trains, the results of vicious hatred and communal fury, have outdone even Belsen and other bestialities created by the warped Nazi mind . . . I do not think I have ever witnessed such cold-bloodedness by any human beings as I witnessed last night . . . [with reference to a specific refugee train killing] . . . In every carriage without exception the dead and dying were mixed up with the wounded – it was certainly a train of death . . . (Aiyar 1994: 26)

In his own discussion of Punjab violence, Brass makes the same connection, placing the Partition experience in the middle of a symbolic chronology linking the Nazi Holocaust and the anti-civil mass

150

murders of more recent time. "The Punjab massacres," he writes, "precede and anticipate contemporary forms of genocide and 'ethnic cleansing' . . . most notably the Hutu–Tutsi killings in Rwanda and the massacres and forced migrations of peoples in ex-Yugoslavia: Croatia, Bosnia and Kosovo." One "cannot help also but think," he continues, "of the mortal cycle of revenge and retribution in contemporary Israel and the occupied West Bank" (Brass 2003: 72). Writing about the troubles from the Pakistani side, Mushirul Hasan draws the anti-civil analogy in the same way.

> It is important to examine why most people, who had so much in common and had lived together for generations, could turn against their neighbors, friends and members of the same caste and class within hours and days. Such tragedies have taken place in the former state of Yugoslavia, but it is unclear why they have gone unnoticed at research centers in the Subcontinent, especially in the areas most affected by gruesome violence and migration. (Hasan 2000: 271)

The Violence Trope and Other Anti-Civil Associations

At once generic signifier and historically specific signified, the postcolonial sign "violence" trips off a series of abstract signifiers and empirical signifieds of an equally anti-democratic kind. For Brass, Partition violence created an anti-civil commitment to religion, by "forcing the displacement of peoples in such a way as to carry the implications of Partition itself to its logical conclusion, namely, the concentration of all peoples defined in categorical terms as belonging to particular religious groups on opposite sides of the partition line" (Brass 2003: 82). Such a "cultural marker," he asserts, is exclusionary, since it "inevitably disregards the legitimate claims and aspirations of those persons and groups who do not fit the prevailing categories" (Bass 2003: 82. Jason Francisco, quoting Alok Bhalla, editor of *Stories about the Partition of India,* similarly complains that "the Partition forced members of both communities 'to leave behind a human world . . . in return [for] an empty allegory of a religious community'" (Bhalla 1994: xxii; Francisco nd: 4). Chakrabarty links Partition violence to "the persistence of religion *and* caste" (Chakrabarty 2002: 6, italics added). Pandey links it to the "narrow and diminishing view of nationalism" that "has elevated the nationstate – indeed, a contingent form of the nation-state as found in India today – to the status of the end of all history" (Pandey 1997: 3). Greenberg connects Partition violence to exclusionary narratives

151

about the sacrality of some specific territory, citing such "Edenic myths" as Palestinian dreams of "old Jaffa," Hindu memories of the "sealed-away sweetness of Lahore," and Jewish settler beliefs about the inalienable Jewishness of ancient Israel's land (Greenberg 2005: 97). Chakrabarty, in his examination of the post-Partition narratives by Hindu Bengali refugees, describes a "devotional attachment to land," in which "the village is variously seen as some form of a mother figure or mother goddess" (Chakrabarty 2002: 122).

Responding to contemporary feminism, postcolonial intellectuals have emphasized the patriarchal character of transition, condemning it as an anti-democratic pollution deeply implicated in Partition violence and the postcolonial society that emerged in its wake. Jasodhara Bagchi asserts that "a woman's body" was "a pawn even in the game of nation building" and condemns the "hypocritical obsession with women's sexual purity" that "marks the patriarchal foundation of the hegemonic class in India" (Bagchi 2003). Brass suggests that "untold numbers of women and children were 'saved' by their own fathers and brothers by being slaughtered to prevent their capture, abduction, rape, and conversion during these raids" (Brass 2003: 89). Dardur argues "that the discursive maintenance of a universalizing definition of nationalist identity elides the experience and agency of women in order to contain the threat they pose to a monolithic patriarchal imaginary in the postcolonial modern nation-state" (Dardur 2006: 14). Women's bodies, she writes, "became sites of violence where different ethnic communities sought to establish their dominance over each other at the time of partition" (Dardur 2006: 66). Modernist forces wanted to "save" women, while traditionalist forces wanted to "keep them pure".

> The suicide, "martyrdom," sexual assault, "abduction," and social death suffered by women at the time of partition underscore how the metaphorical representation of women's chastity as representative of community honour was read as literal in patriarchal competitions for nationalist power. (Dardur 2006: 66)[10]

In the South Asian context, "communalism" is the historically specific term that signifies each of these destructive intrusions into the postcolonial civil sphere. Rhetorically, it is typically linked with extremism and sometimes the trope "communal fanaticism" is deployed. Because "a sentimental conception of community affected the perception and evaluation of inter-community conduct," Rajeev Bhargava suggests, "it left no space for relatively impersonal principles that could prevent reasonable disagreements from degenerating into hostility" (Bhargava 2000: 199). Without such impersonal civil principles, there can be no extended solidarity, so conflict must always lead to polarization. Writing after the Indian government's "vacillation and weak-kneed response" to the 1993 sacking of a sacred Islamic mosque by followers of the Hindu national party, a journalist suggested that the event recalled the traumatizing violence of Partition and "reinforced the impression that Hindu communalists in some sense really do represent the will of the majority." Vehemently denying such a possibility, the journalist attacked the "hatred-driven, jingoistic version of Indian nationalism" as "malign, intolerant, bellicose, obsessively North Indian, male supremacist, 'Aryan,' social Darwinist and casteist" (Bidwai 1993: 87). He attacked, in other words, communalism's anti-civil polarizing quality.

Conclusion: Postcolonial Trauma and Civil Institutions

In this chapter, I have described a trauma process that seeks to rewind the history of postcoloniality, suggesting that it can be seen as an effort to create a more civil form of postcolonial society. Unlike some other efforts at civil repair, this postcolonial effort has not, for the most part, had access to the regulative institutions of a democratic state, whether legal regulations or administrative tribunals.[11] Veena Das bitterly complains that there were not "any court cases in which a theatrical space could have been created for the acknowledgment of the suffering imposed" (Das 1995, quoted in Greenberg 2005: 96). Greenberg acidly observes that "no Israeli court prosecuted any of the Jews responsible for the massacres at Deir Yassin, al-Dawayima, or any other Palestinian village" and "no Arab court prosecuted any of the Palestinians responsible for massacres on the road to Mount Scopus or in Kfar Etzion" (Greenberg 2005: 96).

It has been inside the communicative institutions of civil society, not the regulative ones, that these postcolonial trauma processes have been played out. Among the various communicative possibilities, moreover, it has been the "factual" narratives of academic history and the "fictional" narratives of first-person testimonies and third-person literature that stand out. The narrative form allows psychological identification, and such emotional attachments allow the extension of new cultural-cum-political frames. In reviewing seven volumes of fictional and factual stories that appeared in New Delhi in the middle 1990s, Jason Francisco speaks of the new literary interest in the Partition, even of the emergence of "Partition as a genre." He hails this new genre as finally providing transparency and factual truth. Allowing for the first time "a direct gaze at ugliness and survival," the real experiences of Partition are now "burning brightly." The consequence is "unbridled reclamation" – "a just remembrance mandates a better future" (Francisco nd: 2). The postcolonial intellectuals in their factual historical writing speak in much the same way. They describe their accomplishment as burrowing beneath the nationalist ideologies of founding figures. Recovering the actual record, they have, for the first time, revealed Partition's empirical truth.

While I have honored these factual and fictional efforts, my purpose in this chapter has been to consider them in a very different way. I have tried to demonstrate they are less about exact remembrance than about reconstruction. Their ambition has less to do with producing transparency than about creating empathy. They are about moral, not just cognitive truth. The trauma process does not simply return to buried memory; it creates new ones. It allows events to be seen a different way, and repositions roles and responsibilities of actors, and suggests that the present must be repaired in a manner that makes it consistent with the newly remembered past. It is for these reasons that postcolonial trauma process is pregnant with possibilities. If Francisco has construed the process of trauma too literally, he has certainly got the potential consequences right. "Stories of repair," he suggests, "remind us of the sparks of ethical conscience that dwell in the human soul, even in the most degraded of times, and of the healing power of positive memory" (Francisco nd: 12). The postcolonial trauma process puts new solidarities on the table. If new empathies can be created, then feelings about others can take more extended and inclusive forms.

> [Partition] literature does what religious leaders in each community failed to do: to make communities forces for the affirmation of humanity broadly, and to forge nations – if nations are the destinies of cherished traditions – dedicated to human improvement, dedicated precisely to virtuous conduct with those of different faith. (Francisco nd: 24)

154

— 6 —

GLOBALIZATION AND TRAUMA:
THE DREAM OF COSMOPOLITAN
PEACE

By friends and foes alike, globalization is hailed as a revolutionary, path-breaking, *Weltgeschichte* phenomenon. It solves the world's economic problems or condemns more of the world's people to poverty. It creates equality and cooperation or frightfully deepens inequality and hegemonic domination. It opens the way for world peace or it ushers in a new and nightmarish period of terrorism and war.

Is it possible to pry "globalization" out of the clutches of the rhetorical binaries that define the passionate simplifications of symbolic life?

Globalization is, indeed, one of the central facts of our time. It is a reference that must become central to the social sciences, but has not yet. In this respect, Beck's claim that modern social science is hobbled by methodological nationalism bears serious consideration (Beck 2000).

But globalization is too important to be left to the globalizers, the entrepreneurs of globalization, whether economic, political, or intellectual, who have created what might be called the discourse of globalization. The members of this carrier group make use of the facts of globality to suggest that the rules of the game no longer hold, whether these are the "social laws" that link capitalist markets with economic inequality and undemocratic political power with domination, or some long-standing conceptions of modernity in social science.[1]

About such apocalyptic and utopian claims we must be very cautious. Globalization is not an alternative reality that makes previous knowledge and social reality irrelevant. It is a long emerging if only recently visible and represented reality, a social phenomenon that in

155

itself is neither sacred nor profane. It must be made mundane, and put back inside history and social science.

To begin this process, we might start with globalization marking an unprecedented compression of time and space, the materialist idea David Harvey (1989) introduced and Anthony Giddens (1990) elaborated on his way to becoming one of globalization's leading intellectual ideologists.[2] We need to amend this proposition in a fundamental way. Compression affects not only the pragmatics but also the semantics of communication, the basic meaning units, the symbolic languages upon which interactions depend. There exist not only new technologies of movement and communication but also more condensed and transcendent cultural logics, such as democracy and human rights, which spread common understandings and structures of feeling more widely than before. It is by the compression of space, time, *and* meaning that globalization creates a significantly more expansive field of action and organization.

Does such an expansion mark a new order of magnitude? Giddens and other entrepreneurs of globalization suggest that radically new knowledges are necessary. If this claim is false, as I believe it to be, this question remains: Why has incremental change in scale so frequently been represented as a change of exponential magnitude? Could it be that such a shift in the representational order is itself the fundamental and radical change? If so, it is an aspect of globalization to which globalizing intellectuals have not paid sufficient attention.

We will return later to this shift in the field of representation. Let us speak first of the mundane process of globalization. My hypothesis is that globalization should not be understood as something radically new. It marks rather another step in the millennia-long compression of time/space/meaning, and the corresponding expansion in reach of the institutions that represent them, i.e., the extension of political, economic, and cultural organization and power (Mann 1986).

In fact, far from being a radically new knowledge, this process of compression/expansion already formed the central subject of modernization theory in the middle of the last century. More than any other historical transformation, it was the movement from "particular" and "local" to the "universal" and "national" that fascinated modernization theorists, who framed it as a movement from traditional to modern society. In retrospect, from the perspective of postmodern critique, we can see this binary as both tragic and absurd. The first side of the binary represents a vast simplification, ignoring the extraordinary variation between different forms of earlier societies, for example the giant power reach of early empires. The other side of the binary is also highly exaggerated. Nation and universal are as contradictory as synonymous. As for the much heralded modernity of the twentieth century, it turned out to be as barbaric as any recorded in the annals of traditional history.

None of this postmodern reconsideration, however, suggests that modernization theorists were wrong to conceptualize historical development as an enlargement of scope. Insofar as we are moving toward a more global playing field, we are in the midst of this familiar process. Social organizations and cultural structures alike are expanding their scope and reach.[3]

By emphasizing the familiarity of this process, and how it was a central topic for modernization theory, I mean to suggest that, whether italicized, capitalized, or followed with an exclamation point, globalization does not present an abrupt change. To understand it, we need not invent new or alternative knowledges. Rather, we must better apply the theoretical and empirical ideas already available, which means to orient them in a more global way.

Every process evoked in the globalization literature has already been conceptualized in studies of the transformation of social organization from local to national scale, studies which have traced the sometimes incremental, sometimes abrupt enlargements in economic, political, military, religious, legal, penal, and cultural life. How these processes work has been conceptualized in a manner that has little to do with the scale of the nation as such.

Let us consider, for example, the classical theoretical writings of Marx, Weber, and Durkheim, and their systemic understandings of such social phenomena as class formation, mode of production, division of labor, functional differentiation, bureaucracy, stratification, authority, and power. Were the concepts and propositions created by these writings, in contrast with their more restricted empirical referents, dependent on national scale? The empirical equation of their own societies – identified in terms of nation, civilization, or class – with progress, universalism and rationality was indeed often myopic. But such classical theorizing about the organizational and cultural processes that sustain universalism and particularism can largely still stand. The same is true for much of the modern theorizing we have inherited from such sociological thinkers as Parsons, Elias, Goffman, and Geertz. They, too, dealt centrally with universalizing processes and compressions of temporal, spatial, and cultural scale, and their insights provide foundations for thinking about the globalizing phase we are experiencing today.

But in the impassioned and simplified rhetorics of globalization more is involved than merely empirical claims. There are moral assertions about justice being possible for the first time or no longer being possible again. There is a sense of imminence, of an historical shifting that, for better or for worse, has already transformed, or is about to, the basic meaning of social life. I wonder whether globalization has such normative purchase? Does the compression of space, time, and meaning translate into edicts about justice and the good life?

Let's do a thought experiment. You are a citizen of Florence in the year 1500 and you are visited by the angel of history and vouchsafed a vision of the different, nationally organized world that is to come. Deeply inspired by this new vision of universalism, you turn to your companion in the palazzo and exclaim:

> Hey, you're not going to believe this, but there's going to be, starting in a hundred years or so, the birth of an amazing thing called the nation state, and everything henceforth will be organized on a gigantically different scale. There will be an extraordinary compression of time and space, and everything, I mean everything, will be subject to the new law of nationalization. Someday, everything we take for granted – about economic life, war, science, customs, politics, religion, education – will be based not on this little puny city or even this region, but on the great entity that will be called the nation.

Would you have been right, in that long ago Florentine time, to be so excited? Did nationalization turn out to be anything so great? Certainly it represented a new compression of space, time, and meaning, and it had immense historical significance. But was it liberating in the normative sense? Did it have any particular moral purchase? Should we have heralded it in the apocalyptic or utopian manner that the economic, political, and intellectual entrepreneurs speak about globalization today?

The enthusiasm of our Florentine ancestor may be excused. The movement toward the city-state had once promised enlightenment, freedom, and justice, and he was already beginning to feel its restrictive corruptions full face. The promise of expanding to the national field seemed to provide a way out of that urban cul-de-sac. The promise of the nation made universalism still seem possible, just as the promise of the city had before. But this new promise to make the universal concrete turned out no differently. The social and moral possibilities of nationalization were rather more limited than its ideologists had thought.

Similar caution applies to the phase of time/space/meaning expansion in which we are participating today. Globalization is a mundane process that, in the course of the twentieth century, has created at least as much trouble as possibility. The reach of markets has dramatically expanded, producing and distributing on a wider scale than ever before. These economic processes, however, have contributed as much to exploitation and poverty as to wealth creation and economic participation. Information from distant parts of the world has become increasingly available in real time, but it has not become free floating and universal. Even the most rapidly circulated and easily available information remains attached to particular world views, interests and powers. Rather than having displaced enslaving religious dogmas for liberating reason, such globalizing ideologies as nationalism, communism, fascism, and economic liberalism merely provided secular versions of equally heinous and dogmatic constraint. Like the earlier world-historical belief systems that emerged in the Axial Age, these modern ideologies created supplicants and priests. In the name of purification and world transformation, they justified massive violence and created havoc and mayhem on a global scale.[4] It is hardly surprising, in light of this modernist legacy, that so-called traditional religion has recently found on the global stage a new life.

As the world's territory has been scaled down from empires and up from cities, globalizing rhetorics charged nation-states with the mission of democracy and equality. It has been much more likely, however, for the new nations to become iron cages of suppression, with the universalism of the "people" becoming a camouflage for primordiality of some primitive kind (see Chapter 5, above). If nations represented a new phase of time/space/meaning compression, their expansionary powers have not necessarily been linked to individual freedom or civil rights. The origins of international law in the Treaty of Westphalia brought the destructive wars of religion to an end, but it did so by underscoring national sovereignty (Clark 1999; Lipschutz 1992). The treaty gave freedom and respect not to individuals but to states. We live still within a tradition of international law that has nothing intrinsically to do with human rights (Cushman 2005). With the significant exception of the European Union, which itself remains a regionally restricted power, no larger, more impartial, more universalistic, and more democratic entity has yet taken over from the nation-state.[5]

These sober reflections about twentieth century globalization are underscored when we consider war, the national form of organized violence so conspicuously neglected by classical and modern social theory. Has it not been the very compression of time, space, and meaning that has allowed destructive violence and mass murder

159

to become so world-wide? The utopian vision of a cosmopolitan and boundary-less civil society eloquently espoused by Kant (1970 [1784]) emerged just as the ideal of a more democratic civil sphere was becoming firmly instantiated in the revolutionary nation-state. Napoleon advanced even as Kant wrote. Since that time, the imperial idea of reshaping the world in the name of universal ideals has been related to war, whether waged for a French warrior's vision of Europe, a Russian revolutionary's ideal of communism, a German dictator's scheme for a *Volk Gemeinschaft*, or a new world order envisioned by a democratic and capitalist United States.

Yet, if we must resist the impulse to fold normative aspirations for a global imaginary into some immanent empirical laws about globalization, we must try all the harder, as David Held (2004) quite rightly insists, to steer time/space/meaning compression in normatively more compelling ways. The present phase of globalization does open up new democratic possibilities. If the social and cultural processes involved in contemporary time/space/meaning compression are not radically new but mundane, it may well be that the sense of newness is in the name, in the signifier and not the signified. What I am suggesting is that we understand contemporary "globalization" as a process of social representation.

Why has globalization emerged as a dominant new imaginary? What discourse does it crystallize, what fears does it carry, and what hopes does it represent? "Globalization" appeared in response to the trauma of the twentieth century, in a moment of hope when it seemed, not for the first time, that the possibility for a world-wide civil society was finally at hand. Since before the Enlightenment, the idea of world peace has accompanied the expansion of organizational and cultural power. From the seventeenth century on, the political theory of high and organic intellectuals alike has articulated the idea of peaceful conflict resolution through the concept of civil power. The possibility for civil control, as opposed to military violence or political domination, can be traced back to the idea of the social contract, to the Lockean vision of consensual agreement and persuasion in contrast with the Hobbesian resort to force and fraud. Sociologically, the idea of civil society points to the idea of a liberal discourse at once critical and tolerant, and to institutions, from factual and fictional mass media to voting and law, that allow collectivities to be guided by symbolic communication among independent and rational citizens bound by ties of solidarity and mutual obligation (Alexander 2006).

In what has been called the long nineteenth century, during the "Age of Equipoise" that followed upon the end of the Napoleonic wars, there was the sense, not only among Euro-American elites, that such cosmopolitan peace was finally at hand.[6] It seemed possible to believe that, alongside the expansion of organizational and cultural power, "civilization" was becoming world-wide. That this civil utopian vision of a peaceful world was shadowed by the expansion of colonial conquest outside Europe is a fearful symmetry more visible from our own time.[7]

This dream of reason was shattered by the First World War. For intellectuals and artists, and thoughtful men and women on every side, the war exposed the barbarism that contradicted modernity's promise to create a more civil society.[8] If that first globalizing war exposed the ugly face of military nationalism that threatened cosmopolitan peace, so much more so did the totalitarianisms that emerged during its wake. The Second World War marked a globalizing battle over the very possibility for modern civil life.

In the wake of these war traumas, the victors promised to renew the dream of cosmopolitan peace.[9] The utopian discourse of world civil society was even embedded in formally democratic institutional regimes, the quasi-world governments of first the League of Nations, then the United Nations. The ideas for these repair efforts were provided by such high intellectuals as Bertrand Russell and implemented by such organic intellectuals as Ralph Bunche. Yet, the carrier groups for these efforts at renewing the cosmopolitan dream were the victorious national hegemons themselves. The infrastructure of national power belied aspirations for global civil order. When strains at the level of nation-states became too intense, the League of Nations was destroyed. It had been hobbled from its beginnings, of course, by America's refusal to join. The United Nations was undermined even more quickly, by the division of the postwar "universalizing spirit" into the fighting camps of the Cold War. The rhetoric on both sides of this great divide rang the bells of international peace, but in the background one could always hear the sounds of war.

When the third world war of the short twentieth century was finished, there were once again utopian hopes for the repair of civil society and the creation of world peace. The utopian representation "globalization" first emerged in the late 1980s, as the Cold War wound down. As this new collective representation gained power, in the decade following, it seemed to many that a world civil society was finally at hand. This time around, the high and organic intellectuals were former activists and peaceniks, post-Marxist and liberal leftists who had campaigned for peace against the Vietnam War in the US, for "Europe" and against national boundaries on the continent, and for nuclear disarmament on both sides. International law would be based not on the rights of sovereign nations, but on individual and human rights. National force was pledged to multinational, not national interest, to a new world order in which peace and civil respect would reign. The Security Council of the United Nations was approached as if it were a global democratic forum in which rational discussion could affect the distribution of wealth and the application of power.[10]

Once again, however, this moment of equipoise was underpinned by a national infrastructure. It was the victors in the Cold War who were most excited about globalization; the losers were more interested in national reconstruction and restoring regional strength. It was the President of the United States, Bill Clinton, who gave commencement addresses on civil society as the key to world peace. It was NATO that intervened in Kosovo. It should not be surprising that this most recent dream for cosmopolitan peace reigned for scarcely more than a decade. The postwar collective effervescence in which globalization became such a powerful new representation came to an end with the election in America of George W. Bush, which was accompanied by the neo-conservative discourse of empire. National interest was unabashedly reasserted, global agreements cancelled, and global conferences and institutions boycotted. President Bush and his fellow neo-conservative politicians and intellectuals handled and channeled the national trauma of September 11, 2001. They highlighted anti-civil violence and global fragmentation and constructed a narrative that pointed to a Hobbesian struggle between civilizations. Collective violence once again came to be waged by nations and blocs, with divisive rather than unifying effects for the world scene.[11]

These events were experienced by the intellectuals promoting globality, and by its organized carrier groups, not merely as disappointment but betrayal. For explanation, many turned to anti-Americanism, the long-standing culture structure which divides good and evil by polluting the United States and purifying any collectivity, ideology, or region that comes to represent the other side.[12] No matter how culturally satisfying, this interpretation elides the systemic processes at play. The structures and the ideologies of the world are still primarily organized nationally, and hardly at all in a globally civil way. As long as this organizational structure is maintained, when other states amass extraordinarily asymmetrical power they will undoubtedly act in a similar way.

To accept anti-Americanism as explanation rather than as interpretation, moreover, misses the ambiguous and often productive role that this cultural trope often has played. To pollute America as a hegemon is to make deviant anti-civil actions as such, not merely the United States. By creating a stark if simplifying contrast between "American" action, on the one side, and a more civil sort of global power, this binary has the effect of allowing the purifying power of the globalization representation to be sustained. In February, 2003, in the days just before the American invasion of Iraq, the meaning of this cultural confrontation and the stakes involved were clearly displayed on the front page of the *New York Times*. Reporting the massive demonstrations that had unfolded throughout the world on the previous day, a *Times* correspondent wrote: "The fracturing of the Western alliance over Iraq and the huge anti-war demonstrations around the world this weekend are reminders that there may still be two superpowers on the planet: the United States and world public opinion" (Tyler 2003). Apparently factual, this statement is also an interpretive reconstruction. It framed unfolding empirical events in a globally civil way. They are presented as transpiring on the public stage of the world, and America is portrayed not as an elect but as a particularistic nation, confronting not the evil of an Iraqi dictator but the world as a civil, rationally organized society: "President Bush appears to be eyeball to eyeball with a tenacious new adversary: millions of people who flooded the streets of New York and dozens of world cities to say they are against war based on the evidence at hand" (Tyler 2003).

There is no world government that can curb a hegemonic state bent on defending its interests as nationally conceived. The nascent global civil sphere has none of the institutions that, in a fully functioning democracy, allow public opinion to produce civil power and thus regulate the state, such as independent courts, party competition, and elections. Yet this nascent global civil sphere does have access to institutions of a more communicative kind. Despite different languages and separated ownership and organization, national news stories construct extra-national events in a manner that often reveals a high level of intertextuality, creating the common understandings and interpretations that allow there to be putatively global events. These "factual" understandings are sustained by the intense circulation around the globe of "fictional" mass media, which are far from being merely entertaining in their cultural effects. These fictional media are movies, television dramas, novels, music, and the international brands whose consumption is creating a more common material culture world-wide.

It is within this symbolic and institutionally constructed sea of global public opinion that there emerges the world stage, on which transpire polls, demonstrations, social movements, scandals, corruptions, terrorism, electoral triumphs, and tragedies, performances that palpably create the very sense that there is a supra-national life.[13] It is within this febrile and often highly unstable membrane of global consciousness that international institutions and nongovernmental organizations create forms not of governance in the state-political sense, but of governmentality, from agreements over labor conditions and world health to regulations about the environment and land mines. The rules and resources that sustain governmentality, as opposed to government, rest on consensus and agreement rather than on the violence-backed power of a state.[14]

The dream of cosmopolitan peace has not died. The forceful hope for creating a global civil sphere remains. It is embodied in the collective representation of globalization, which has organizational integuments and political and economic effects. There is a global stage on which local events are evaluated, not only nationally or ethnically, but according to the standards of the civil sphere. Before this stage, sits an idealized audience of world citizens. Sometimes the performances projected to this audience are initiated by avowedly global actors. More often, they reflect local scripts of national actors, which are projected on the world stage and evaluated according to the principles of cosmopolitan peace and by the discourse and interactions of civil life.

Since the first national institutionalizations of civil societies, there has been imagined the possibility for a civil sphere on a supra-national scale. In the seventeenth century, the trope of "oriental despotism" emerged, reconfiguring colonialism into a fight for civil power on a global scale. In the middle of the eighteenth century, the Lisbon earthquake became a trauma for Europe and offered a sentimental education for "all mankind." In the early nineteenth century, the moral movement against anti-slavery achieved political success by generating moral empathy, extending solidarity and psychological identification to nonwhite Others for the first time. In the mid-twentieth century, the narration and memorialization of the Holocaust formed a powerful basis for expanding moral universalism, establishing genocide as a principle for evaluating national, ethnic, and religious power. At the end of the twentieth century, globalization emerged as a new representation on the fragile public stage of world life.

Globalization refers to a process of space/time/meaning compression that is ongoing. These expansions have not yet, by any means, created the basis for globality in the sense of a supra-national civil society, as the recent revival of nation-centered rhetorics and practices of national hegemony have demonstrated. Nonetheless, globalization is a new and powerful social representation. It has performative force, and it has emerged for good sociological reasons. Even if it is sharply contested, the dream of cosmopolitan peace can never be entirely suppressed.

NOTES

1 Whether the lay perception of events as "traumatic" was at some point in historical time confined to the West, or whether the language was also intrinsic to the pre-globalization cultural discourse of non-Western societies, is an issue that merits further investigation. It does not, however, concern us directly here. I suggest in the conclusion to this chapter that, in the context of modern globalization, members of both Western and non-Western collectivities do employ such a framework. The claim, then, is that the theory of cultural trauma presented here is universal in a post-foundational sense, and in the following chapters I employ the model to understand processes in both Western and non-Western societies.

2 The ultimate example of such naturalization is the recent effort to locate trauma in a specific part of the brain through PET scanning, the brain color imaging that has become a research tool of neurology. Such images are taken as proof that trauma "really exists" because it has a physical, material dimension. I would not wish to suggest that trauma does not, in fact, have a material component. Every component of social life exists on multifold levels. What I object to is reduction, the idea that trauma is a symptom produced by a physical or natural base. In this sense, trauma theory bears marked resemblance to another naturalistic understanding that has permeated contemporary social life, namely the notion of "stress." According to contemporary lingo, persons are "placed under stress," i.e., it is a matter of their environments, not of the mediation of actors who construct an environment as stressful according to their social position and cultural frame.

3 A more distinctively sociological representation of the psychoanalytic approach to trauma is Jeffrey Prager's (1998) study of repression and displacement in the case of a patient who claimed sexual harassment by her father. Prager goes beyond lay trauma theory by demonstrating how the individual's memory of trauma was the product not only of her actual experience, but also of the contemporary cultural milieu, which by its emphasis on "lost memory syndrome" actually presented the possibility of trauma to her.

166

4 For a nonpsychoanalytic, emphatically sociological approach to memory, derived from the Durkheimian tradition, see Paul Connerton, *How Societies Remember* (1989).

5 For an analysis of Lacan in the psychoanalytically informed humanities, see specifically Caruth's "Traumatic Awakenings: Freud, Lacan, and the Ethics of Memory," 91–112 in Caruth (1996).

6 For another illuminating and influential work in this tradition, see Dominick LaCapra, *Representing the Holocaust: History, Theory, Trauma* (1994).

7 All quotations are from pp. 5–7.

8 Piotr Sztompka emphasizes the importance of "agency" for theorizing social change in *Sociology in Action: The Theory of Social Becoming* (1991) and in *The Sociology of Social Change* (1993). See also Alexander (1987) and Alexander, Giesen, Munch, and Smelser (1987).

9 The concept of "claims" is drawn from the sociological literature on moral panics. See Kenneth Thompson (1998).

10 In relation to issues of cultural change and conflict, Weber's concept has been developed further by S. N. Eisenstadt in "The Axial Age: The Emergence of Transcendental Visions and the Rise of Clerics" (1982), and, most recently, by Bernhard Giesen in *Intellectuals and the Nation* (1998). Claim-making groups correspond also to the concept of "movement intellectuals" developed, in a different context, by Ron Eyerman and Andrew Jamison in *Social Movements: A Cognitive Approach* (1994). Smelser (1974) illuminated the group basis for claim making in his reformulation of Tocqueville's notion of "estate." See also Bjorn Wittrock (1991).

11 Thompson also speaks of a "representational process."

12 For the contingency of this process of establishing the nature of the pain, the nature of the victim, and the appropriate response in the aftermath of the "trauma" created by the Vietnam War, see Gibson (1994).

13 Maillot's representation of the difficulties of the Northern Ireland peace process combines these different aspects of the classifying process:

> None of the "agents of violence" would agree on the reasons for the violence and on its nature. In fact, only the supporters of the IRA and, to a much less extent, part of the nationalist community, would agree that there was an actual "war" going on. For a substantial section of the Unionist community, the IRA is entirely to blame. "Our whole community, indeed our whole country, has been the victim of the IRA for over 30 years," said Ian Paisley Jr. . . . As all the other issues discussed in the run-up to the signing of the Good Friday Agreement, the question of victims proved highly emotional and controversial . . . one that enabled all participants to vent their frustration and their anger, and one that revealed the different approaches each side was to take. Indeed, the very term victim has proved controversial, as participants disagreed on the people who constituted this group.

14 The notion of transparency, so necessary for creating a normative, or philosophical, theory of what Habermas has called his "discourse ethics," is debilitating for creating a sociological one.

15 Smelser (1962) described how state agencies and other agents of social control make efforts to "handle and channel" what we are here calling the trauma process.

16 Insofar as such memorializations are not created, the traumatic suffering has

either not been persuasively narrated or has not been generalized beyond the immediately affected population. This is markedly the case, for example, with the 350-year enslavement of Africans in the United States. Ron Eyerman (2004) demonstrates how this experience came to form the traumatic basis for black identity in the United States. However, despite the fact that white Americans initiated what has been called the "second Reconstruction" in the 1960s and 1970s, and despite the permeation among not only black but white American publics of fictional and factual media representations of slavery and postslavery trauma, white power centers in American society have not dedicated themselves to creating museums to memorialize the slavery trauma. A letter to the editor in the *New York Times* points eloquently to this absence and to the lack of black–white solidarity it implies:

> To the Editor: The worthy suggestion that the Tweed Courthouse in Lower Manhattan be used as a museum to memorialize New York City's slave history . . . evokes a broader question: Why is there no national museum dedicated to the history of slavery? One can only imagine the profound educational and emotional effect a major institution recounting this period of our history would have on all Americans. Perhaps President-elect George W. Bush, in striving to be a uniter of people, would consider promoting such a project in our capital? (*New York Times*, December 19, 2000, sec. 1)

17 For example, the routinization of the traumatic transitions to democracy of the 1990s produced a body of specialists who, far from being desiccated and instrumental, worked to spread a new message of moral responsibility and inclusion. Under the headline "For Nations Traumatized by the Past, New Remedies," the *New York Times* reported that:

> From temporary offices on Wall Street, a new international human rights group has plunged into work with 14 countries, helping them come to terms with the oppressions that mark their recent past. The International Center for Transitional Justice opened its doors on March 1, incubated by the Ford Foundation and led by Alex Boraine, an architect of South Africa's Truth and Reconciliation Commission. The South African commission was the first to hold public hearings where both victims and perpetrators told their stories of human rights abuses in the era of apartheid. With a growing number of countries turning to truth commissions to heal the wounds of their past, many governments and human rights groups in Asia, South America, Africa and Europe are now asking for advice, information and technical assistance from those that have been through the process . . . The foundation . . . asked Mr Boraine . . . to develop a proposal for a center that would conduct research in the field and help countries emerging from state sponsored terrorism or civil war . . . "The day we got our funds, we were actually in Peru, and it has been a deluge ever since." (July 29, 2001: A5)

18 This insightful work, by one of the most important contemporary French sociologists, develops a strong case for the moral relevance of mediated global images of mass suffering, but does not present a complex causal explanation for **why** and where such images might be compelling, and where not.

2 HOLOCAUST AND TRAUMA: MORAL UNIVERSALISM IN THE WEST

1 In the inaugural conference of the United States Holocaust Research Institute, the Israeli historian Yehuda Bauer made a critical observation and posted a fundamental question to the opening session.

> About two decades ago, Professor Robert Alter of California published a piece in *Commentary* that argued that we had had enough of the Holocaust, that a concentration of Jewish intellectual and emotional efforts around it was counterproductive, that the Holocaust should always be remembered, but that there were new agendas that had to be confronted ... Elie Wiesel has expressed the view that with the passing on of the generation of Holocaust survivors, the Holocaust may be forgotten ... But the memory is not going away; on the contrary, the Holocaust has become a cultural code, a symbol of evil in Western civilization. Why should this be so? There are other genocides: Hutu and Tutsi in Rwanda, possibly Ibos in Nigeria, Biharis in Bangladesh, Cambodia, and of course the dozens of millions of victims of the Maoist purges in China, the Gulag, and so forth. Yet it is the murder of the Jews that brings forth a growing avalanche of films, plays, fiction, poetry, TV series, sculpture, paintings, and historical, sociological, psychological and other research. (Quoted in Berenbaum and Peck 1998: 12)

> The same opening session was also addressed by Raul Hilberg. As the editors of the conference book suggest, Hilberg's "magisterial work, *The Destruction of the European Jews*," which had been "written in virtual isolation and in opposition to the academic establishment nearly four decades earlier," had since "come to define the field" of Holocaust studies (Berenbaum and Peck 1998: 1). Hilberg began his address as follows:

> When the question is posed about where, as academic researchers of the Holocaust, we stand today, the simple answer is: in the limelight. Never before has so much public attention been lavished on our subject, be it in North America or in Western Europe ... Interest in our topic is manifest in college courses, which are developed in one institution or another virtually every semester; or conferences, which take place almost every month; or new titles of books, which appear practically every week. The demand for output is seemingly inexhaustible. The media celebrate our discoveries, and when an event in some part of the world reminds someone of the Holocaust, our researchers are often asked to explain or supply a connection instantaneously. (Quoted in Berenbaum and Peck 1998: 5)

> This chapter may be viewed as an effort to explain where the "limelight" to which Hilberg refers has come from and to answer Bauer's question "Why should this be so?"

2 Of course, to be defined as a traumatic event for all humankind does not mean that the event is literally experienced or even represented as such by all humankind. As I suggest in the conclusion of this chapter, indeed, only one part of contemporary humankind has even the normative aspiration of experiencing the originating event as a trauma – the "Western" versus the "Eastern" part of humankind – and this cultural–geographical difference itself may have fateful consequences for international relations, definitions of legal–moral responsibility, and the project of global understanding today.

169

3 Once an "atrocity" had involved murderous actions against civilians, but this definition was wiped out during the course of the Second World War.

4 The report continued in a manner that reveals the relation between such particularistic, war-and-nation-related definitions of atrocity and justifications for nationalistic military escalation of brutality in response: "Even though the truth of Japan's tribal viciousness had been spattered over the pages of history down through the centuries and repeated in the modern slaughters of Nanjing and Hong Kong, word of this new crime had been a shock . . . Secretary of State Cordell Hull speaking with bitter self-restraint [sic] excoriated the 'demons' and 'fiendishness' of Japan. Senator Alben W. Barkley exclaimed: 'Retribution [must] be meted out to these heathens – brutes and beasts in the form of man.' Lister Hill of Alabama was practically monosyllabic: 'Gut the heart of Japan with fire!'" The connection of such attributions of war atrocity to pledges of future military revenge illuminates the lack of indignation that later greeted the atomic bombing of Hiroshima and Nagaski. This kind of particularistic framing of mass civilian murder would be lifted only decades later – after the Jewish mass murder had itself become generalized as a crime that went beyond national and war-related justifications. I discuss this later.

5 For a detailed "thick description" of these first encounters, see Robert Abzug, *Inside the Vicious Heart* (1985).

6 During April, under the entry "German Camps," the *New York Times Index* (1945: 1184) employed the noun eight times.

7 For a broad discussion of the role played by such analogies with alleged German First World War atrocities in creating initial unbelief, see Laqueur (1980). The notion of moral panic suggests, of course, a fantasied and distorted object or belief (Thompson 1998). In this sense, trauma is different from panic. (See Alexander 2003b).

8 This is not to say that the fact of the Nazis' anti-Jewish atrocities was accepted all at once but that the Allies' discovery of the concentration camps, relayed by reporters and photographers, soon did put an end to the doubts, which had not been nearly as thoroughly erased by revelations about the Majdanek death camp liberated by Soviets months earlier. For a detailed discussion of this changing relationship between acceptance and doubt, see Zelizer (1998: 49–140).

9 In early October 1945, General George Patton, the much-heralded chief of the US Third Army, became embroiled in controversy over what were taken to be anti-Semitic representations of the Jewish survivors in the camps Patton administered. The general had contrasted them pejoratively with the German and other non-German camp prisoners and given them markedly worse treatment. In light of the argument I will make hereafter, it is revealing that what was represented as intolerable about this conspicuous mistreatment of Jewish survivors was its implied equation of American and Nazi relations to Jews. The *New Republic* headlined its account of the affair "The Same as the Nazis."

> Only on the last day of September did the nation learn that on the last day of August, President Truman had sent a sharp letter to General Eisenhower regarding the treatment of Jews in Germany. The President told the General bluntly that according to a report made by his special investigator, Earl Harrison, "we appear to be treating the Jews as the Nazi treated them, except that we do not

exterminate them." Thousands of displaced Jews are still crowded in badly run concentration camps, improperly fed, clothed and housed, while comfortable homes nearby are occupied by former Nazis or Nazi sympathizers. These Jews are still not permitted to leave the camps except with passes, which are doled out to them on the absolutely incomprehensible policy that they should be treated as prisoners . . . Americans will be profoundly disturbed to learn that anti-Semitism is rife in the American occupation forces just as is tenderness to Nazis. (October 8, 1945: 453)

Time reported the event in the same way:

Plain G.I.s had their problems, too. Ever since they had come to Germany, the soldiers had fraternized – not only with *Fraulein* but with a philosophy. Many now began to say that the Germans were really O.K., that they had been forced into the war, that the atrocity stories were fakes. Familiarity with the eager German women, the free-faced German young, bred forgetfulness of Belsen and Buchenwald and Oswieczim. (October 8, 1945: 31–2)

In a story headlined "The Case of General Patton," the *New York Times* wrote that Patton's transfer from his Bavarian post "can have and should have just one meaning," which was that the US government "will not tolerate in high positions . . . any officers, however brave, however honest, who are inclined to be easy on known Nazis and indifferent or hard to the surviving victims of the Nazi terror" (October 3, 1945: 18). For more details on Patton's treatment of the Jewish camp survivors, see Abzug (1985).

10 In "Radical Evil: Kant at War with Himself" (Bernstein 2001), Richard Bernstein has provided an illuminating discussion of Kant's use of this term. While Kant intended the term to indicate an unusual, and almost inhuman, desire not to fulfill the imperatives of moral behavior, Bernstein demonstrates that Kant contributed little to the possibility of providing standards of evaluation for what, according to post-Holocaust morality, is called radical evil today. Nonetheless, the term itself was an important addition to moral philosophy. I want to emphasize here that I am speaking about social representations of the Holocaust, not its actual nature. I do not intend, in other words, either here or elsewhere in this chapter, to enter into the debate about the uniqueness of the Holocaust in Western history. As Norman Naimark (2001) and many others have usefully pointed out, there have been other terrible ethnically inspired bloodlettings that arguably can be compared with it – for example, the Armenian massacre by the Turks, the killing fields in Cambodia, which claimed three million of a seven million-person population, the Rwanda massacre. My point here is not to make claims about the objective reality of what would later come to be called the Holocaust but about the sociological processes that *allowed estimations* of its reality to shift over time. For an analysis of the discourse about uniqueness, see the section below on "The Dilemma of Uniqueness."

11 This commonsense link is repeated time and again, exemplifying not empirical reality but the semantic exigencies of what I will call the progressive narrative of the Holocaust. For example, in his influential account of the postwar attack on anti-Semitism, Leonard Dinnerstein (1981–2: 149) suggests that "perhaps the sinking in of the knowledge that six million Jews perished in the Holocaust" was a critical factor in creating the identification

with American Jews. A similarly rationalist approach is exhibited by Edward Shapiro (1992) in his book-length study of the changing position of Jews in postwar America. Shapiro observes that "after the Holocaust, anti-Semitism meant not merely the exclusion of Jews from clubs [etc.] but mass murder" (Shapiro 1992: 16). The issue here is what "meant" means. It is not obvious and rational but highly contextual, and that context is culturally established. The distinguished historian of American history John Higham represents this Enlightenment version of lay trauma theory when he points to the reaction to the Holocaust as explaining the lessening of prejudice in the United States between the mid-1930s and the mid-1950s, which he calls "the broadest, most powerful movement for ethnic democracy in American history." Higham suggests that "in the 30s and 40s, the Holocaust in Germany threw a blazing light on every sort of bigotry," thus explaining the "traumatic impact of Hitlerism on the consciousness of the Western world" (Higham 1984: 154). Movements for ethnic and religious tolerance in the United States, Higham adds, came only later, "only as the war drew to a close and the full horrors of the Nazi concentration camp spilled out to an aghast world" (171). Such Enlightenment versions of lay trauma theory seem eminently reasonable, but they simply do not capture the contingent, sociologically freighted nature of the trauma process. As I try to demonstrate hereafter, complex symbolic processes of coding, weighting, and narrating were decisive in the unpredicted postwar effort to stamp out anti-Semitism in the United States.

12 See the observation by the sociological theorist Gerard Delanty (2001: 43): "What I am drawing attention to is the need to address basic questions concerning cultural values, since violence is not always an empirical objective reality, but a matter of cultural construction in the context of publicly shaped discourses and is generally defined by reference to an issue."

13 Access to the "means of symbolic production" is one of the key elements in determining the success of social performances (Alexander 2006a).

14 To think of what might have been, it is necessary to engage in a counterfactual thought experiment. The most successful effort to do so has occurred in a best-selling piece of middlebrow fiction called *Fatherland*, by Robert Harris (1992), a reporter for the London *Times*. The narrative takes place in 1967, in Berlin, during the celebrations of Adolf Hitler's seventieth birthday. The former Soviet Union and the United Kingdom were both conquered in the early 1940s, primarily because Hitler's general staff had overruled his decision to launch the Russian invasion before he had completed his effort to subjugate Great Britain. The story's plot revolves around the protagonists' efforts to reveal the hidden events of the Holocaust. Rumors had circulated of the mass killings, but no objective truth had ever been available. As for the other contention of this paragraph – that Soviet control over the camps' discoveries would also have made it impossible for the story to be told – one may merely consult the Soviets' presentation of the Auschwitz death camp outside Krakow, Poland. While Jewish deaths are not denied, the focus is on class warfare, Polish national resistance, and communist and Polish deaths. It is well known, for example, that the East Germans, under the Soviet regime, never took responsibility for their anti-Semitic past and its central role in the mass killing of Jews, focusing instead on the Nazis as non-national, class-based, reactionary social forces.

15 In her detailed reconstruction of the shifting balance between doubt and

belief among Western publics, Zelizer demonstrates that the Soviets' discovery of the Majdanek death camp in 1944 failed to quell disbelief because of broad skepticism about Russian reporters, particularly a dislike for the Russian literary news-writing style and tendency to exaggerate: "Skepticism made the Western press regard the liberation of the eastern camps as a story in need of additional confirmation. Its dismissive attitude was exacerbated by the fact that the US and British forces by and large had been denied access to the camps of the eastern front [which made it] easier to regard the information trickling out as Russian propaganda" (Zelizer 1998: 51).

16 In modern sociology, the great empirical student of typification is Harold Garfinkel, who, drawing upon Husserl and Schutz, developed a series of supple operationalizations such as *ad-hocing*, *indexicality*, and the "etc. clause" to describe how typification is carried out empirically.

17 See Brooks (1995) for a literary approach to social transformation that is apposite Fussell's in terms of both method and history. Brooks describes the connection between the literary genre of melodrama and more general cultural romanticism in key literary works of the nineteenth century. Fussell observes how this romantic faith was shattered by the First World War, and how the ironic genre deeply affected literary and popular work that followed.

18 See Herf (1984) and also Philip Smith's (1998) investigations of the coding of Nazism and Communism as variations on the modernist discourse of civil society.

19 For how the coding of an adversary as radical evil has compelled the sacrifice of life in modern war, see Alexander (1998) and Smith (2005).

20 Just so, the earlier failure of such nations as France to vigorously prepare for war against Germans had reflected an internal disagreement about the evility of Nazism, a disagreement fuelled by the long-standing anti-Semitism and anti-Republicanism triggered by the Dreyfus affair. For a discussion of this, see William Shirer's classic, *The Collapse of the Third Republic* (1969).

21 Statements and programs supporting better treatment of Jews were often, in fact, wittingly or unwittingly accompanied by anti-Semitic stereotypes. In the months before the United States entered the war against Germany, *Time* reported: "A statesmanlike program to get a better deal for the Jews after the war was launched last week by the American Jewish Congress and the World Jewish Congress, of which the not invariably statesmanlike, emotional, and politics dabbling Rabbi Steven S. Wise is respectively president and chairman" (July 7, 1941: 44). Indeed, in his statistical compilation of shifting poll data on the personal attitudes of Americans during this period, Stember (1966) shows that the percentage of Americans expressing anti-Semitic attitudes actually increased immediately before and during the early years of the anti-Nazi war, though it remained a minority. For a helpful discussion of anti-Semitism in the early twentieth century, see Hollinger (1996).

22 Higham (1984) shows how left-leaning intellectuals, artists, academics, and journalists set out to oppose the nativism of the 1920s and viewed the rise of Nazism in this context. While they focused particularly on the Jewish problem, they also discussed issues of race.

23 From the phrase of Clifford Geertz (1984): "anti-anti-relativism," which he traced to the phrase from the McCarthy era, "anti-anti-Communism." Geertz writes that his point was not to embrace relativism but to reject anti-relativism, just as anti-McCarthyites had not wanted to embrace

173

Communism but to reject anti-Communism. Just so, progressive Americans of that time did not wish to identify with Jews but to reject anti-Semitism because, I am contending, of its association with Nazism.

24 The premise of the following argument is that "salvation" can continue to be a massive social concern even in a secular age. I have made this theoretical argument in relation to a reconsideration of the routinization thesis in Max Weber's sociology of religion (Alexander 1983) and employed this perspective in empirical studies of secular culture (Alexander 2003b, 2010).

25 See Turner's introduction of "liminality" via his reconstruction of Van Gennep's ritual process (Turner 1969).

26 In regard to the eventual peace treaty that would allow progress, the reference was, of course, to the disastrous Versailles Treaty of 1919, which was viewed in the interwar period as having thwarted the progressive narrative that had motivated the Allied side during the First World War. President Woodrow Wilson had presented the progressive narrative of that earlier struggle by promising that this "war to end all wars" would "make the world safe for democracy."

27 I should add by the Jewish *and non-Jewish* victims as well, for millions of persons were victims of Nazi mass murder in addition to the Jews – Poles, "gypsies" or Roma, homosexuals, disabled persons, and political opponents of all types. That virtually all of these non-Jewish victims were filtered out of the emerging collective representation of the Holocaust underlines the arbitrary quality of trauma representations. By *arbitrary*, I mean to refer to Saussure's foundational argument, in his *Course in General Linguistics*, that the relation between signifier and signified is not based on some intrinsically truthful or accurate relationship. The definition of the signifier – what we normally mean by the symbol or representation – comes not from its actual or "real" social referent per se but from its position within the field of other signifiers, which is itself structured by the broader sign system, or language, already in place. This is essentially the same sense of arbitrariness that is invoked by Wittgenstein's argument against Augustine's language theory in the opening pages of *Philosophical Investigations*. This notion of arbitrariness does not mean, of course, that representation is unaffected by noncultural developments, hence the extensive effort here to contextualize this analysis in historical terms.

28 In February 1943 the widely read popular magazine *American Mercury* published a lengthy story by Ben Hecht, called "The Extermination of the Jews" (February 1943: 194–203), that described in accurate detail the events that had already unfolded and would occur in the future. The following report also appeared in *Time:*

> In a report drawn from German broadcasts and newspapers, Nazi statements, smuggled accounts and the stories of survivors who have reached the free world, the [World Jewish] Congress told what was happening in Poland, slaughterhouse of Europe's Jews. By late 1942, the Congress reported, 2,000,000 had been massacred. *Vernichtungskolonnen* (extermination squads) rounded them up and killed them with machine guns, lethal gas, high-voltage electricity, and hunger. Almost all were stripped before they died; their clothes were needed by the Nazis. ("Total Murder," March 8, 1943: 29)

Two months later, *Newsweek* reported the Nazi destruction of the Warsaw Ghetto: "When [the] Gestapo men and Elite Guard were through with the job, Warsaw, once the home of 450,000 Jews, was 'judenrein' (free of Jews). By last week all had been killed or deported" (May 24, 1943: 54). In October 1944 the widely popular journalist Edgar Snow published details about the "Nazi murder factory" in the Soviet liberated town of Majdanek, Poland, in the *Saturday Evening Post* (October 28, 1944: 18–19).

Abzug (1985: 17) agrees that "the more sordid facts of mass slaughter, labor and death camps, Nazi policies of enslavement of peoples deemed inferior and extermination of Europe's Jews" were facts that were "known through news sources and widely publicized since 1942." In the manner of Enlightenment lay trauma theory – which would suggest that knowledge leads to redemptive action – Abzug qualifies his assertion of this popular knowledge by insisting that the American soldiers who opened up the camps and the American audience alike suffered from a failure of "imagination" in regard to the Nazi terror (17). According to the theory of cultural trauma that informs our analysis, however, this was less a failure of imagination than a matter of collective imagination being narrated in a certain way. It points not to an absence of perception but to the presence of the contemporary, progressive narrative framework, a framework that was brought into disrepute by later developments, which made it appear insensitive and even inhumane.

29 Another historian, Peter Novick, makes the same point:

> For most Gentiles, and a great many Jews as well, [the Holocaust] was seen as simply one among many dimensions of the horrors of Nazism. Looking at World War II retrospectively, we are inclined to stress what was distinctive in the murderous zeal with which European Jewry was destroyed. Things often appeared differently to contemporaries . . . Jews did not stand out as the Nazis' prime victims until near the end of the Third Reich. Until 1938 there were hardly any Jews, qua Jews, in concentration camps, which were populated largely by Socialists, Communists, trade unionists, dissident intellectuals, and the like. Even when news of mass killings of Jews during the war reached the West, their murder was framed as one atrocity, albeit the largest, in a long list of crimes, such as the massacre of Czechs at Lidice, the French at Oradour, and American prisoners of war at Malmedy. (Novick 1994: 160)

30 The term was introduced in 1944 by American author Ralph Lemkin, in his book *Axis Rule in Occupied Europe* (1994). As Lemkin defined it, genocide applied to efforts to destroy the foundations of national and ethnic groups and referred to a wide range of antagonistic activities, including attacks on political and social institutions, culture, language, national feelings, religion, economic existence, and personal security and dignity. It was intended to cover all of the anti-national activities carried out by the Nazis against the occupied nations inside Hitler's Reich. In other words, when first coined, the term definitely did not focus on the element of mass murder that after the discovery of the death camps came to be attributed to it.

31 The author, Frank Kingdon, was a former Methodist minister.

32 In an article on the success of *Gentleman's Agreement*, in the *Saturday Review of Literature* (December 13, 1947: 20), the author asserted that "the Jewish people are the world symbol of [the] evil that is tearing civilization apart" and suggested that the book and movie's success "may mean that the conscience of America is awakening and that something at least will be done about it."

33 Short makes this Jewish exceptionalism clear when he writes that "with war raging in the Pacific, in Europe and in the shipping lanes of the Atlantic, Hollywood made a conscious effort to create a sense of solidarity among the nation's racial and ethnic groups (*excepting* the Japanese-Americans and the blacks)" (Short, 1981: 157, italics added).

34 See also Higham (1984) and Silk (1984).

35 It remains an empirical question whether American Jews were themselves traumatized by contemporary revelations about the Nazi concentration camps. Susan Sontag's remembered reactions as a California teenager to the revelatory photographs of the Belsen and Dachau death camps are often pointed to as typical of American Jewish reaction more generally: "I felt irrevocably grieved, wounded, but a part of my feelings started to tighten; something went dead; something still is crying" (quoted in Shapiro 1992: 3, and in Abzug 1985: vii). Yet that this and other oft-quoted retrospective reactions were shared by the wider Jewish public in the United States has been more of a working assumption by scholars of this period, particularly but by no means exclusively Jewish ones. Not yet subject to empirical demonstration, the assumption that American Jews were immediately traumatized by the revelations reflects Enlightenment lay trauma theory. It might also represent an effort at post hoc exculpation vis-à-vis possible guilt feelings that many American and British Jews later experienced about their lack of effort or even their inability to block or draw attention to the mass murders.

36 *Symbolic action* is a term developed by Kenneth Burke to indicate that understanding is also a form of human activity, relating action to expressive form and to the goal of parsing meaning. The term became popularized and elaborated in the two now classical essays published by Clifford Geertz in the early 1960s, "Religion as a Cultural System" and "Ideology as a Cultural System" (1973). Reference to "culture structure" refers to my effort to treat culture as a structure in itself. Only by analytically differentiating culture from social structure – treating it as a structure in its own right – does it move from being a dependent to an independent variable (Alexander 2003a). For related discussions of "culture structure," see Alexander and Smith (2003); Kane (1992); Rambo and Chan (1990) and Magnuson (2008). This discussion of historical transformations in the symbolization of Jewish mass murder is also informed by my work in social performance, which conceptualizes a clear separation between symbolic action, on the one hand, and audience reception, on the other, and suggests a number of relatively independent cultural and institutional mediations that lay inbetween – such as social and hermeneutic power, means of symbolic production, and *mise-en-scène*. (Alexander 2006a and Alexander, Giesen and Mast 2006).

37 See Wilhelm Dilthey, "The Construction of the Historical World in the Human Sciences" (1976).

38 By the early 1990s, knowledge of the Holocaust among American citizens greatly exceeded knowledge about the Second World War. According to public opinion polls, while 97 percent of Americans knew about the Holocaust, far fewer could identity "Pearl Harbor" or the fact that the United States had unleashed an atomic bomb on Japan. Only 49 percent of those polled realized that the Soviets had fought with Americans during that war. In fact, the detachment of the Jewish mass killings from particular historical events had proceeded to the point that, according to an even more recent survey, more

than one-third of Americans either didn't know that the Holocaust took place during the Second World War or insisted that they "knew" it did not (Novick 1999: 232).

39 Yehuda Bauer, in his editor's introduction to the first issue of *Holocaust and Genocide Studies*, suggested this new, *weltgeschichte* (world-historical) sensibility:

> There is not much point in dealing with one aspect of the Holocaust, because that traumatic event encompasses all of our attention; therefore, no concentration on one discipline only would meet the needs ... We arrived at the conclusion that we would aim at a number of readers' constituencies: students, survivors, high school and college teachers, academics generally, and that *very large number of people who feel that the Holocaust is something that has changed our century, perhaps all centuries*, and needs to be investigated. (1986: 1, italics added)

This journal not only embodied the newly emerging generalization and universalization I am describing here but also can be viewed as an institutional carrier that aimed to promote its continuation. Thus, two years later, in an issue of the journal dedicated to papers from a conference entitled, "Remembering for the Future," held at Oxford University in July 1988, Bauer pointedly observed that "one half of the authors of the papers *are not Jewish*, bearing witness to the fact that among academics, at least, there exists a growing realization of the importance of the event to our civilization, *a realization that is becoming more widespread among those whose families and peoples were not affected by the Holocaust*" (1986: 255, italics added).

40 The historian Peter Gay, who coedited the *Columbia History of the World* in 1972, was reportedly embarrassed to find later that the enormous volume contained no mention of Auschwitz or of the murder of 6 million Jews, an embarrassment exacerbated by the fact that he himself was a Jewish refugee from Germany (Zelizer 1998: 164–5).

41

> In 1949, there was no "Holocaust" in the English language in the sense that word is used today. Scholars and writers have used "permanent pogrom" ... or "recent catastrophe," or "disaster," or "the disaster." Sometimes writers spoke about annihilation and destruction without use of any of these terms. In 1953, the state of Israel formally injected itself into the study of the destruction of European Jewry, and so became involved in the transformation [by] establish[ing] Yad Vashem as a "Martyrs" and "Heroes' Remembrance Authority" ... Two years later Yad Vashem translated *shoah* into "Disaster" ... But then the change occurred quickly. When catastrophe had lived side-by-side with disaster the word holocaust had appeared now and then ... Between 1957 and 1959, however, "Holocaust" took on ... a specific meaning. It was used at the Second World Congress of Jewish Studies held in Jerusalem, and when Yad Vashem published its third yearbook, one of the articles dealt with "Problems Relating to a Questionnaire on the Holocaust." Afterwards Yad Vashem switched from "Disaster" to "Holocaust" ... Within the Jewish world the word became commonplace, in part because Elie Wiesel and other gifted writers and speakers, in public meetings or in articles ... made it coin of the realm. (Korman 1972: 259–61)

42 On *shoah*, see Ofer (1996). In telling the story of linguistic transformation inside the Hebrew language, Ofer shows that inside of Israel there was a similar narrative shift from a more progressive to a more tragic narrative frame and that this shift was reflected in the adoption of the word *shoah*, which had strong biblical connotations related to apocalyptic events in Jewish history, such as the flood and Job's sufferings: *shoah* was conspicuously not applied to such "everyday" disasters as pogroms and other repeated forms of anti-Semitic oppression. On the relative newness of the American use of the term *Holocaust* – its emergence only in the postprogressive narrative period – see John Higham's acute observation that "the word does not appear in the index to Richard H. Pells, *The Liberal Mind in a Conservative Age: American Intellectuals in the 1940s and 1950s* – in spite of the attention he gives to European influence and Jewish intellectuals" (Higham, personal communication). According to Garber and Zuckerman (1989: 202), the English term was introduced by Elie Wiesel, in the *New York Times Book Review* of October 27, 1963, in relation to the Jewish mass murder, but there is some debate about the originality of Wiesel's usage. Novick, for example, relates that the American journalist Paul Jacobs employed the term in an article on the Eichmann trial, in 1961, that he filed from Jerusalem for the American liberal magazine *New Leader*. Significantly, Jacobs wrote of "the Holocaust, as the Nazi annihilation of European Jewry is called in Israel." Whatever its precise origins – and Wiesel's 1963 usage may well have marked the beginning of a common usage – the symbolically freighted semantic transition, which first occurred in Israel and then in America, had wide ramifications for the universalization of meaning vis-à-vis the Jewish mass killing. Until the late 1970s, for example, Germans still used bureaucratic euphemisms to describe the events, such as the "Final Solution." After the German showing of the American television miniseries *Holocaust,* however, *Holocaust* replaced these terms, passing into common German usage. One German scholar, Jean Paul Bier, described *Holocaust* as an "American word" (1986: 203); another testified that, after the television series, the term "'Holocaust' became a metaphor for unhumanity" (Zielinski 1986: 273).

43 For the central role of "our time" in the tropes of contemporary historical narratives, see Alexander (2003c).

44 This is not to say, however, that Christological themes of redemption through suffering played no part in the tragic dramatization. As anti-Semitic agitation increased in the late nineteenth century, Jesus frequently was portrayed by Jewish artists as a Jew and his persecution presented as emblematic not only of Jewish suffering but also of the Christian community's hypocrisy in relation to it. During this same period, important Christian artists like Goya and Grosz began to develop "a new approach to Christ, using the Passion scenes outside their usual biblical context as archetypical of the sufferings of modern man, especially in times of war" (Amishai-Maisels 1988: 457). As the Nazi persecution intensified before and during the Second World War, this theme emerged with increasing frequency – for example in the despairing paintings of Marc Chagall. Again, the aim was to provide a mythically powerful icon of Jewish martyrdom and, at the same time, "to reproach the Christian world for their deeds" (464). With the liberation of the camps, there emerged a far more powerful way to establish this icon – through the images of emaciated, tortured bodies of the victims themselves. Immediately after the war, artists such as Corrado Cagli and Hans Grundig stressed the similarity between the

camp corpses and Holbein's "Dead Christ," and Grundig even set the corpses on a gold background, emphasizing their similarity to medieval representations of martyrs. The most telling similarity between Christ and the corpses was not, however, invented by artists but was found in news photographs of those corpses whose arms were spread out in a cruciform pose. One such photograph, published under the title "Ecce Homo-Bergen Belsen," is said to have had an immediate and lasting effect on the artistic representation of the Holocaust (467). It was undoubtedly the case that, for many religious Christians, the transition of Jews from killers of Christ to persecuted victims of evil was facilitated by such iconographic analogies. Nonetheless, even here, in the pictorial equation of Jesus with the Nazi victims, the theme was tragedy but not redemption in the eschatological sense of Christianity. The symbolization held the pathos but not the promise of the crucifixion, and it was employed more as a criticism of the promises of Christianity than as an identification with its theodicy of hope. It should also be mentioned, of course, that the religious mythology and ritual surrounding the death of Christ draw heavily from the classical aesthetic genre of tragedy.

45 "Pity involves both distance and proximity. If the sufferer is too close to ourselves, his impending misfortune evokes horror and terror. If he is too distant, his fate does not affect us ... The ethical and political questions are: whom should we pity? ... The tragic hero? Ourselves? Humanity? All three, and three in one" (Rorty 1992: 12–13). Against Adorno's claim that the Holocaust must not be aestheticized in any way, Hartman (1996) insists that "art creates an unreality effect in a way that is not alienating or desensitizing. At best, it also provides something of a sage-house for emotion and empathy. The tears we shed, like those of Aeneas when he sees the destruction of Troy depicted on the walls of Carthage, are an acknowledgment and not an exploitation of the past" (157).

46 In these psychological terms, a progressive narrative inclines the audience toward projection and scapegoating, defense mechanisms that allow the actor to experience no responsibility for the crime. This distinction also points to the difference between the genres of melodrama and tragedy, which otherwise have much in common. By breaking the world completely into black and white, and by providing assurance of the victory of the good, melodrama encourages the same kind of projection and scapegoating as progressive narratives; in fact, melodramatic narratives often drive progressive ones. For the significance of melodramatic narratives in the nineteenth century and their connection to stories, both fictional and realistic, of ethical triumph, see Brooks (1995). In practice, however, dramatizations of the Holocaust trauma, like virtually every other dramatization of tragedy in modern and postmodern society, often overlap with the melodramatic.

47 By the early 1940s, the Polish Ministry of Information, independent journalists, and underground groups released photos of corpses tumbled into graves or stacked onto carts. One such depiction, which appeared in the *Illustrated London News* in March 1941 under the headline "Where Germans Rule: Death Dance before Polish Mass Execution," portrayed victims digging their own graves or facing the death squad. The journal told its readers that "behind these pictures is a story of cold-blooded horror reminiscent of the Middle Ages" (quoted in Zelizer 1998: 43).

48 This is the radical and corrosive theme of Bauman's provocative *Modernity*

and the Holocaust (1989). While Bauman himself professes to eschew any broader universalizing aims, the ethical message of such a perspective seems clear all the same. I am convinced that the distrust of abstract normative theories of justice, as expressed in such postmodern efforts as Bauman's *Postmodern Ethics* (1993), can be understood as a response to the Holocaust, as well, of course, as a response to Stalinism and elements of the capitalist West. In contrast to some other prominent postmodern positions, Bauman's ethics is just as strongly opposed to communitarian as to modernist positions, an orientation that can be understood by the centrality of the Holocaust in his critical understanding of modernity. Bauman's wife, Janina, is a survivor and author of a moving Holocaust memoir, *Winter in the Morning* (1986). The dedication of *Modernity and the Holocaust* reads: "To Janina, and all the others who survived to tell the truth."

49 "Lachrymose" was the characterization given to the historical perspective on Jewish history developed by Salo Baron. The most important early academic chronicler of Jewish history in the United States (Liberles 1995), Baron held the first Chair of Jewish History at Harvard. Baron was deeply affected by what seemed, at the time, to be the reversal of Jewish assimilation in the *fin-de-siècle* period. In response to this growth of modern anti-Semitism, he began to suggest that the medieval period of Jewish–Gentile relations – the long period that preceded Jewish "emancipation" in the Enlightenment and nineteenth century – actually may have been better for the Jewish people, culturally, politically, economically, and even demographically, than the post-emancipation period. Postwar Jewish historiography, not only in the United States but also in Israel, often criticized Baron's perspective, but as the progressive narrative of the Holocaust gave way to the tragic frame, his lachrymose view became if not widely accepted then at least much more positively evaluated as part of the whole reconsideration of the effects of the Enlightenment on modern history. See Liberles (1995). For a broader analysis of the contradictory processes of Jewish "incorporation" into the civil spheres of Europe and the US see Alexander (2006b: 459–548).

50 This has, of course, been the complaint of some intellectuals, from the very beginning of the entrance of the Holocaust into popular culture, from *The Diary of Anne Frank* to Spielberg's later dramas. As I will suggest below, however, the real issue is not dramatization per se but the nature of the dramatic form. If the comic frame replaces the tragic or melodramatic one, then the "lessons" of the Holocaust are, indeed, being trivialized.

51 She adds that "The appeal to pity is . . . also an appeal to fellow feeling."

52 Tragedy . . . provides us with the appropriate objects towards which to feel pity and fear. Tragedy, one might say, trains us or habituates us in feeling pity and fear in response to events that are worthy of those emotions. Since our emotions are being evoked in the proper circumstances, they are also being educated, refined, or clarified . . . Since virtue partially consists in having the appropriate emotional responses to circumstances, tragedy can be considered part of an ethical education. (Lear 1992: 318)

Is it necessary to add the caveat that to be "capable" of exercising such an ethical judgment is not the same thing as actually exercising it? This cultural shift to which I am referring is about capability, which, while clearly a prerequisite of action, does not determine it.

53 Such a notion of further universalization is not, of course, consistent with postmodern social theory or philosophy, and the intent here is not to suggest that it is.

54 My aim in this section should not be misunderstood as an effort to aestheticize and demoralize the inhuman mass murders that the Nazis carried out. I am trying to denaturalize, and therefore sociologize, our contemporary understanding of these awful events. Despite their heinous quality, they could be interpreted in various ways. Their nature did not dictate their interpretation. As Robert Braun (1994) suggests: "Historical narratives do not necessarily emplot past events in the form of tragedy and this form of emplotment is not the only node of narration for tragic events" (182).

What I am suggesting here is a transparent and eerie homology between the tragic genre – whose emotional, moral, and aesthetic qualities have been studied since Aristotle – and how we and others have come to understand what the Holocaust "really was." Cultural sociology carries out the same kind of "bracketing" that Husserl suggested for his new science of phenomenology: the ontological reality of perceived objects is temporarily repressed in order to search for those subjective elements in the actor's intentionality that establish the *sense* of verisimilitude. What the Holocaust "really was" is not the issue for this sociological investigation. My subject is the social processes that allowed the events now identified by this name to be seen as different things at different times. For the lay actor, by contrast, the reality of the Holocaust must be taken as an objective and absolute. Moral responsibility and moral action can be established and institutionalized only on this basis.

In historical and literary studies, there has developed over the last two decades an intense controversy over the relevance of the kinds of cultural methods I employ here. Scholars associated with the moral lessons of the Holocaust – for example, Saul Friedlander – have lambasted the deconstructive methods of narrativists like Hayden White for eliminating the hard-and-fast line between "representation" (fiction) and "reality" (fact). Friedlander organized the tempestuous scholarly conference that gave birth to the collective volume *Probing the Limits of Representation* (1992a). In the conference and the book he drew an analogy between cultural historians' questioning of reality and the politically motivated efforts by contemporary Italian fascists, and all the so-called revisionists since then, to deny the mass murder of the Jews. While I would strongly disagree with Friedlander's line of criticism, there is no doubt that it has been stimulated by the way the aestheticizing, debunking quality of deconstructive criticism has, from Nietzsche on, sought to present itself as a replacement for, rather than a qualification of, the traditional political and moral criticism of the rationalist tradition. By contrast, I am trying here to demonstrate that the aesthetic and the critical approach must be combined.

55 Each national case is, of course, different, and the stories of France, the United Kingdom, Italy, the Netherlands and the Scandinavian countries (e.g., Eyerman 2008) would depart from this account in significant ways. Nonetheless, as Diner (2000) remarks, insofar as "the Holocaust has increasingly become a universal moral icon in the realm of political and historical discourse," the "impact of the catastrophe can be felt in various European cultures, with their disparate legacies [and] even within the realm of collective . . . identities" (218). Non-Western countries, even the democratic ones,

181

have entirely different traumas to contend with, as I have pointed out in my introduction (cf. Alexander and Gao 2007).

56 In fact, I believe that it is because of the symbolic centrality of Jews in the progressive narrative that so relatively little attention has been paid to the Nazis' equally immoral and unconscionable extermination policies directed against other groups – for example, Poles, homosexuals, Roma ("gypsies"), and the disabled. Some frustrated representatives of these aggrieved groups – sometimes for good reasons, other times for anti-Semitic ones – have attributed this lack of attention to Jewish economic and political power in the United States. The present analysis suggests, however, that cultural logic is the immediate and efficient cause for such a focus. This logic is also propelled, of course, by geopolitical and economic forces, but such considerations would apply more to the power and position of the United States in the world system of the postwar world than to the position of Jews in the United States.

As I have shown, it was not the actual power of Jews in the United States but the centrality of "Jews" in the progressive American imagination that defined the crimes of Nazis in a manner that focused on anti-Semitism. In terms of later developments, moreover, it was only because of the imaginative reconfiguring of the Jews that political and economic restrictions were eliminated in a manner that eventually allowed Jews to gain influence in mainstream American institutions. As I will show below, moreover, as American power declined, so did the exclusive focus on Jews as a unique class of Holocaust victims. This suggests, as I will elaborate later, that the contemporary omnipresence of the Holocaust symbol has more to do with "enlarging the circle of victims" than with focusing exclusively on Jewish suffering.

The most significant scholarly example of this tendentious focus on "Jewish power" as the key for explaining the telling of the Holocaust story is Peter Novick's book *The Holocaust in American Life* (1999). To employ the categories of classical sociological theory, Novick might be described as offering an instrumentally oriented "status group" explanation à la Weber, in contrast to the more culturally oriented late-Durkheimian approach taken here. Novick suggests that the Holocaust became central to contemporary history because it became central to America, that it became central to America because it became central to America's Jewish community, and that it became central to Jews because it became central to the ambitions of Jewish organizations that were central to the mass media in all its forms (207). Jewish organizations first began to emphasize the Holocaust because they wanted to "shore up Jewish identity, particularly among the assimilating and intermarrying younger generations" (186) and to maintain the Jews' "victim status" in what Novick sees as the identity-politics shell game of the 1980s – "Jews were intent on permanent possession of the gold medal in the Victimization Olympics" (185). Despite acknowledging that it is "impossible to disentangle the spontaneous from the controlled" (152), he emphasizes the "strategic calculations" (152) of Jewish organizations, which are said to have motivated them to emphasize the Holocaust in response to "market forces" (187).

The analysis here fundamentally departs from Novick's. Whereas Novick describes a particularization of the Holocaust – its being captured by Jewish identity politics – I describe its universalization. Where Novick describes a nationalization, I trace internationalization. Where Novick expresses skepticism about the metaphorical transferability of the "Holocaust," I describe such metaphorical bridging as essential to the social process of moral engagement. In terms of sociological theory, the point is not to deny that status groups are significant. As Weber clarified in his sociology of religion, however, such groups must be seen not as creators of interest per se but as "carrier groups." All broad cultural currents are carried by – articulated by, lodged within – particular material and ideal interests. Even ideal interests, in other words, are represented by groups – in this case status groups rather than classes. But, as Weber emphasized, ideal and material interests can be pursued only along the "tracks" that have been laid out by larger cultural ideas.

The sense of the articulation between these elements in the Holocaust construction is much more accurately represented in Edward T. Linenthal's book *Preserving Memory: The Struggle to Create the Holocaust Museum* (1995). Linenthal carefully and powerfully documents the role of status group interests in the fifteen-year process involved in the creation of the Holocaust Museum in Washington, DC. He demonstrates, at the same time, that the particular parties were deeply affected by the broader cultural context of Holocaust symbolization. President Carter, for example, initially proposed the idea of such a museum partly on political grounds – in order to mollify a key democratic constituency, the Jews, as he was making unprecedented gestures to Palestinians in the diplomatic conflicts of the Middle East (17–28). Yet, when a Carter adviser, Stuart Eizenstat, first made the written proposal to the president, in April 1978, he pointed to the great popularity of the recently broadcast *Holocaust* miniseries on NBC. It was in terms of this broader context – in which the Holocaust was already being universalized – that Eizenstat also warned the president that other American cities, and other nations, were already engaged in constructing what could be competing Holocaust commemorative sites. Even Linenthal, however, sometimes loses sight of the broader context. Describing the contentious struggles over representation of non-Jewish victims, for example, he speaks of "those committed to Jewish ownership of Holocaust memory" (39), a provocative phrasing that invites the kind of reductionist, status-group interpretation of strategic motivation that Novick employs. As I have shown in this chapter, the Holocaust as a universalizing symbol of human suffering was, in a fundamental sense, inextricably related to the Jews, for the symbol was constructed directly in relationship to the Jewish mass murder. This was not a matter of ownership but a matter of narrative construction and intensely experienced social drama, which had been crystallized long before the struggles over representation in the museum took place. As a result of the early, progressive narrative of the Nazis' mass murder, non-Jewish Americans had given to Jews a central pride of place and had greatly altered their attitudes and social relation to Jews as a result. The conflicts that Linenthal documents came long after this crystallization of Jewish centrality. They were about positioning vis-à-vis an already firmly crystallized symbol, which had by then become renarrated in a tragic manner. Engorged with evil and universalized in its meaning, the Holocaust could not possibly be "owned" by any one particular social group or by any particular nation. The Holocaust museum was able to gain consensual support precisely because the symbol of evil had already become highly

NOTES TO PAGES 64–8

generalized such that other, non-Jewish groups could, and did, associate and reframe their own subjugation in ways that strengthened the justice of their causes. See my discussion of metonymy, analogy, and legality later in the chapter.

Norman G. Finkelstein's book *The Holocaust Industry: Reflections on the Exploitation of Jewish Suffering* (2000) represents an even more tendentious and decidedly more egregious treatment of Holocaust centrality than Novick's, in a sense representing a long and highly polemical asterisk to that earlier, more scholarly book. Finkelstein bothers not at all with the ambiguity of motives, flatly saying that the Jewish concentration on the Holocaust, beginning in the late 1960s, was "a ploy to delegitimize all criticism of Jews" (37). The growing crystallization of the Holocaust as a metaphor for evil invites from Finkelstein only ridicule and ideology-critique: "The abnormality of the Nazi holocaust springs not from the event itself but from the exploitive industry that has grown up around it . . . 'The Holocaust' is an ideological representation of the Nazi holocaust. Like most ideologies, it bears a connection, if tenuous, with reality . . . Its central dogmas sustain significant political and class interests. Indeed, The Holocaust has proven to be an indispensable ideological weapon" (150–51).

57 Higham (1984) rightly notes that a range of factors involving what might be called the "modernization" of America's Jewish population – increasingly high rates of urbanization and education, growing professionalization – also facilitated the identification with them of non-Jews. Other, more specifically cultural processes, however, were also fundamentally involved.

58 According to a 1990 survey, when Americans were presented with a list of well-known catastrophic events, a clear majority said that the Holocaust "was *the* worst tragedy in history" (quoted in Novick 1999: 232, italics in original).

59 The tragic and personal qualities of the *Diary*, which set it against the "progressive narrative" structure of the early postwar period, initially had made it difficult to find a publisher.

Queriod, the literary publishing house in Amsterdam, rejected the manuscript of *Het Achterhuis*, giving as its reasons the fact that "in 1947 it was certain that war and everything to do with it was stone dead . . . Immediately as the terror was over and the anxieties of that pitch-black night were banished, people did not want to venture again into the darkness. They wished to give all their attention to the new day that was dawning" (Strenghold 1988: 337).

60 Doneson's helpful historical reconstruction of the dramatization of the *Diary* also emphasizes the personal focus. Like many other commentators (e.g., Rosenfeld 1995), however, she suggests that this focus undermines the tragic message of the Holocaust rather than generalizing it. In this, she joins the ranks of those who decry the "Americanization" of the Holocaust, an interpretation with which my approach strongly disagrees.

61 This clash of genres was demonstrated by the storm of controversy inside Germany that greeted the 1995 decision by a new German cable company to broadcast old episodes of *Hogan's Heroes*.

62 See the extensive social scientific discussion in Zielinski (1986), from which this discussion is derived.

63 It was after this crystallizing event that some of the intellectuals who had been

most associated with focusing public discussion on the Holocaust began to criticize its transformation into a mass collective representation. Elie Wiesel made his famous declaration (quoted earlier) that the ontological nature of Holocaust evil made it impossible to dramatize. Complaining, in effect, that such dramatization stole the Holocaust from those who had actually suffered from it, Wiesel described the television series as "an insult to those who perished, and those who survived" (quoted in Morrow 1978). Such criticism only intensified in response to the subsequent flood of movie and television dramatizations. In *One, by One, by One: Facing the Holocaust,* for example, Judith Miller issued a fervent critique of the appropriation of the original event by the mass media culture of the "Holocaust industry" (1990: 232). Rather than seeing the widespread distribution of the mass-mediated experience as allowing universalization, she complained about its particularization via "Americanization," presumably because it was in the United States that most of these mass media items were produced: "Europe's most terrible genocide is transformed into an American version of kitsch" (232).

Aside from knee-jerk anti-Americanism, which has continued to inform critiques of the "Holocaust industry" in the years since, such a perspective also reflects the anti-popular culture, hermeneutic tone-deafness of the Frankfurt School's "culture industry" approach to meaning. (See Docker [1994] for a vigorous postmodern criticism in this regard.) Such attacks stand outside the interpretive processes of mass culture. In place of interpretations of meaning, they issue moral condemnations: "This vulgarization is a new form of historical titillation . . . In societies like America's, where the public attention span is measured in seconds and minutes rather than years or decades, where sentimentality replaces insight and empathy, it represents a considerable threat to dignified remembrance" (Miller 1990: 232). Such complaints fundamentally misapprehend cultural processes in general and cultural trauma in particular. (See my later discussion of the "dilemma of uniqueness.")

While such typically leftist complaints are well intended, it is revealing that their "anti-commodification" arguments overlap quite neatly with the conservative, sometimes anti-Semitic language that German conservatives employed in their effort to prevent the *Holocaust* miniseries from being shown in their country. Franz Joseph Strauss, the right-wing, nationalist leader of the Bavarian Christian Democrats, called the series "a fast-buck operation." The German television executives opposed to airing the series condemned it as "a cultural commodity . . . not in keeping with the memory of the victims." *Der Spiegel* railed against "the destruction of the Jews as soap opera . . . a commercial horror show . . . an imported cheap commodity . . . genocide shrunken to the level of *Bonanza* with music appropriate to *Love Story*." After the series was televised and its great impact revealed, one German journalist ascribed its effect to its personal dramatization: "No other film has ever made the Jews' road of suffering leading to the gas chambers so vivid . . . Only since and as a result of 'Holocaust' does a majority of the nation know what lay behind the horrible and vacuous formula 'Final Solution of the Jewish Question.' They know it because a US film maker had the courage to break with the paralyzing dogma . . . that mass murder must not be represented in art" (quoted in Herf 1986: 214, 217).

64 See the Arendt–Jaspers correspondence on these issues and the astute analysis by Richard J. Bernstein in *Hannah Arendt and the Jewish Question* (1996).

65 "The capture and trial of Eichmann and, in the following years, the controversies surrounding Hannah Arendt's *Eichmann in Jerusalem* were something of a curtain raiser to the era of transition. For the mass public this was the first time the Holocaust was framed as a distinct and separate process, separate from Nazi criminality in general" (Novick 1994: 161). It was only as a result of this separation that the poet A. Alvarez could have made his much-noted remark in the *Atlantic Monthly*, to the effect that "while all miseries of World War II have faded, the image of the concentration camp persists" (quoted in Zelizer 1998: 155).

66 Novick (161) goes on to observe that "it was in large part as a result of the acceptance of Arendt's portrait of Eichmann (with an assist from Milgram) that 'just following orders' changed, in the American lexicon, from a plea in extenuation to a damning indictment."

67 See, in more depth, Browning, "Ordinary Germans or Ordinary Men? A Reply to the Critics," in Berenbaum and Peck (1998: 252–65), and Goldhagen, "Ordinary Men or Ordinary Germans?" in Berenbaum and Peck (1998: 301–8).

68 "Spielberg does not show what 'Germans' did but what *individual* Germans did, offering hope that one of them – Schindler – would become one of many. Unlike *Holocaust* . . . Spielberg can tell a 'true tale' that must seem doubly strange. While the events in *Schindler's List* may contradict the idea of the Nazi state as the perfect machine, the State's and Schindler's deficiencies provide a paradox of choice – 'the other Nazi,' the German who did good" (Wiessberg 1997: 178, italics in original).

69 By "force of arms" I refer to the ability of the North Vietnamese to successfully resist the United States and South Vietnamese on the ground. David Kaiser's *American Tragedy* (1999) demonstrates that, in purely military terms, the Americans and South Vietnamese forces were never really in the game and that, in fact, the kind of interventionist war the United States benightedly launched could not have been won short of using nuclear arms. If the United States had not intervened militarily in Vietnam, America might not have lost control over the means of symbolic production, and the Holocaust might not have been universalized in the same way.

70 The power of this symbolic reversal is attested to by the fact that, two decades later, an American psychologist, Herbert C. Kelman, and a sociologist, V. Lee Hamilton, published *Crimes of Obedience: Toward a Social Psychology of Authority and Responsibility* (1989), which in developing a theory of "sanctioned massacre" drew explicit connections between American military behavior at My Lai and German Nazi behavior during the Holocaust.

71 One demonstration of this polluting association was provided by the *New York Times* review of a much-trumpeted televised program called *Nuremberg*. "Here's the defining problem with *Nuremberg*, TNT's ambitious, well-meaning two-part miniseries about the trial of Nazi war criminals: the 'best' character in the movie is Hermann Goring. Through Brian Cox's complex performance, Goring (founder of the Gestapo, Hitler's no. 2) becomes his finest self. He is urbane, loyal, and courageous – and he gets the best lines. The victors will always be the judges, the vanquished always the accused," he says with world-weary knowingness (Julie Salamon, "Humanized, but Not Whitewashed, at Nuremberg," July 14, 2000: B 22).

72 In 1995, the Smithsonian Museum in Washington, DC, had planned to

186

mount an exhibition commemorating the Allies' defeat of Japan and the successful conclusion of the Second World War. The plans included highlighting the plane that had dropped the atomic bomb on Hiroshima. The public uproar that greeted these plans eventually had the effect of preventing the exhibition from ever going forward. See Linenthal (1995).

73 These suggestions were made, for example, in both Laqueur (1980) and Dawidowicz (1982). The scholarly arguments along these lines culminated with the publication of David S. Wyman's book *The Abandonment of the Jews: America and the Holocaust, 1941–1945* (1984).

74 Unfortunately, Linenthal's otherwise helpful discussion implies that, in this case as in others, there is a disjunction, perhaps a morally reprehensible one, between the dissensus about empirical facts and the interpretive frame. I would suggest (Alexander 2003b) that these are different arenas for the mediation of cultural trauma, and each arena has its own framework of justification.

75 See, for example, the brilliant but mythologizing biography of Jean Lacouture, *De Gaulle: The Rebel 1890–1944* (1990). After the Allied armies, primarily British and American, had allowed the relatively small remnant of the French army under De Gaulle to enter first into Paris, as a symbolic gesture, De Gaulle dramatically announced to an evening rally that Paris "has risen to free itself" and that it had "succeeded in doing so with its own hands."

76 Max Ophuls's film *The Sorrow and the Pity* exercised a profound expressive effect in this regard, as did the American historian Robert O. Paxton's book *La France de Vichy*. For an overview of these developments, see Hartman, "The Voice of Vichy" (Hartman 1996: 72–81).

77 How many Austrians themselves – or Swiss, or Dutch for that matter (Eyerman 2008) – have come to accept this new position in the Holocaust story is not the issue, and there certainly is a new right movement in Continental Europe that often takes on anti-Semitic tones and minimizes Nazi atrocities against Jews. That said, there have definitely been deep and significant cultural processes inside various European nations that have transformed former victims into quasi-perpetrators. This process of symbolic inversion is well illustrated by the emergence of a new association in Austria, the Gedenkdienst, or Commemorative Service Program. This government-sponsored but privately organized program allows young men to perform alternative service by volunteering in a Holocaust-related institution somewhere in the world: "The interns are challenging their country's traditional notion of its wartime victimization – that Austria simply fell prey to Nazi aggression. In fact, thousands of Austrians acted as Nazi collaborators and likely committed war crimes against Jews . . . 'I want to tell [people] that I acknowledge it,' Zotti [a Gedenkdienst volunteer] says, 'It's important for me. It's my country. It's my roots. I want to put it in the light of what it is'" (*Los Angeles Times*, July 30, 2000: E3).

78 The phrase has been evoked innumerable times over the last three decades in both theological and secular contexts – for example, Vigen Guroian's "Post-Holocaust Political Morality" (1988).

79 According to a poll taken during the 1990s, between 80 and 90 percent of Americans agreed that the need to protect the rights of minorities, and not "going along with everybody else," were lessons to be drawn from the Holocaust. The same proportion also agreed that "it is important the people

keep hearing about the Holocaust so that it will not happen again" (quoted in Novick 1999: 232).

80 On May 20, 1999, the *San Francisco Chronicle* ran the following story from the *Los Angeles Times* wire service:

> The Justice Department renewed its long legal battle yesterday against alleged Nazi death camp guard John Demjanjuk, seeking to strip the retired Cleveland autoworker of his US citizenship. For Demjanjuk, 79, the action marks the latest in a 22–year-old case with many twists and turns . . . The Justice Department first accused Demjanjuk of being Ivan the Terrible in 1977, and four years later a federal judge concurred. Demjanjuk was stripped of his US citizenship and extradited in 1986 to Israel, where he was convicted of crimes against humanity by an Israeli trial court and sentenced to death. But Israel's Supreme Court found that reasonable doubt existed on whether Demjanjuk was Ivan the Terrible, a guard [in Treblinka] who hacked and tortured his victims before running the engines that pumped lethal gas into the chambers where more than 800,000 men, women and children were executed . . . Returning to a quiet existence in Cleveland, Demjanjuk won a second court victory last year when [a] US District Judge – citing criticism of government lawyers by an appellate court panel – declared that government lawyers acted "with reckless disregard for their duty to the court" by withholding evidence in 1981 that could have helped Demjanjuk's attorneys . . . The Justice Department [will] reinstitute denaturalization proceedings based on other evidence. ("US Reopens 22-Year Case against Retiree Accused of Being Nazi Guard": A4)

The proceedings were reinstated in 2001, and Demjanjuk was ordered deported from the US in 2005. No country agreed to receive him until 2009, when he was sent to Germany. On May 12, 2011, a Munich court convicted Demjanjuk of being an accessory to the murder of 27,900 Jews, sentencing him to five years of prison. Released pending appeal, Demjanjuk resides, at the time of this writing, in a German nursing home.

81 The first issue of the journal *Holocaust and Genocide Studies* carried an article by Seena B. Kohl entitled "Ethnocide and Ethnogenesis: A Case Study of the Mississippi Band of Choctaw, a Genocide Avoided" (1986: 91–100). After the publication of his *American Holocaust: The Conquest of the New World* (1991) David E. Stannard wrote:

> Compared with Jews in the Holocaust . . . some groups have suffered greater *numerical* loss of life from genocide. The victims of the Spanish slaughter of the indigenous people of Mesoamerica in the sixteenth century numbered in the tens of millions . . . Other groups also have suffered greater proportional loss of life from genocide than did the Jews under Hitler. The Nazis killed 60 to 65 per cent of Europe's Jews, compared with the destruction by the Spanish, British, and Americans of 95 per cent or more of numerous ethnically and culturally distinct peoples in North and South America from the sixteenth through the nineteenth centuries . . . Among other instances of clear genocidal intent, the first governor of the State of California openly urged his legislature in 1851 to wage war against the Indians of the region "until the Indian race becomes extinct." (2, italics in original)

Stannard is ostensibly here denying the uniqueness of the Holocaust, even while he makes of it a pivotal reference for moral determinations of evil.

82 Delanty (2001) makes an apposite observation, suggesting that "the discourse of war around the Kosovo episode was one of uncertainty about the cognitive status of war and how it should be viewed in relation to other historical events of large-scale violence" (43). Delanty directly links this discursive conflict, which he locates in what he calls the "global public sphere," to the ethical questions of what kind of interventionist action, if any, outsiders were morally obligated to take: "The implications of this debate in fact went beyond the ethical level in highlighting cultural questions concerning the nature of war and legitimate violence . . . about what exactly constitutes violence [and] who was the victim and who was perpetrator [and] the constitution of the 'we' who are responsible" (43). Yet because Delanty views this discursive conflict as primarily cognitive, between more or less similarly valued "cognitive models," he fails sufficiently to appreciate the moral force that the Holocaust's engorged evility lent to the metaphors of ethnic cleansing and genocide. This leads Delanty to make the perplexing observation that "as the war progressed, the nature of the subject of responsibility, the object of politics and whether moral obligations must lead to political obligation became more and more uncertain," with the result that the "obligation to intervene was severely limited" (43). Yet, if the analysis in the present chapter is correct, it would seem to suggest precisely the opposite: Given the uneven weighting of the polluted symbols of violence, as the Yugoslavian wars progressed, during the decade of the 1990s, the Holocaust symbol gained increasing authority with the result that the immanent moral obligations became increasingly certain and the political obligation to intervene increasingly available.

83 The very same day, Germany's deputy foreign minister for US relations, a Social Democrat, "suggested why Germany was able to participate in the NATO assault on Yugoslavia: The '68ers,' veterans of the student movement, used to tell their elders, 'We will not stand by, as you did while minority rights are trampled and massacres take place.' Slobodan Milosevic gave them a chance to prove it" (*San Francisco Chronicle*, May 14: A1).

84 For a detailed discussion of the fundamental analogizing role played during media construction of the Balkan crisis by recycled Holocaust photos, see Zelizer (1998: 210–30).

85 The date was December 11, 1946.

86 On the fiftieth anniversary of that proclamation, Michael Ignatieff recalled that "the Holocaust made the Declaration possible," that it was composed in "the shadow of the Holocaust," and that "the Declaration may still be a child of the Enlightenment, but it was written when faith in the Enlightenment faced its deepest crisis of confidence" (1999: 58).

87 The World War II trials [should] receive credit for helping to launch an international movement for human rights and for the legal institutions needed to implement such rights. Domestic trials, inspired in part by the Nuremberg trials, include Israel's prosecution of Adolf Eichmann for this conduct during World War II; Argentina's prosecution of 5,000 members of the military junta involved in state terrorism and the murder of 10,000 to 30,000 people; Germany's prosecution of border guards and their supervisors involved in shooting escapees from East Germany; and Poland's trial of General Jaruzelski for his imposition of martial law . . . Nuremberg launched a remarkable

189

international movement for human rights founded in the rule of law; inspired the development of the United Nations and of nongovernmental organizations around the world; encouraged national trials for human rights violations; and etched a set of ground rules about human entitlement that circulate in local, national, and international settings. Ideas and, notably, ideas about basic human rights spread through formal and informal institutions. Especially when framed in terms of universality, the language of rights and the vision of trials following their violation equip people to call for accountability even where it is not achievable. (Minow 1998: 27, 47–8)

88 The scholar was Yehuda Bauer. See note 39.

89 Despite his misleading polemics against what he pejoratively terms the "Holocaust industry," it is revealing that even such a critic of popularization as Finkelstein realizes that the uniqueness of Holocaust evil does not preclude, and should not preclude, the event's generalization and universalization:

> For those committed to human betterment, a touchstone of evil does not preclude but rather invites comparisons. Slavery occupied roughly the same place in the moral universe of the late nineteenth century as the Nazi holocaust does today. Accordingly, it was often invoked to illuminate evils not fully appreciated. John Stuart Mill compared the condition of women in that most hallowed Victorian institution, the family, to slavery. He even ventured that in crucial respects it was worse. (Finkelstein 2000: 148)

Citing a specific example of this wider moral effect, Finkelstein observes that, "seen through the lens of Auschwitz, what previously was taken for granted – for example, bigotry – no longer can be. In fact, it was the Nazi holocaust that discredited the scientific racism that was so pervasive a feature of American intellectual life before World War II" (2000: 148).

90 This instrumentalizing, desacralizing, demagicalizing approach to routinization is captured in the quotation with which Max Weber famously concluded *The Protestant Ethic and the Spirit of Capitalism* (1958 [1904]: 182). Observing that modernity brought with it the very distinct possibility of "mechanized petrification, embellished with a sort of convulsive self-importance," Weber added this apposite passage: "Specialists without spirit, sensualists without heart; this nullity imagines that it has attained a level of civilization never before achieved." This understanding has been applied to the memorialization process – as kind of inevitable, "developmental" sequence – by a number of commentators, and, most critically, in Ian Buruma, *The Wages of Guilt* (1994), and Peter Novick, *The Holocaust in American Life* (1999).

91 I am grateful to the author for sharing his findings with me.

92 Internal memo from Alice Greenwald, one of the museum's consultants, and Susan Morgenstein, the former curator and subsequently director of temporary exhibits, February 23, 1989.

93 Interview with Ralph Applebaum, chief designer of the Holocaust Museum.

94 Internal memo from Cindy Miller, project director, March 1, 1989.

95 This is Linenthal's own observation.

96 A *Los Angeles Times* description of the museum brings together its tragic dramatization, its participatory experiential emphasis, and its universalizing ambition:

The 7-year-old West Los Angeles museum is internationally acclaimed for its high-tech exhibits, for pushing ideas instead of artifacts. You know right away that this is not the kind of museum where you parade past exhibits on the walls. The place is dark and windowless with a concrete bunker kind of feel, lit by flashes from a 16-screen video wall featuring images of civil rights struggles and blinking list of words: *Retard. Spic. Queen.* (July 30, 2000: E1, italics in original)

The exhibition at the Los Angeles museum begins by asking visitors to pass through one of two doors marked "unprejudiced" and "prejudiced."

3 HOLOCAUST AND TRAUMA: MORAL RESTRICTION IN ISRAEL

1 The complaint that caused Itamar Shapira to be fired from Yad Vashem came from a group of students from Efrat, a large settlement in formerly Palestinian, now Israeli occupied territory. While this is revealing of the very divisions inside contemporary Israel which we discuss below, the origins of the complaint are not significant in terms of the point we are making here. What we are emphasizing is not where the complaint came from, but how this central communicative institution in Israel reacted to it.

2 In a series of influential studies, the psychiatrist Vamik Volkan has explored such narrowing and particularistic responses to trauma and the manner in which they fuel violence and revenge, e.g., Volkan (2001). From an historical and cultural sociological perspective, Volkan's work is limited by the individualistic and naturalizing assumptions that so often detract from psychoanalytic perspectives on collective life. These problems also affect, but in a less restrictive manner, the wide-ranging, politically engaged studies by Dan Bar-On and his colleagues, e.g., Shamir, Yitzhaki-Verner and Bar-On (1996) and Bar-On (1997).

3 It is paradoxical that in her searching and original investigation, Idith Zertal (2005) insists on contrasting what she views as the truly "historical dimension of the events" with their "out-of-context use" in the new nation's collective memory, which she condemns for having "transmuted" the facts (4–5). The position that informs our own approach is that history is never accessible as such. To make it seem so is to provide resources for the kind of ideology critique in which Zertal is so powerfully engaged.

4 For an account of this emancipation, its fateful disappointments, and the rise of Zionism as one among several Jewish responses, see Alexander 2006, chapter 18. The idea of returning to Jerusalem had, of course, long been an essential idiom of diasporic Judaism.

5 For an account of this situation, see Khalidi (1997).

6 For a synthetic account of the significant contrast between the mentalities and fighting strategies of the left- and right-wing Jewish forces fighting for the creation of the Jewish state, see Bickerton and Klausner (2002), pp. 100–115.

7 For many contemporary friends of Israel – and we certainly count ourselves among them – such a characterization will appear harsh. It seems to us, however, the ineluctable conclusion from two decades of Israel's own deeply revisionist, self-critical historiography. As such writers as Benny Morris (1987) and Ilan Pappe (1992) have documented in painstaking and painful

191

empirical detail, the independence conflict involved not just Palestinian residents' voluntary flight but massive, Israeli-instigated population transfers, pushing hundreds of thousands of Palestinians off their land and wiping out the Palestinian identities of hundreds of once-Arab villages. This is not to say that the historical events triggered by the UN's two-state resolution were inevitable, nor is it to absolve the Palestinian and Arab parties of their own fateful responsibilities. For a collection of archival-based essays by Arab and Jewish scholars exploring this complex and deeply contradictory period, see Rogan and Shlaim (2001). That collection is also notable for Edward Said's "Afterword: The Consequences of 1948" (2001). In this, one of the radical Palestinian critic's last published essays, Said lashes out at the repressive, anti-Semitic, and militaristic conditions that, in his view, have marked so much of Arab and Palestinian political and cultural life during the post-independence period. For an insightful overview of the polarizing, if delayed, effects of Israeli's "history wars" over its collective identity – and an argument for it as psychologically overdetermined – see Brunner (2002).

8 This specifically Israeli–Jewish frame complemented the more broadly polluting binary of Western Orientalism. Though sweeping and polemical, Said was not wrong when he suggested, thirty years ago in *The Palestinian Question*, that "between Zionism and the West there was and still is a community of language and of ideology [that] depends heavily on a remarkable tradition in the West of enmity toward Islam in particular and the Orient in general." Asserting that Arabs were "practically the *only* ethnic group about whom in the West racial slurs are tolerated, even encouraged," Said suggested that "the Arabs and Islam represent viciousness, veniality, degenerate vice, lechery, and stupidity in popular and scholarly discourse" (Said 1979: 26, italics in source).

9 See also Bilu and Witztum (2000); Bar (2005); Ofer (2000).

10 Zertal (2005): 39, and Handelman and Katz (1990). Handelman and Katz interpret this juxtaposition as having suggested that, for the Israelis, Holocaust Day signified an exit from the suffering of diasporic Jewry, framing the tragedy, in a progressive manner, as adumbrating the emergence of the Jewish state.

11 As Zertal notes, it has even been proposed that all six million Jewish casualties be granted Israeli citizenships (Zertal 2005: 3).

12 The phrase "From Holocaust to Revival" (in Hebrew *M'shoah L'tkuma*) is polysemic. The word *Tkuma* can be translated both as "revival" and as "establishment" (specifically regarding the establishment of the state of Israel).

13 For an elaborate discussion of the privatization of the Holocaust memory in Israeli society, see Shapira (1998).

14 Bilu and Witztum note, for example, that the psychiatric diagnosis of post-traumatic-stress disorder could only emerge in the wake of the Yom Kippur War, for it implied a weakening of the indomitable Israeli protagonist's military strength: "The myth of heroism, and with it the layers of disregard and denial that had hidden combat stress reactions from the public eye in the preceding wars, were extensively eroded in the 1973 War. Following the utter surprise and confusion at the onset of the war, the military defeats in the first days of fighting, and the heavy toll of casualties – more than 2,500 soldiers

killed and about 7,000 wounded – the war was inscribed in the national consciousness as a massive trauma" (Bilu and Witztum 2000: 20).

15 For a detailed account of this change in the Israeli attitude toward the memory of the Holocaust, see Yablonka (2008).

16 A collection of testimonies and experiences from the Six-Day War provides numerous examples, see A. Shapira (1968).

17 Examples include Azarya and Kimmerling (1985–6), Kimmerling (1993 and 1999).

18 While this protest is popularly known in Israel as the "400,000 protest," sources disagree on the exact number of demonstrators who participated. More conservative estimates put the number at half of that, while others claim that the square in which it was held, including the adjoining streets, could not have held even a third (Azaryahu 2007).

19 The empathy-creating possibilities of Holocaust memory is ignored by Zertal's reconstruction, whose cultural history has no place for the peace movement.

20 For an elaborate account of the first years of *Gush Emunim* and of the religious and political context out of which it had emerged, see Newman (1985). The turn from a messianic religious discourse to a militaristic discourse in the political culture of *Gush Emunim* is discussed in Taub (2010). If the polarizing effects of the Israeli trauma-drama's shifting retellings were deepened by more "fundamentalist," and often more eschatological, versions of Jewish religion, the same can be said for the Palestinian trauma. More radical and rejectionist elements, publicly dedicated to the annihilation of Israel, increasingly experienced the sources of their trauma, and its possible resolution, through Islamicist faith. For this intertwining of the religious extremes, see Friedland and Hecht (1996, 168–70 and 355ff).

21 Due to the multipartisan structure of the Israeli political map, the definitions of "right wing" and "left wing" are rather slippery. Whereas political parties differ according to their socioeconomic policies, ranging from socialism to extreme liberalism, these positions do not necessarily align with their positions regarding the Arab–Israeli conflict. Further complications arise when one takes into account these parties' stances regarding the relations between religion and the state, which range from orthodoxy to extreme secularism, as well as minority parties.

22 It should be emphasized that not all Jewish residents of the territories conquered by Israel in 1967 are part of this movement. While the original postwar settlers were characterized by a religious and ideological commitment to the settlement project, a significant part of the Jewish migrants to these territories were motivated by economic considerations. The ideology described here represents the more audacious and activist "settlement movement" and does not extend to all Jewish residents of the occupied territories.

23 *Israel Studies* 14, no. 1 (Spring 2009).

4 MASS MURDER AND TRAUMA: NANJING AND THE SILENCE OF MAOISM

1 Communist and fascist revolutions can be thought of in this manner, allowing the aggrieved collectivity, whether the proletariat or the folk, or more specifically its political and intellectual representatives, to take power and fashion a

new social system that supposedly will prevent such traumas from occurring in the future. We will develop this theme in the latter part of this chapter in regard to the Chinese revolution of 1949.

2 Chang's book has inevitably become a lightning rod for controversy, and this is apparently true, for reasons that should be evident, in some quarters of Japanese politics and scholarship. In terms of its reception in the Anglophone world, we are not aware of serious challenges to the general empirical claims advanced in Chang's work. In his foreword to the book, William C. Kirby, Professor of Modern Chinese History at Harvard University (Kirby 1997) attests that "Ms Chang shows more clearly than any previous account" the "bestial behavior" committed by "Japanese commanders and troops" during the seven weeks of confrontation at Nanjing. Other expert analysts agree. Peter Li (2000: 57) later called the Nanjing Massacre the "best kept secret about World War II." Referring to such events as the Nanjing Massacre, Eugene Sledge (1998) claims that "the best secret of World War II is the truth about Japanese atrocities." See also James Yin and Shi Young (1996) and Siyun Lin, *Nan Jing Bao Wei Zhan yu Nan Jing Da Tu Sha* [*The Battle in Defense of Nanjing and the Massacre in Nanjing*] (2011), available at http://www.china-week.com/html/548.htm. While Lin's motives are more political and ideological than scientific – he is a right-wing amateur historian who has, on many occasions, attempted to defend the Jingoistic Japanese war policy – this does not necessarily invalidate his findings. In this case, Rui Gao's subsequent research in her Yale PhD dissertation, *Eclipse and Memory: Public Representation of the War of Resistance in Maoist China and its Official Revision in Post-Mao Era*, has confirmed that what Lin has claimed about the contents of history books in CCP China is generally correct. See also note 3 below.

3 After the conclusion of the Pacific War, the International Military Tribunal of the Far East estimated that there were more than 260,000 non-combatants murdered. Some experts place the total at over 350,000 (Chang 1997: 4). When presenting the paper on which this chapter is based at Sophia University in Tokyo Japan, we were informed that some respected Japanese scholars have challenged these estimates, placing the number of victims at "only" 200,000. There is, inevitably, some controversy about such factual assertions in regard to long past historical events, and it is not the intention of this chapter to offer definitive empirical estimates in quantitative terms. We believe, nonetheless, that the available historical evidence does not challenge our basic presupposition here – that mass murder on a "world-historical" scale did occur during these weeks in Nanjing. Assuming these historical events to have taken place, our aim in this chapter is to offer new interpretations of the reaction to them.

4 The reference to the atomic bombings as traumas that helped define postwar Japanese identity raises the obvious question of where, in this process of Japanese identity construction, a sense of responsibility for the Nanjing Massacre might lie. The answer, many observers have suggested, is close to "nowhere at all." Chang provides a bitingly critical overview of Japanese denials, not only of their responsibility for the massacre, but also of its very empirical existence, characterizing this process as Japan's "second rape" of Nanjing (Chang 1997: 199–214). To speak of the Japanese nation as a collectivity in this manner clearly runs the risk, however, of effacing the

controversies that divide the country in the struggles over how to remember its militarist past, as Akiko Hashimoto has made clear in "The Cultural Trauma of a Fallen Nation: Japan, 1945" (Eyerman et al. 2011). That said, the relative insensitivity of the Japanese government to such issues as the Nanjing Massacre has indeed played a powerful role in textbook, scholarly, and media trauma construction for the Chinese people and plays some role in Japan's interstate relations in Asia today. Yet, while the case of Japan's relation to the massacre is increasingly debated (see Schwartz 2011), China's relation to the massacre has rarely been thematized, despite the fact that China's own attitude to the massacre in the decades after 1937 had enormous repercussions, even for the Japanese. See note 17 below and Appendix I for further discussion of the contemporary Japanese relation to the massacre.

5 Chang treats this German involvement as evidence of the factual transparency of the massacre, but it can also, at the same time, be taken as evidence of the widespread appeal of the Orientalist frame, such that it could even provide a framework for bridging the gulf between Nazis and anti-Nazis. For the concept of Orientalism, see Edward Said's classic, *Orientalism* (Vintage, New York, 1979).

6 The original Chinese title is *Ri Kou de Can Sha Jian Yin Mie Jue Ren Xing!*

7 The original Chinese title is *Ren Lei Suo Gong Qi de Bao Xing.*

8 See note 33 below. We must acknowledge, however, that our investigation of KMT representations of the massacre is far from complete. We were able to look only at *Zhong Yang Ri Bao* (the *Central Daily*), the major news daily published by the KMT government, and for this source only for the dates before 1937 and after 1945. While we did closely examine this newspaper on the three memorial day periods of the massacre – on December 13 from 1945 to 1948 – it is certainly possible that, in the period preceding, significant representations of the trauma at Nanjing were made. We would expect, however, that such representations would reveal how, and why, the Nanjing Massacre did *not* enter centrally into the KMT's version of Chinese identity. Because it estimated the CCP enemy to be as insidious as the Japanese, and ultimately, indeed, a much greater danger, this Kuomintang carrier group could not weigh perpetrator evil in the manner required by trauma construction. Our reasoning on this question is further elaborated below, in note 33.

9 In earlier drafts of this chapter, we primarily depended on secondary data for the case of school textbooks. For the current draft, we have had access to original data as made available by the Library of the People's Education Press in PRC, the central publishing institution that was exclusively in charge of compiling, editing, and distributing school textbooks in the PRC. According to the librarian of the Press, for at least two decades after the building of PRC began in 1949, the press monopolized control over textbook publishing. This means that the textbooks edited and published by the press were widely adopted in elementary and middle schools throughout the China of Mao's era; in fact, they provide very likely the only versions of events that were made available for students around the time. For the purpose of this research, we checked all the history textbooks for elementary, junior, and senior middle schools and their respective teacher's reference books. Except for one "new" edition of 1961 – which did not, it turned out, ever enter into circulation – our data pool represents all the history textbooks circulating in PRC during the two decades after 1949. While history texts for elementary

and junior middle school displayed deep silence about the massacre, we did find exceptions in the 1958 edition of history texts for senior middle school and some of the teacher reference books. Mitigating these exceptions are three considerations. First, extra materials offered in to teachers were in principle only supplementary to history texts; they were not required to be taught to students or memorized by them. Second, in the sole history text where the incident was mentioned, the 1958 edition of a senior middle school text, the enormous horror of Nanjing was confined to a one-sentence narrative: "In Nanjing, the Japanese invading forces conducted an inhuman killing, raping and looting, and in more than one month, the number of civilians being murdered amounted to no less than 300,000" (*Senior Middle School Textbook for Chinese History,* Book 4, Beijing, People's Education Press, 1958, p. 40). While the incident is identified here with "horror," it is not symbolically heightened by such metaphors as "massacre," "mass killing," or "mass murder," terms that were applied to murderous events in which the Kuomintang were involved during the "White Terror" period (see note 26 below for such semiotic hierarchy). Third, the number of readers who would ever be able to read the sentence, namely, the students receiving senior middle education in China in the 1950s and 1960s, remained small in comparison with elementary or junior middle school. As for the ten years known as the era of the "Cultural Revolution," the People's Education Press dissipated, and therefore stopped publishing textbooks. Schools were mostly closed during the first three years, and, when they resumed, the use of textbooks was chaotic. Without a standardized system, each province or region had its own edition of textbooks published. While we do not have access to most of the dozens of editions of history textbook published during this period, we expect that they gave intense class struggle supreme social significance, with the result that there would not have been symbolic space for the incident in Nanjing to assume historical significance. As in the case of the articles in *People's Daily* that we discuss shortly, there was throughout this period an effort to focus on the impotence and negligence of the Kuomintang, which featured as a general representation of class enemies.

10 *New Edition of History Textbook for Senior Elementary School,* Book 4, ed. Compiling and Editing Committee for Textbooks of Ministry of Education, People's Government of North Central China, Xin Hua Bookstore, 1950, p. 24. The history textbooks for elementary and junior middle school that were published by the People's Education Press during the two decades of Mao's China, which were also examined in our research, include: *New Edition of History Textbook for Senior Elementary School,* Book 4, ed. Compiling and Editing Committee for Textbooks of Ministry of Education, People's Government of North Central China, Xin Hua Bookstore, 1950; *Senior Elementary School Textbook History,* Book 4, People's Education Press, 1956; *Senior Elementary School Textbook History,* Book 2, People's Education Press, 1961; *Junior Middle School Textbook Chinese History,* Book 4, People's Education Press, 1956; *Senior Middle School Textbook for Chinese History,* Book 4, People's Education Press, 1958; *Teacher's Reference Guide for Senior Middle School Textbook for Chinese History,* Book 4, People's Education Press, 1958; *Full-Time Ten Year School Junior Middle Textbook (Experimental Edition) Chinese History,* Book 4, ed. History Edition Team for General Textbooks for Elementary and Middle School,

People's Education Press, 1979; and *Elementary Textbook History,* Book 2, ed. Division of History of People's Education Press, People's Education Press, 1992.

11 *Junior Middle School Textbook for Chinese History,* Book 4, ed. and pub. People's Education Press, 1956, p. 74.

12 In the 1959 edition of the teachers' reference guide for junior middle school, for example, the section devoted to the Kuomintang's struggle with Japanese forces in 1937 was limited to one short paragraph, and, again, it seemed to be intended more as evidence for the cowardice and impotence of the Kuomintang regime. This reference to Nanjing consisted of five words: "In December, Nanjing was lost." *See Teacher's Reference Guide for Junior Middle School Textbook for Chinese History,* Book 4, ed. People's Education Press, People's Education Press, 1959, p. 83.

13 See *Full-Time Ten Year School Junior Middle Textbook (Experimental Edition) Chinese History,* Book 4, ed. History Edition Team for General Textbooks for Elementary and Middle School, People's Education Press, 1979, and *Elementary Textbook History,* Book 2, ed. Division of History of People's Education Press, People's Education Press, 1992.

14 These findings are the result of a computer search through the archives of *People's Daily* for references to "Nanjing Massacre" in the thirty-six years between 1946 and 1982. There were two mentions in the *People's Daily* in 1950: March 14 (p. 1) and December 8 (p. 2); six mentions in 1951: February 24 (p. 3), February 27 (p. 1), March 4 (p. 4), April 21 (p. 4), May 1 (p. 5); two mentions in 1952: April 9 (p. 1), September 7 (p. 1); and six mentions in 1960: May 16 (pp. 1, 2), May 23 (p. 4), May 26 (p. 3), May 30 (p. 6). In note 32 below, in the context of our explanation of why the Nanjing Massacre did not enter centrally into Chinese collective identity, we will discuss the content of this handful of references and offer an interpretation of why they occurred when they did. In 1982, this long silence was broken with a surge of new articles and references, which continued over the course of the decade, for reasons which will become clear.

15 See Chang's (1997) discussions of "Japanese Damage Control" (p. 147), "Japanese Propaganda" (pp. 149–53), and "The Occupation of Nanjing" (pp. 159–67).

16 For this concept, "the means of symbolic production," and a systematic discussion of the broad range of elements required for successful symbolic performances vis-à-vis social audiences, see Alexander, Giesen, and Mast (2006).

17 In April 2005, large-scale anti-Japanese demonstrations broke out in major cities throughout China. Among the major rhetorical protests of these demonstrations was the accusation that Japanese elementary and high school textbooks narrated Japan's military history against China in a distorted manner, one that neglects or denies Japan's wartime atrocities against Asian nations, including the Nanjing Massacre. While these actions were, of course, stimulated and controlled by the Communist state, they also responded to mass sentiment. Whatever the source of the protests, that official Japanese accounts have avoided responsibility for the massacre cannot be denied. See Appendix I.

18 "Among the big and small contradictions determined or influenced by the basic contradiction," Mao writes, "some become intensified, some are temporarily or partially solved or mitigated, and some emerge anew;

197

consequently the process reveals itself as consisting of different stages" (Mao 1962: 225).

19 See *New Edition of History Textbook for Senior Elementary School*, Book 4, ed. Compiling and Editing Committee for Textbooks of Ministry of Education, People's Government of North Central China, Xin Hua Bookstore, 1950, p. 14; *Junior Middle School Textbook for Chinese History*, Book 4, People's Education Press, 1956, pp. 31–32; *Senior Middle School Textbook for Chinese History*, Book 4, People's Education Press, 1958, p. 21; *Teacher's Reference Guide for Senior Middle School Textbook for Chinese History*, Book 4, People's Education Press, 1958, p. 52.

20 *Junior Middle School Textbook for Chinese History*, Book 4, People's Education Press, 1956, p. 32.

21 The major figure that initiated the incident was known to be Wang Jingwei, a political figure of Kuomintang who later collaborated with Japan and became the head of the puppet government in Nanjing. His famous anti-Communist slogan as proposed during the incident – "better to kill one thousand non-Communists by mistake than allow a true Communist to slip through the net" – later became a monumental piece of evidence for CCP in its narrative construction of the suffering of its members at the hands of Kuomintang reactionaries.

22 *Junior Middle School Textbook for Chinese History*, Book 4, People's Education Press, 1956, p. 32.

23 *Senior Middle School Textbook for Chinese History*, Book 4, People's Education Press, 1958, p. 21.

24 Ibid.: 23.

25 One could refer to *Junior Middle School Textbook for Chinese History*, Book 4, People's Education Press, 1956, pp. 79–80 for the original text. One could also find such text sections in all the other editions listed in note 10.

26 Because Lin was a military and political guru whose rank and prestige was second only to Chairman Mao's, his commemoration monograph from which these quotations were drawn can be regarded as an authoritative version that sets the overall tone for the narration of the War of Resistance as well as shapes the interpretation and collective memoires among the public. In her article on memorization of the war and the Communist trauma, Gao (2011) has reconstructed the narrative elements of Lin's article. Among its other salient features, she has discovered a semiotic hierarchy between the conspicuous enemy of the war, the Japanese invading forces, and the true evil of all time, the Kuomintang regime as the general representative of class enemies. In this semiotic ranking, the Japanese were not only portrayed as a much lesser evil than the Kuomintang regime but are generously endowed with likelihood of symbolic redemption to which the latter is completely denied. See Gao (2011).

27 In "Revolutionary Trauma and Representation of the War," Gao (2011) traces the narrative construction of the Communist trauma as established in Mao's China (1949–76), which defined the class enemy as the ultimate evil and the proletarian masses as the traumatized and trampled victims. Gao suggests that the overwhelming success of this narrative construction, along with the sacred new collectivity of revolutionary China, was based on the universal class victimhood that prevented the War of Resistance from emerging as a collective trauma. The vertical nature of the Chinese resistance conflict, Gao

finds, posed an inconvenient contradiction of the horizontal symbolic demarcation of the world of the oppressed, as entailed by class trauma.

28 The original Chinese title is *Jiang Jun Dao Chu An Wu Tian Ri, Jian Sha Jie Lue Tu Tan Ren Min.*

29 The original Chinese title is *Jiang Zheng Fu Jian Chi Du Cai Nei Zhan, Jing Ji Mian Lin Quan Mian Beng Kui.*

30 The original Chinese title is *Tuan Jie Di Guo Fan Zhan Ren Min.*

31 The original Chinese title is *Ri Ben Ren Min de Fan Zhan Hu Sheng.*

32 It was, in fact, under the camouflaging cover of such references to the polluted American enemy that the brief references noted earlier (note 14 above) to the Nanjing Massacre in postrevolutionary China appeared. Both mentions of the massacre in 1950 in *People's Daily*, for example, appeared in news reports decrying the evil-doings of the "American imperialists" who had not only robbed the "world's people" of postwar victory but now threatened the hard-won world peace. One article (*People's Daily*, 3/14/1950: 1), entitled "The Monstrous Crimes of MacArthur" (*Mai Ke A Se de Tao Tian Zui Xing*) accuses the American general of abusing power in the proceedings of the International Military Tribunal of the Far East by shielding the Japanese war criminals – including those who were perpetrators in Nanjing, which is where the massacre was mentioned. In 1951, the massacre was briefly mentioned in an article (*People's Daily*, 5/1/1951: 5) entitled "Oppose Invasion by the US and Defend World Peace" (*Fan Dui Mei Guo Qin Lue, Bao Wei Shi Jie He Ping*). The point was that such a tragedy would be repeated if the Americans got their way and were able to rearm the Japanese imperialists. Both these stories tellingly demonstrate how the postrevolutionary focus of attention had effectively shifted to the new enemy of the nation, the American imperialists. The Nanjing Massacre was relevant only as a piece of indirect evidence for the evilness of this new target.

Just as the massacre was recruited as part of the war propaganda in the Korean War in the early 1950s, it was incorporated, and subordinated into the larger framework of class struggle in news coverage about the Japanese student movement against the US-Japan Security Treaty in 1960. In each of the six articles that mentioned the massacre during this year, the dominant motif was the student movement and, more broadly, the Chinese people's positive responses to it. The point, in other words, was not to make the massacre a trauma-drama for the Chinese people, but to make use of its memory to recall the trauma of the anti-Japanese struggle and to transform the memories of that trauma into a struggle against the Japanese alliance with the United States. The war crimes were constructed as having been committed by the Japanese imperialists, so that the proletariat, the Japanese "people," remained innocent victims. The more evil the Japanese imperialists, as powerfully illustrated by their unforgivable crimes in the massacre, the more justified the current struggle of the Japanese people against them. Therefore, to fight against the current Japanese imperialists, who were supported by the most dangerous enemy of all, the American imperialists, the Chinese people must ally themselves with the righteous struggle of the Japanese people – as one of the articles suggested, "Let's unite and fight together!" (*Hu Xiang Tuan Jie, Hu Xiang Zhi Chi, Gong Tong Dou Zheng*) (*People's Daily*, 5/16/1960: 2).

33 The same can probably be said, more conditionally, for trauma construction

by the KMT. We have not, as we mentioned earlier, had sufficient access to Kuomintang media to make a secure judgment on this matter. Certainly, we have reason to believe that the conservative side paid more attention to the mass murder. They were, after all, in control of Nanjing, then the Chinese capital, when the massacre took place. Nonetheless, it does not appear that the Kuomintang widely publicized the massacre; they did not make it central to their collective identity, to the identity of (one national variant of) modern "Chinese." On the tenth anniversary of the massacre, on December 13, 1947, on the second page of *Central Daily*, we found a feature story titled "This Day of Nanjing Ten Years Ago: Massacre! Massacre!" With the help of accompanying photos, this article communicated a traumatic event replete with vivid and gruesome details of atrocities, and was filled with phrases such as "tragic beyond compare in this human world," "atrocities of unparalleled savage," and "unprecedented in the human history."

At the same time, however, and we believe this marks a telling parallel with the cultural logic of the CCP, this Kuomintang construction of "atrocities" linked them to enemies whose evil was weighted just as heavily as the Japanese perpetrators. These were the civil enemies inside China. Only one week after the anniversary issue, on the third page of the *Central Daily* of December 19, 1947, there appeared an essay that depicted the means of killing and torturing in as gruesome detail as the descriptions employed in the story about the massacre. This time, however, the antagonists in the plot were the "Communist bandits," not the Japanese. This parallel version of the Kuomintang narrative was just as powerfully bifurcated into good and evil; it employed the image of hell on earth and even evoked the language of class struggle: "The North-Western Part of Shangxi Province Has been Transformed into Hell: People were Moaning under the Class Struggle." There was even a sensational news report that these "Communist bandits" in Shangxi province had forced their Kuomintang POWs to eat the bodies of their fellow prisoners (*Central Daily*, 12/21/1947: 4). The displacing effect of such a construction seems clear. The construction of trauma-drama depends on weighting evil; the perpetrator must be constructed as such having committed a unique and unparalleled crime that it becomes engorged with evil, a sacred monster set apart from everything human. This cannot happen if a traumatic event is relativized by placing it side-by-side with another, committed by an entirely different party, but which is constructed in very similar terms. When one asks, which protagonist is truly evil – the one who tortures, kills, and commits cannibalism against individuals or small groups, or the one who commits mass massacre? – the answer is not so clear.

34 *The East is Red* was a song and dance epic of the Chinese revolution, a gigantic performance project proposed and coordinated by no less than Zhou Enlai, the premier of the PRC in Mao's era. The words introduce Act Four, which is devoted to the depiction of the War of Resistance. The performance debuted in Beijing in October 1964. In celebration of the fifteenth anniversary of the founding of the new republic, the epic performance presents a vivid depiction of the Chinese revolution in the form of songs, dance, opera, and ballet and thus offers an ideal text for interpreting how the nation represents its own past and defines its collective identity to the public, including the representation of the War of Resistance in the public arena. To a certain extent, the textual part of this theatrical performance, including both its verse

and its song lyrics, composes a highly condensed version of modern Chinese history as seen from the perspective of the CCP. The entire script of the performance and its English translation may be found at the following website: http://www.wyzxsx.com/Article/Class12/201007/165476.html (last accessed on September 30, 2010). We modified the English translation found on this website.

35 Ibid. While these words are meant to introduce Act II, which is devoted to the first Great Revolution Period and the anti-Communist massacres committed by the Kuomintang regime that brought this time to a tragic end, its figurative language and emotional expression vividly illustrate the thematic "goriness" with which the CCP constructed its trauma of revolution.

36 Ibid.

37 The CCP's Ministry of Propaganda obviously played a critical role in this crystallization and memorialization process, initiating a series of large-scale artistic and literary projects since 1949 to strengthen "propaganda" work. According to Cheng (2002), one of the most influential of these projects was to publicize and advocate for *San Hong* (the Three Reds) among younger generations. These refer to three revolutionary novels that were singled out as the most important materials for ideological inculcation. Each was devoted to depicting the heroic feats of Chinese Communists during their long-time struggle before 1949, and all had in their titles a Chinese character that means "red," the color regarded as representing Communism: *Hong Qi Pu* (*Keep the Red Flags Flying*), *Hong Ri* (*The Red Sun*), and *Hong Yan* (*The Red Crag*). These novels were not only published and distributed exclusively by the Youth Press of China, under direct supervision of the Central Committee of Chinese Communist Youth League, but also formed an essential component of the required reading collections for tens of millions of school kids and young people for generations. Among the three, the most influential, *The Red Crag*, was based on the experience of Communist martyrs who were jailed and eventually killed in a prison conglomerate controlled by Kuomintang in the suburb of Chongqing. The novel was republished more than twenty times between 1961 and the 1980s, with a total distribution of 8 million (Cheng 2002). It was also adapted into a movie *Lie Huo Zhong Yong Sheng* (*To Acquire Eternal Life in the Raging Fire*), and an opera titled "Sister Jiang," the name of a major female CCP figure. The characters in the novel have become such an important component of the social imagination in contemporary China that the name of a CCP traitor portrayed in it, Pu Zhigao, has become an alternative expression for traitor in the Chinese language, and one of its major female CCP martyr figures, Jiang Jie (Sister Jiang), has become a consecrated heroine whose name is often used as a metonymy for the entire Communist martyr group. As a now deified embodiment of Communist virtue and loyalty, her holiness might be compared with that of France's Joan of Arc. The prison conglomerate where these CCP figures were portrayed as having been incarcerated and murdered became a revolutionary museum, as we mention in the notes following. See Guangbin Luo and Yiyan Yang, *Hong Yan* (*The Red Crag*) (Beijing: Youth Press of China, 1961); and Bin Liang, *Hong Qi Pu* (*Keep the Red Flag Flying*) (Beijing: Youth Press of China, 1957).

38 This refers to the Geleshan Cemetery of Revolutionary Martyrs in Chongqing, later known as the Revolutionary Museum of Geleshan, built on the base of

the prison conglomerate where the story in *The Red Crag* happened. The museum not only exhibits the "original" torture chamber but also offers a vivid reenactment of the primal torture scene for visitors. According to a pamphlet dedicated to the museum (Li et al. 1998), it remains one of the important heritage sites under state protection, and also one of the One Hundred Model Patriotic Education Bases under the direct supervision of the CCP's Ministry of Propaganda. It claims to be "one of the most visited museums in the country," with the number of visitors in 1997 amounting to more than two million (ibid.: 126–44).

39 See Qiang Wu, *Hong Ri* (*The Red Sun*) (Beijing: Youth Press of China, [1957] 2004). The novel was published first in 1957, and has been frequently republished for subsequent generations of Chinese, right up until today. While there are no official statistics on the number and distribution of readers of this novel, that it belongs to "The Three Reds" should put the broadness of circulation beyond doubt. See note 37.

40 Tragically and ironically, Zhang's polluted figure as a perpetrator in Communist trauma seems to have been perpetuated by the building of a "memorial" – more accurately, a line of carving on the wall in celebration of the victory of the PLA – at the site of his death in the cave of the Meng Liang Gu mountain. It coldly reads: "This is the Site Where Zhang Lingfu Was Shot to Death."

41 Examples abound. Consider an issue of the *People's Daily* published in 1985. This year marked the 40th anniversary of the victory in the war and there had been large-scale commemoration activities in the public sphere of the PRC, including the building and opening of the memorial for the Nanjing Massacre. In the commemoration discourse, the Japanese ruling party was condemned as being guilty of undermining world peace, while Japanese people were portrayed as brothers and sisters of the sacred camp of peace-lovers. In an article titled "Japanese Public Figures Talk on the 40th Anniversary of Victory in the War of Resistance; People from Japan and China Unite to Defend Peace in Asia as well as in the World," it was asserted that the Japanese ruling party and politicians "kept on behaving in opposition to the will of Japanese people, hurting the feelings of the people in countries that had been occupied by Japanese Jingoists" (*People's Daily*, 9/2/1985: 7). On page 6 of the same paper, an article with the title "Treasure the Present while Remember the Past" appeared. In this article, the reporter interviewed some famous "Japanese friendly personnel" and veterans who were formerly stationed in China. These representatives of the Japanese people all enthusiastically pledged to continue promoting Sino–Japanese friendship. It is particularly illuminating that at the end of the article, a statistic is presented as evidence for the reassuring conclusion that "the absolute majority of Japanese people had drawn profound historic lessons from the distressful war experience":

> According to the survey conducted by Asahi News on Japanese people's attitude towards the issue of Yasukuni Shrine: among all the 624 letters from the readers, 544 showed disapproval to visits to the shrine, which compose 87% of the sample, and only 49 letters showed approval. This demonstrates the strong wish of Japanese people to learn from history. (P. 6)

Two weeks from the day after news reports covering the building of the memorial for the Nanjing Massacre were published, an article appeared, on

August 27th (p. 6), with the title "Not to Let the Tragedy Repeat Itself!" It was reported in detail how the "Japanese mass people" made efforts to avoid "making the same mistake"; "would gather each year on August 15th, to commemorate the day, to oppose war and to advocate for world peace"; how they would put on anti-war exhibitions and build memorials for Chinese slave laborers who had died in Japan; and avow that they would "never go into war again."

42 Besides the media coverage, increasing internet space has been dedicated to the massacre and its memorization. Such websites include www.nj1937.org, www.njmassacre.org, www.china918.org, and www.china918.net; though not singularly devoted to the massacre, all specialize in the War of Resistance. Many are radically nationalistic, and they seem to represent a spontaneous collective attempt to build a new sacred national identity that is negatively rooted in the profaned memory of the war.

5 PARTITION AND TRAUMA: REPAIRING INDIA AND PAKISTAN

1 This chapter was first presented at the conference "Historical Trauma between Family, Civil Society, and State in Israel and Palestine" hosted by the Mediterranean Programme, RSCAS, European University Institute, Florence, September 28–9, 2007. I am grateful to t00he conference organizers, Benoit Challand and Marcella Simoni, for having stimulating my initial investigation. I wish also gratefully to acknowledge Je0ffrey Guhin for his excellent research assistance.

2 For this perspective on the contradictory qualities of the civil sphere, the intertwining of particularism and universalism, see Alexander 2006, especially Chapter 8.

3 For an historical account of such efforts in the context of disappointed idealism, see Jay Winter's helpful *Dreams of Peace and Freedom: Utopian Moments in the 20th Century* (Durham, Duke University Press, 2006). Winter's argument provides an antidote to claims that such globalizing efforts were simply attempts to institutionalize Western domination or secure super-power domination – though they were these as well.

4 For a searing critique of recent sociological theorizing about globalization from a subaltern perspective, see Ramaswami Harindranath, 2006.

5 In regions occupied by such highly developed imperial civilizations as the Indian, Chinese, Mogul, and Ottoman empires, the aboriginal peoples had already been colonized, a process of subjugation and incorporation that involved what we would today call ethnic cleansing. This layering of colonialism, and its prior existence outside the West, is often neglected in the romantic-cum-ideological criticisms that describe European colonialism as the equivalent of original sin. For example, Berber studies has opposed the naturalization of Arab identity and the Magreb. Nomadic tribal societies had peopled the North African and Middle Eastern regions before the military, religious, and economic expansion of Islam in the eighth and ninth centuries. Five centuries later, Ibn Kaldun developed a cyclical model to explain the struggle between Berbers and Arabs, explaining it as a cycle of between desert tribe and urban civilization.

6 Of course, this manner of remembering, which suppresses the traumas of

203

postcolonial transition and the wide and varied responsibilities associated therein (see below), continues to mark the contemporary intellectual scene. Consider, for example, narratives that accept the failures of postcolonial states but place blame exclusively on the colonizers themselves, e.g., because of how they established postcolonial boundaries, their postcolonial interference, or the exigencies of world capitalist system.

7 This is not to say that these critics of new national leaders let the earlier colonialists off the hook (see n. 6, above). The degree to which anti-civil structures and meanings were rooted in precolonial societies, how much was the effect of errors of the anti-colonial movement, and how much simply the result of the transition are matters of intense debate in the postcolonial literature.

> Historians of Muslim politics in north India have a list of significant dates and events that go back to 1857 or even earlier that represent steps on the road to Pakistan, opportunities lost for a Hindu–Muslim settlement, and the decisive moment or moments when Pakistan became inevitable. The further back the date is placed, the more likely it is that the historian providing the date accepts the view that there was an underlying problem or fault line of Hindu–Muslim relations running throughout the subcontinent that required a solution, failing which the creation of two separate nation-states, one predominantly Muslim, one Hindu, was inevitable. The later the date is placed, the more likely it is that the historian rejects the latter view and argues that the differences between Hindus and Muslims are modern political inventions – either of the British rulers or the Indian politicians – and that the creation of Pakistan was a consequence of political, not religious, struggles for power that could have been compromised. In this view, the fateful steps towards partition were all taken between 1937 and 1946. (Brass 2003: 73)

For a typical argument that colonialism itself created these anti-civil tensions, see Hamza Alavi (2002), who shows how British Anglo-vernacular policy intensified communalism by undermining the ability for Muslims to teach religion in their own schools.

8 The positivist, purely "factual" approaches to Partition – as compared to the emphasis on trauma, meaning, and civil society I am developing here – have continued to appear, of course, even in recent times. See, e.g., Bharadwaj et al., unpublished manuscript.

9 This broadly democratic rather than narrowly socialist vision is one reason for these revisionist historians to have adopted the Gramscian term subaltern in the first place, instead of employing the more traditional Marxist notion of working class. Gramsci had introduced the term in part to avoid economism and to describe the coalition-like, more democratic nature of struggles for hegemony in capitalist civil society. On the two sides of civil society discourse, individual autonomy and collective obligations, see Alexander, *The Civil Sphere* (2006b).

10 See also, e.g., Debali Mookerjea-Leonard (2004); Ananya Jahanara Kabir (2005); J. Edward Mallot (2006); Erin O'Donnel (2004).

11 When new, postcolonial regimes have been established, of course, regulative institutions do become involved, e.g., as in South Africa's Truth and Reconciliation Commission, which became an iconic form of organized intervention inspiring many successors as well as such international institutions

as the Center for Transitional Justice. Even when such efforts at rethinking do take the organized form of regulating institutions, however, they remain deeply imbedded in communicative and performative processes. For an exploration of this embeddedness in the case of the South African TRC, see Tanya Goodman (2009).

6 GLOBALIZATION AND TRAUMA: THE DREAM OF COSMOPOLITAN PEACE

1 I have in mind such globalizing intellectuals as Giddens, Held, Beck, Keane, and Kaldor (see note 10). See later in this chapter for a discussion of the intellectual carrier group and their theoretical and empirical claims.

2 By "time-space compression," Harvey signals "processes that so revolutionize the objective qualities of space and time that we are forced to alter, sometimes in quite radical ways, how we represent the world to ourselves." (1989:240)

3 For a sympathetic reading of the progressive elements of modernization theory, and the contextualization of its critics, see Alexander (1995).

4 Eisenstadt's (1982) Weberian perspective on the manner in which free floating intellectuals and transcendental, world-transforming ideologies emerged on a global level in the first millennium BC forms an important, relativizing perspective for the current claims that are made for the newly emergent representation of globalization.

5 On how some of Europe's leading democratic intellectuals have recently employed the particularistic and simplistic tropes of "orientalism" to suggest European cultural and political superiority to America, see Heins (2005).

6 For the long nineteenth and short twentieth centuries, see Eric Hobsbawm (1990, 1994); for the Age of Equipoise that followed the Napoleonic wars and lasted nearly to the end of the nineteenth century, see Burn (1964).

7 For the self-deceptive conflation of the model of democratic citizen with patrimonial subject during the colonial era, see Mamdani (1996).

8 For how twentieth-century social theory responded to the ennui and traumas of the century's first half, see Alexander (1990).

9 In the following, I draw upon Alexander et al. (2004), which suggests that the construction of cultural trauma – defining the pain, the perpetrators, the victims, and the antidote – is a central path by which collectivities sustain and develop collective identity.

10 It was Giddens' *Consequences of Modernity*, in 1990, that most forcefully introduced the idea that "globalization" characterized contemporary late modernity. Giddens brought Ulrich Beck, another intellectual central to this discourse, to the LSE, and it has primarily been a group of post-Marxist British intellectuals, including, with Giddens and Beck, Mary Kaldor, John Keane, and David Held, who brought the idea of civil globality into centrality in the fifteen years since. Mary Kaldor emphasizes the importance of the 1980s European disarmament and peace movements in "The Ideas of 1989: The Origins of the Concept of Global Civil Society" (Kaldor 2003a), and she points to such early collaborations as Kaldor and Falk, *The New Détente* (1989). The work of hers that discusses globalization in a manner that can most clearly be seen as casting it as an idealistic "collective representation" is *Global Civil Society: An Answer to War* (2003b). The representation process

emerging from the end of the Cold War can be seen in Keane's work (1988, 1991, 2003). Moving into this arena of representation slightly later, Held's influential writings have clarified and highlighted the democratic dimensions of Giddens' globalization concept (e.g., 1995, 2004; and Held and McGrew 2002). All these writings mix normative elaborations about the scope and desirability of a global civil society with empirical data about its structural processes and analytic dimensions. Held's work is especially striking in this regard, for, while it makes broad incursions into the empirical domain, it is explicitly imbedded in normative political theory. At the other end of the empirical/normative continuum is the Global Civil Society project, the edited volumes that, since 2001, have been produced annually at the London School of Economics by Mary Kaldor, Helmut Anheier, and Marlies Glasius. This tightly organized and highly collaborative project, funded in large part by the Ford Foundation, has projected the "representation" of democratic globalization from London to activists, students, and intellectuals throughout the world.

11 For the neo-conservative discourse of empire, see, e.g., Boot (2001); D'Souza (2002); Kagan (2003). For an overview of this revival and an ironic yet forceful liberal-realist case for American imperial power as, in principle, the only viable force for progressive transformation in a Hobbesian world, see Ferguson (2004). The most sophisticated and influential conservative argument against the very possibility for a global civil society is undoubtedly Huntington's (1996), which made its first appearance as a widely influential article in *Foreign Affairs* (1993). Huntington employs a primordial understanding of culture to develop a seemingly scientific case that the world's distinctive civilizations are based on religions that can never be reconciled, which means that, rather than moving toward global civil order, the future of international politics will revolve around prolonged conflict for hegemony.

12 For a systematic empirical interpretation of French anti-Americanism during the postwar period, see Kuisel (1993) and, more generally, Buruma and Margalit (2004).

13 The cultural power of this communicative dimension of a "global civil sphere" was markedly on display during the January 25 Revolution in Egypt in the winter of 2011. Western media engaged sympathetically with the revolution against the dictatorial regime, and these representations powerfully constrained and directed interventions by European nations and the United States. See Alexander (2011).

14 For this distinction, see, particularly, Held and McGrew (2002).

REFERENCES

Abzug, R. H. (1985) *Inside the Vicious Heart: Americans and the Liberation of Nazi Concentration Camps*. Oxford University Press, New York.

Ahmed, I. (2002) The 1947 Partition of India: A paradigm for Pathological Politics in India and Pakistan. *Asian Ethnicity* 4(3), 9–28.

Aiyar, S. (1994) *Violence and the State in the Partition of Punjab, 1947–48*. PhD thesis, University of Cambridge.

Alavi, H. (2002) Misreading Partition Road Signs. *Economic and Political Weekly*. November 2–9.

Alexander, J. C. (2011) *Performative Revolution in Egypt: An Essay in Cultural Power*. Bloomsbury Academic, London.

Alexander, J. C. (2010) *The Performance of Politics: Obama's Victory and the Democratic Struggle for Power*. Oxford University Press, New York.

Alexander, J. C. (2009) *Remembering the Holocaust: A Debate*. Oxford University Press, New York.

Alexander, J. C. (2009) Postcolonialism, Trauma, and Civil Society: A New Understanding. In K. Sokratis et al. (eds). *Conflict, Citizenship and Civil Society*. Routledge, London, pp. 221–40.

Alexander, J. C. (2007) Remembrance of Things Past: Cultural Trauma, the "Nanjing Massacre" and Chinese Identity (with Gao, R.). In Y. Shaodang et al. (eds) *Tradition and Modernity: Comparative Perspective*. Peking University Press, Beijing.

Alexander, J. C. (2007) "Globalization" as Collective Representation: The New Dream of a Cosmopolitan Civil Sphere. In I. Rossi (ed.) *Frontiers of Globalization Research: Theoretical and Methodological Approach*. Springer, New York, pp. 371–82.

Alexander, J. C. (2006a) Cultural Pragmatics: Social Performance between Ritual and Strategy. In J. C. Alexander, B. Giesen, and J. Mast (eds) *Social Performance: Symbolic Action, Cultural Pragmatics, and Ritual*. Cambridge University Press, Cambridge, UK, pp. 29–90.

Alexander, J. C. (2006b) *The Civil Sphere*. Oxford University Press, New York.

Alexander, J. C. (2004) On the Social Construction of Moral Universals: The "Holocaust" from War Crime to Trauma Drama. In J. C. Alexander et al.

(eds) *Cultural Trauma and Collective Identity*. University of California Press, Berkeley.

Alexander, J. C. (2004) Cultural Pragmatics: Social Performance between Ritual and Strategy. *Sociological Theory* 22(4), 527–73.

Alexander, J. C. et al. (2004) *Cultural Trauma and Collective Identity*. University of California Press, Berkeley.

Alexander, J. C. (2003a) *The Meanings of Social Life: A Cultural Sociology*. Oxford University Press, New York.

Alexander, J. C. (2003b) Cultural Trauma and Collective Identity. In J. C. Alexander, *The Meanings of Social Life*. Oxford University Press, New York, pp. 85–108.

Alexander, J. C. (2003c) Modern, Anti-, Post, and Neo: How Intellectuals Explain "Our Time". In J. C. Alexander, *The Meanings of Social Life*. Oxford University Press, New York, pp. 193–228.

Alexander, J. C. (1998) Bush, Hussein, and the Cultural Preparation for War: Toward a More Symbolic Theory of Political Legitimation. *Epoche* 21(1), 1–14.

Alexander, J. C. (1995) Modern, Ante, Post and Neo: How Intellectuals Have Tried to Understand the Crisis of Our Time. In J. Alexander *Fin-de-Siecle Social Theory: Relativism, Reduction, and the Problem of Reason*. Verso, London, pp. 6–64.

Alexander, J. C. (1990) Between Progress and Apocalypse: Social Theory and the Dream of Reason in the Twentieth Century. In J. C. Alexander, and Sztompka, P. (eds) *Rethinking Progress: Movements, Forces, and Ideas at the End of the Twentieth Century*. Unwin Hyman Limited, London, pp. 15–39.

Alexander, J. C. (1987) *Twenty Lectures: Sociological Theory Since World War II*. Columbia University Press, New York.

Alexander, J. C. (1983) Max Weber: The Classical Attempt at Synthesis. In J. C. Alexander, *Theoretical Logic in Sociology, Vol. 3*. University of California Press, Berkeley.

Alexander, J. C. and Smith, P. (2003) The Strong Program in Cultural Sociology: Elements of a Structural Hermeneutics. In J. C. Alexander, *The Meanings of Social Life*. Oxford University Press, New York, pp. 11–26.

Alexander, J. C. et al. (eds) (2006) *Social Performance: Symbolic Action, Cultural Pragmatics, and Ritual*. Cambridge University Press, Cambridge, UK.

Alexander, J. C. et al. (eds) (2004) *Cultural Trauma and Collective Identity*. University of California Press, Berkeley.

Alexander, J. C. et al. (eds) (1987) *The Micro–Macro Link*. University of California Press, Berkeley.

Amishai-Maisels, Z. (1988) Christological Symbolism of the Holocaust. *Holocaust and Genocide Studies* 3(4), 457–81.

Anderson, B. (1991) *Imagined Communities*. Verso, London.

Arendt, H. (1951) *The Origins of Totalitarianism*. Harcourt Brace Jovanowich, New York.

Aristotle (1987) *Poetics I* (trans. R. Janko). Hackett, Indianapolis.

Aron, R. (1990) *Memoirs: Fifty Years of Political Reflection*. Holmes and Meier, New York.

Austin, J. L. (1962) *How to Do Things with Words*. Clarendon Press, Oxford.

Azarya, V. and Kimmerling, B. (1985–6) Cognitive Permeability of Civil–Military

Boundaries: Draftee Expectations from Military Service in Israel. *Studies in Comparative International Development* 20(4), 42–63.

Azaryahu, M. (2007) *Tel Aviv: Mythography of a City*. Syracuse University Press, Syracuse, NY.

Baer, A. (1999) Visual Testimonies and High-Tech Museums: The Changing Embodiment of Holocaust History and Memorialization. Department of Sociology, University of Madrid, unpublished manuscript.

Bagchi, J. (2003) Freedom in an Idiom of Loss. In J. Bagchi and S. Dasgupta (eds) *The Trauma and the Triumph: Gender and Partition in Eastern India*. Stree, Kolkata, pp. 17–29.

Bakhtin, M. M. (1986) *Speech Genres and Other Late Essays*. University of Texas Press, Austin, TX.

Bar, D. (2005) Holocaust Commemoration in Israel during the 1950s: The Holocaust Cellar on Mount Zion. *Jewish Social Studies: History, Culture, Society* 12(1), 16–38.

Bar-On, D. (1997) Israeli Society between the Culture of Death and the Culture of Life. *Israel Studies* 2(2), 88–112.

Bauer, Y. (1986) Editor's Introduction. *Holocaust and Genocide Studies* 1(1), 1–2.

Bauman, J. (1986) *Winter in the Morning*. Virago, London.

Bauman, Z. (1993) *Postmodern Ethics*. Blackwell, Oxford.

Bauman, Z. (1989) *Modernity and the Holocaust*. Polity, Cambridge, UK.

Bauman, Z. (1968) *State and Society*. University of California Press, Berkeley.

Beck, U. (2000) The Cosmopolitan Perspective: Sociology in the Second Age of Modernity. *British Journal of Sociology* 51(1), 79–105.

Ben-Amos, A. and Bet-El, I. (1999) Holocaust Day and Memorial Day in Israeli Schools: Ceremonies, Education and History. *Israel Studies* 4(1), 258–84.

Benn, D. W. (1995) Perceptions of the Holocaust: Then and Now. *World Today*, June 5, 102–103.

Berenbaum, M. (1998) Preface. In M. Berenbaum and A. J. Peck (eds) *The Holocaust and History: The Known, the Unknown, the Disputed, and the Reexamined*. Indiana University Press, Bloomington, pp. xi–xii.

Berenbaum, M. and Peck, A. J. (eds) (1998) *The Holocaust and History: The Known, the Unknown, the Disputed, and the Reexamined*. Indiana University Press, Bloomington.

Bernstein, R. J. (2001) Radical Evil: Kant at War with Himself. In M. Pia Lara (ed.) *Rethinking Evil*. Berkeley: University of California Press, Berkeley, pp. 55–85.

Bernstein, R. J. (1996) *Hannah Arendt and the Jewish Question*. Polity, Cambridge, UK.

Bhalla, A. (ed.) (1994) *Stories about the Partition of India*. Indus/Harper Collins, Delhi.

Bharadwaj, P., Khwaja, A. and Mian, A. (Unpublished manuscript) The Partition of British India: Impact on Gender, Literacy and Occupation.

Bhargava, R. (2000) History, Nation and Community: Reflections on Nationalist Historiography of India and Pakistan. *Economic and Political Weekly*, January 22, p. 199.

Bickerton, I. J. and Klausner, C. L. (2002) *A Concise History of the Arab–Israeli Conflict*. 4th edn. Prentice Hall, Upper Saddle River, NJ.

Bidwai, P. (1993) BJP Does Not Represent India. *The Nation*, January 25, p. 87.

Bier, J. (1986) The Holocaust, West Germany, and Strategies of Oblivion, 1947–1979. In A. Rabinbach and J. Zipes (eds) *Germans and Jews since the Holocaust: The Changing Situation in West Germany.* New York: Holmes and Meier, New York, pp. 185–207.

Bilu, Y. and Witztum, E. (2000) War-Related Loss and Suffering in Israeli Society: An Historical Perspective. *Israel Studies* 5(2), 1–31.

Boltanski, L. (1999) *Distant Suffering.* Cambridge University Press, New York.

Boot, M. (2001) The Case for an American Empire. *Weekly Standard*, October 15, pp. 27–30.

Brass, P. R. (2003) The Partition of India and Retributive Genocide in the Punjab, 1946–7: Means, Methods, and Purposes. *Journal of Genocide Research.* 5(1), 71–101, quoting p. 73.

Braun, R. (1994) The Holocaust and Problems of Historical Representation. *History and Theory* 33(2), 172–97.

Brooks, P. (1995) *The Melodramatic Imagination.* Columbia University Press, New York.

Browning, C. (1996) Human Nature, Culture, and the Holocaust. *The Chronicle of Higher Education*, A72, October 18.

Browning, C. (1992) *Ordinary Men: Reserve Police Battalion 101 and the Final Solution in Poland.* HarperCollins, New York.

Brunner, J. (2002) Contentious Origins: Psychoanalytic Comments on the Debate over Israel's Creation. In J. Bunzl and B. Beit-Hallahmi (eds) *Psychoanalysis, identity, and ideology: Critical Essays on the Israel/Palestine Case.* Kluwer Academic Publishers, Boston, MA, pp. 107–35.

Buck, P S. (1947) Do You Want Your Children to Be Tolerant? *Better Homes and Gardens*, 33, February.

Burn, W. L. (1964) *The Age of Equipoise: A Study of The Mid-Victorian Generation.* Norton, New York.

Buruma, I. and Margalit, A. (2004) *Occidentalism: A Short History of Anti-Westernism.* Atlantic Books, London.

Buruma, I. (1994) *The Wages of Guilt: Memories of War in Germany and Japan.* Farrar Straus Giroux, New York.

Carter, H. (1947) How to Stop the Hate Mongers in Your Home Town. *Better Homes and Gardens*, 45, November.

Caruth, C. (1996) *Unclaimed Experience: Trauma, Narrative, and History.* Johns Hopkins University Press, Baltimore, MD.

Caruth, C. (ed.) (1995) *Trauma: Explorations in Memory.* Johns Hopkins University Press, Baltimore, MD.

Chakrabarty, D. (2002) *Habitations of Modernity: Essays in the Wake of Subaltern Studies.* University of Chicago Press, Chicago, IL.

Chang, I. (1997) *The Rape of Nanjing: The Forgotten Holocaust of World War II.* Basic Books, New York.

Chatterjee, P. (1993) *The Nation and its Fragments: Colonial and Postcolonial Histories.* Princeton University Press, Princeton, NJ.

Cheng, G. (2002) Reconstructing Narratives of China: the Artistic Creation. In Keep the Red Flag Flying, the Red Sun and the Red Crag. *Southern Cultural Forum* (Nan Fang Wen Tan), 3, 22–6.

Clark, I. (1999) *Globalization and International Relations Theory.* Oxford University Press, Oxford.

Clendinnen, I. (1999) *Reading the Holocaust*. Cambridge University Press, Cambridge, UK.

Cohen, E. (1995) Israel as a Post-Zionist Society. *Israel Affairs* 1(3), 203–14.

Cohen, R. (1999) Berlin Holocaust Memorial Approved. *New York Times*, A3, June 26.

Connerton, P. (1989) *How Societies Remember*. Cambridge University Press, Cambridge, UK.

Cushman, T. (2005) The Conflict of the Rationalities: International Law, Human Rights and the War in Iraq. *Deakin Law Review* 10(2), 546–570.

Dardur, J. (2006) *Unsettling Partition: Literature, Gender, Memory*. University of Toronto Press, Toronto.

Das, V. (1995) *Critical Events: An Anthropological Perspective on Contemporary India*. Oxford University Press, Oxford, UK.

Dawidowicz, L. (1982) *On Equal Terms: Jews in America, 1881–1981*. Holt, Rinehart, and Winston, New York.

Delanty, G. (2001) Cosmopolitanism and Violence. *European Journal of Social Theory* 4(1), 41–52.

Deutscher, I. (1968) The Jewish Tragedy and the Historian. In T. Deutscher (ed.) *The Non-Jewish Jew and Other Essays*. Oxford University Press, London, pp. 163–4.

Diamond, S. A. (1969) The Kristallnacht and the Reaction in America. *Yivo Annual of Jewish Social Science*. 14, 196–208.

Dilthey, W. (1976) The Construction of the Historical World in the Human Sciences. In *Dilthey: Selected Writings*. Cambridge University, Cambridge, UK, pp. 168–245.

Dilthey, W. (1962) *Pattern and Meaning in History*. Harper and Row, New York.

Diner, D. (2000) *Beyond the Conceivable: Studies on Germany, Nazism, and the Holocaust*. University of California Press, Berkeley.

Dinnerstein, L. (1981–2) Anti-Semitism Exposed and Attacked, 1945–1950. *American Jewish History* 71, 134–49, September–June.

Dodson, D. W. (1946) College Quotas and American Democracy. *American Scholar*, July, 15(3), 267–76.

Doneson, J. E. (1987) The American History of Anne Frank's Diary. *Holocaust and Genocide Studies* 2(1), 149–60.

Drinan, R. F. (1987) Review of Ann Tusa and John Tusa, The Nuremberg Trial. *Holocaust and Genocide Studies* 3(2), 333–4.

D'Souza, D. (2002) In Praise of American Empire. *Christian Science Monitor*, April 26, p. 11.

Durkheim, E. (1996 [1912]) *The Elementary Forms of Religious Life*. Free Press, New York.

Ebihara, M. and Ledgerwood, J. (2002) Aftermaths of Genocide: Cambodian Villagers. In A. Hinton (ed.) *Annihilating Difference: The Anthropology of Genocide*. University of California Press, Berkeley.

Eisenstadt, S. N. (1982) The Axial Age: The Emergence of Transcendental Visions and the Rise of Clerics. *European Journal of Sociology* 23, 294–314.

Elder, G. H., Jr. (1974) *Children of the Great Depression*. University of Chicago Press, Chicago, IL.

Erikson, K. (1976) *Everything in its Path: Destruction of Community in the Buffalo Creek Flood*. Simon and Schuster, New York.

211

Erlanger, S. (2001) *After the Arrest: Wider Debate about the Role of Milosevic, and of Serbia. New York Times*, A8, April 2.

Eyerman, R. (2008) *The Assassination of Theo van Gogh: From Social Drama to Cultural Trauma.* Duke University Press, Durham, NC.

Eyerman, R. (2004) Cultural Trauma: Slavery and the Formation of African American Identity. In J. Alexander et al. (eds) *Cultural Trauma and Collective Identity.* University of California Press, Berkeley.

Eyerman, R. (2001) *Cultural Trauma: Slavery and the Formation of African American Identity.* Cambridge University Press, New York.

Eyerman, R. and Jamison, A. (1990) *Social Movements: A Cognitive Approach.* Polity, London.

Eyerman, R., Alexander, J. C. and Breese, E. (eds) (2011) *Narrating Trauma: On the Impact of Collective Suffering.* Paradigm Publishers, Boulder, CO.

Feingold, H. L. (1974) *Zion in America: the Jewish Experience from Colonial Times to the Present.* Twayne, Boston, MA.

Feldman, J. (2002) Marking the Boundaries of the Enclave: Defining the Israeli Collective through the Poland Experience. *Israel Studies* 7(2), 84–114.

Ferguson, N. (2004) *The Rise and Fall of the American Empire.* Penguin, London.

Finkelstein, N. G. (2000) *The Holocaust Industry: Reflections on the Exploitation of Jewish Suffering.* Verso, London.

Francisco, J. (nd) In the Heat of Fratricide: The Literature of India's Partition Burning Freshly. *The Annual of Urdu Studies*, p. 4.

French, H. W. (2000) Japanese Veteran Testifies in War Atrocity Lawsuit. *The New York Times,* December 21, AI-6.

Friedland, R. and Hecht, R. (1996) *To Rule Jerusalem.* Cambridge University Press, New York.

Friedlander, S. (1992) Trauma, Transference, and "Working through" in Writing the History of the Shoah. *History and Memory* 4(1): 39–59.

Friedlander, S. (1992a) *Probing the Limits of Representation.* University of California Press, Berkeley.

Friedlander, S. (1979) *When Memory Comes.* Farrar, Strauss, and Giroux, New York.

Friedlander, S. (1978) *History and Psychoanalysis.* Holmes and Meier, New York.

Frye, N. (1971 [1957]) *Anatomy of Criticism.* Princeton University Press, Princeton, NJ, p. 82.

Fussell, P. (1975) *The Great War and Modern Memory.* Oxford University Press, Oxford, UK.

Gao, R. (2011) Revolutionary Trauma and Representation of the War: the Case of China in Mao's Era. In R. Eyerman, J. C. Alexander, and E. Breese (eds) *Narrating Trauma: On the Impact of Collective Suffering.* Paradigm Publishers, Boulder, CO, pp. 53–80.

Garber, Z. and Zuckerman, B. (1989) Why Do We Call the Holocaust "The Holocaust"? An Inquiry into the Psychology of Labels. *Modern Judaism* 9(2),197–211.

Gavish, D. (2005) *A Survey of Palestine under the British Mandate, 1920–1948.* Routledge, London and New York.

Geertz, C. (1984) Distinguished Lecture: Anti Anti-Relativism. *American Anthropologist* 86, 263–78.

Geertz, C. (1973) *The Interpretation of Cultures*. Basic Books, New York.

Gibson, J. W. (1994) *Warrior Dreams: Violence and Manhood in Post-Vietnam America*. Hill and Wang, New York.

Giddens, A. (1990) *Consequences of Modernity*. Polity, Cambridge, UK.

Giesen, B. (2009) From Denial to Confessions of Guilt: The German Case. In J. C. Alexander, *Remembering the Holocaust: A Debate*. Oxford University Press, Oxford and New York, pp. 114–22.

Giesen, B. (2004) The Trauma of Perpetrators: The Holocaust as the Traumatic Reference of German National Identity. In J. C. Alexander et al. (eds) *Cultural Trauma and Collective Identity*. University of California Press, Berkeley.

Giesen, B. (1998) *Intellectuals and the Nation: Collective Identity in a German Axial Age*. Cambridge University Press, New York.

Gleason, P. (1981) Americans All: World War II and the Shaping of American Identity. *Review of Politics* 43(4), 483–518.

Goldhagen, D. J. (1996) *Hitler's Willing Executioners: Ordinary Germans and the Holocaust*. Knopf, New York.

Goodman, T. (2009) *Staging Solidarity: Truth and Reconciliation in a New South Africa*. Paradigm Publishers, Boulder, CO.

Greenberg, J. D. (2005) Generations of Memory: Remembering Partition in India/Pakistan and Israel/Palestine. *Comparative Studies of South Asia, Africa and the Middle East* 25(1), 89–110.

Greene, J. M. and Kumar, S. (2000) Editors' Introduction. In J. M. Greene and S. Kumar (eds) *Witness: Voices from the Holocaust*. Free Press, New York, pp. xxi–xxviii.

Guha, R. (1997) Introduction. In R. Guha (ed.) *A Subaltern Studies Reader, 1986–1995*. University of Minnesota Press, Minneapolis, MN, pp. ix–xxiii.

Guha, R. (1982) On Some Aspects of the Historiography of Colonial India. In R. Guha (ed.) *Subaltern Studies I: Writings on South Asian History and Society*. Oxford University Press, Delhi.

Guroian, V. (1988) Post-Holocaust Political Morality: The Litmus of Bitburg and the Armenian Genocide Resolution. *Holocaust and Genocide Studies* 3(3), 305–22.

Haaretz. (2009) Yad Vashem Fires Employee who Compared Holocaust to Nakba. April 23.

Haaretz. (2009) Rabbis Meet Yasuf Leaders to Calm Tensions after Mosque Arson. December 14.

Habermas, J. (1984) *The Theory of Communicative Action*. Beacon Press, Boston.

Handelman, D. and Katz, E. (1990) State Ceremonies of Israel–Remembrance Day and Independence Day. In D. Handelman, *Models and Mirrors: Towards an Anthropology of Public Events*. Cambridge University Press, Cambridge, UK, pp.191–233

Harindranath, R. (2006) *Perspectives on Global Cultures*. Open University Press, Berkshire, UK.

Harris, R. (1992) *Fatherland*. Hutchinson, London.

Hart, W. R. (1947) Anti-Semitism in NY Medical Schools. *American Mercury*, July, 65: 53–63.

Hartman, G. H. (2000) Memory.com: Tel-Suffering and Testimony in the Dot Com Era. *Raritan* 19, 1–18.

Hartman, G. H. (1996) *The Longest Shadow: In the Aftermath of the Holocaust*. Indiana University Press, Bloomington.

Harvey, David. (1989) *The Conditions of Postmodernity*. Oxford, UK: Blackwell.

Hasan, M. (2000) Memories of a Fragmented Nation: Rewriting the Histories of India's Partition. *The Annual of Urdu Studies*, pp. 263–85.

Hashimoto , A. (2011) The Cultural Trauma of a Fallen Nation: Japan, 1945. In R. Eyerman, J. C. Alexander, and E. Breese (eds) *Narrating Trauma: On the Impact of Collective Suffering*. Paradigm Publishers, Boulder, CO, pp. 29–52.

Hayes, P. (ed.) (1999) *Lessons and Legacies, Vol. 3: Memory, Memorialization and Denial*. Northwestern University Press, Evanston, IL.

Heins, V. (2011) *On Social Suffering and its Cultural Construction*. Brill, Boston, MA.

Heins, V. (2005) Orientalising America? Continental Intellectuals and the Search for Europe's Identity. *Millennium: Journal of International Studies* 34(2), 433–48.

Held, D. (2004) *Global Covenant: The Social-Democratic Alternative to the Washington Consensus*. Polity, Cambridge, UK.

Held, D. (1995) *Democracy and the Global Order: From the Modern State to Cosmopolitan Governance*. Polity, Cambridge, UK.

Held, D. and McGrew, A. (2002) *Governing Globalization: Power, Authority, and Global Governance*. Polity, London.

Herf, J. (1986) The "Holocaust" Reception in West Germany. In A. Rabinbach and J. Zipes (eds) *Germans and Jews since the Holocaust: The Changing Situation in Western Germany*. Holmes and Meier, New York, pp. 208–33.

Herf, J. (1984) *Reactionary Modernism*. Cambridge University Press, New York.

Higham, J. (1984) *Send These to Me*. Johns Hopkins University Press, Baltimore, MD.

Hinton, A. (2002) The Dark Side of Modernity. In Hinton, A. (eds) *Annihilating Difference: The Anthropology of Genocide*. University of California Press, Berkeley.

Hobsbawm, E. (1994) *The Age of Extremes: The Short Twentieth Century, 1914–1991*. Michael Joseph, London.

Hobsbawm, E. (1990) *Nations and Nationalism since 1780*. Cambridge University Press, Cambridge, UK.

Hollinger, D. (1996) *Science, Jews, and Secular Culture: Studies in Mid-Twentieth-Century American Intellectual History*. Princeton University Press, Princeton, NJ.

Huntington, S. (1996) *The Clash of Civilizations and the Remaking of World Order*. Touchstone, New York.

Huntington, S. (1993) The Clash of Civilizations? *Foreign Affairs* 72 (Summer), 22–49.

Huo, A. (2008) *The Military Commander Zhang Lingfu: Early Career and the War of Resistance*. Lao Zhan You Press, Taipei, China.

Ignatieff, M. (1999) Human Rights: The Midlife Crisis. *New York Review of Books*, May, 20, 58–62.

Jalal, A. (1996) Secularists, Subalterns and the Stigma of "Communalism": Partition Historiography Revisited. *Modern Asian Studies*, 30(3), 681–789.

Jalal, A. (1985) *The Sole Spokesman: Jinnah, the Muslim League, and the Demand for Pakistan*. Cambridge University Press, Cambridge, UK.

Jelin, E. and Kaufman, S. (nd) Layers of Memories: Twenty Years After in Argentina. In *Memory and Narrativity*. Unpublished manuscript.

Kabir, A. J. (2005) Gender Memory, Trauma: Women's Novels on the Partition of India. *Comparative Studies of South Asia, Africa and the Middle East.* 25(1), 177–90.

Kagan, R. (2003) *Of Paradise and Power: America and Europe in the New World Order.* Knopf, New York.

Kahan Commission. (1983) *The Beirut Massacre: the Complete Kahan Commission Report.* Karz-Cohl, Princeton, NJ.

Kaiser, D. (1999) *American Tragedy.* Harvard University Press, Cambridge, MA.

Kaldor, M. (2003a) The Ideas of 1989: The Origins of the Concept of Global Civil Society. In *Global Civil Society: An Answer to War.* Polity, Cambridge, UK, pp. 50–78.

Kaldor, M. (2003b) *Global Civil Society: An Answer to War.* Polity, Cambridge, UK.

Kaldor, M., Holden, G. and. Falk, R. (1989) *The New Détente: Rethinking East West Relations.* Verso, London.

Kampe, N. (1987) Normalizing the Holocaust? The Recent Historians' Debate in the Federal Republic of Germany. *Holocaust and Genocide Studies* 2(1), 61–80.

Kane, A. (1992) Cultural Analysis in Historical Sociology: The Analytic and Concrete Forms of the Autonomy of Culture. *Sociological Theory* 9(1), 53–69.

Kant, I. (1970 [1784]). Idea for a Universal History with a Cosmopolitan Purpose. In *Political Writings.* Cambridge University Press, Cambridge, UK, pp. 41–53.

Karsh, E. (2000) Preface. In P. R. Kumaraswamy (ed.) *Revisiting the Yom Kippur War.* Frank Cass, London and Portland, OR, pp. ix–x.

Keane, J. (2003) *Global Civil Society?* Cambridge University Press, Cambridge, UK.

Keane, J. (1991) *The Media and Democracy.* Polity, Cambridge, UK.

Keane, J. (1988) *Democracy and Civil Society: On the Predicaments of European Socialism, the Prospects for Democracy, and the Problem of Controlling Social and Political Power.* Verso, New York.

Keller, S. (1963) *Beyond the Ruling Class.* Random House, New York.

Kelman, H. C. and Hamilton, V. L. (1989) *Crimes of Obedience: Toward a Social Psychology of Authority and Responsibility.* Yale University Press, New Haven.

Khalidi, R. (1997) *Palestinian Identity: The Construction of Modern National Consciousness.* Columbia University Press, New York.

Kimmerling, B. (1998) Political Subcultures and Civilian Militarism in a Settler-Immigrant Society. In D. Bar-Tal, D. Jacobson and A Klieman (eds) *Security Concerns: Insights from the Israeli Experience.* JAI Press, Stamford CT, pp. 395–416.

Kimmerling, B. (1993) *Patterns of Militarism in Israel.* European Journal of Sociology 34(2), 196–223.

Kirby, W. C. (1997) Foreword. In I. Chang, *The Rape of Nanjing: The Forgotten Holocaust of World War II.* Basic Books, New York, pp. ix–xi.

Kleinman, A., Das, V. and Lock, M. (eds) (1997) *Social Suffering.* University of California Press, Berkeley.

Kohl, S. B. (1986) Ethnocide and Ethnogenesis: A Case Study of the Mississippi Band of Choctaw, a Genocide Avoided. *Holocaust and Genocide Studies* 1(1), 91–100.

Korman, G. (1972) The Holocaust in American Historical Writing. *Societas, Vol* 2, 251–70.

Kuisel, R. (1993) *Seducing the French: The Dilemma of Americanization.* University of California Press, Berkeley.

Kuper, L. (1981) *Genocide: Its Political Use in the Twentieth Century.* Yale University Press, New Haven, CT.

LaCapra, D. (1994) *Representing the Holocaust: History, Theory, Trauma.* Cornell University Press, Ithaca, NY.

Lacouture, J. (1990) *De Gaulle: The Rebel, 1890–1944* (trans. P. O'Brien). HarperCollins, New York.

Langer, L. L. (2000) Foreword. In J. M. Greene and S. Kumar (eds) *Witness: Voices from the Holocaust.* Free Press, New York, pp. xi–xx.

Laqueur, W. (1980) *The Terrible Secret: Suppression of the Truth about Hitler's "Final Solution."* Little, Brown, Boston.

Lara, M. P. (1999) *Feminist Narratives in the Public Sphere.* University of California Press, Berkeley.

Lear, J. (1992) Katharsis. In A. O. Rorty (ed.) *Essays on Aristotle's Poetics.* Princeton University Press, Princeton, NJ, pp. 315–40.

Lemkin, R. (1994) *Axis Rule in Occupied Europe.* Carnegie Endowment for International Peace, Washington, DC.

Lentin, R. (2000) *Israel and the Daughters of the Shoah: Reoccupying the Territories of Silence.* Berghahn Books, New York.

Li, H. et al. (1998) *Hong Yan Hun: Chongqing Geleshan Geming Jinianguan* (*The Soul of the Red Crag: Geleshan Revolutionary Museum*). Encyclopedia Press, Beijing.

Li, P. (2000) The Nanjing Holocaust Tragedy, Trauma and Reconciliation. *Society* 37, 56–66.

Liang, B. (1957) *Hong Qi Pu* (*Keep the Red Flag Flying*). Youth Press of China, Beijing.

Liberles, R. (1995) *Salo Wittmayer Baron: Architect of Jewish History.* New York University Press, New York.

Lin, P. (1965) *Long Live the Victory of People's War! In Commemoration of the 20th Anniversary of Victory in the Chinese People's War of Resistance Against Japan.* Foreign Language Press, Beijing.

Linenthal, E. T. (1995) *Preserving Memory: The Struggle to Create the Holocaust Museum.* Viking Books, New York.

Lipschutz, R. (1992) Reconstructing World Politics: The Emergence of Global Civil Society. *Millennium* 21 (3), 389–420.

Lipstadt, D. E. (1996) America and the Memory of the Holocaust, 1950–1965. *Modern Judaism* 16, 195–214.

Luo, G. and Yang, Y. (1961) *Hong Yan* (*The Red Crag*). Youth Press of China, Beijing.

Ma, S. M. Contrasting Two Survival Literatures: On the Jewish Holocaust and the Chinese Cultural Revolution. *Holocaust and Genocide Studies* 2(1), 81–93.

Maariv. (2004) Moving to a New Home is not Similar to Crematoriums and Gas Chambers [Hebrew]. December 21.

Maariv. (2005) The Difficult Scenes that will Never Relent [Hebrew]. August 8.

Magnuson, E. (2008) *Changing Men, Transforming culture: Inside the Men's Movement.* Paradigm Publishers, Boulder, CO.

216

Maillot, A. (2000) Shaping New Identities: The Peace Process and Post-Conflict Reconciliation, Unpublished manuscript, presented at City College Dublin.

Mallot, J. E. (2006) Body Politics and the Body Politic: Memory as Human Inscription in What the Body Remembers. *Interventions* 8(2),165–77.

Mamdani, M. (1996) *Citizen and Subject: Contemporary Africa and the Legacy of Late Colonialism*. Princeton University Press, Princeton.

Mann, M. (1986) *The Sources of Social Power, Vol. 1*. Cambridge University Press, New York.

Manz, B. (2002) Terror, Grief, and Recovery: Genocidal Trauma in a Mayan Village in Guatemala. In A. Hinton (ed.) *Annihilating Difference: The Anthropology of Genocide*. University of California Press, Berkeley.

Miller, J. (1990) *One, by One, by One: Facing the Holocaust*. Simon and Schuster, New York.

Minow, M. (1998) *Between Vengeance and Forgiveness: Facing History after Genocide and Mass Violence*. Beacon Press, Boston, MA.

Mookerjea-Leonard, D. (2004) Quarantined: Women and the Partition. *Comparative Studies of South Asia, Africa and the Middle East* 24(1), 33–46.

Morris, B. (1994) *1948 and After: Israel and the Palestinians*. Oxford University Press, Oxford, UK.

Morris, B. (1987) *Birth of the Palestinian Refugee Problem, 1947–1949*. Cambridge University Press, Cambridge and New York, NY.

Naimark, N. (2001) *Fires of Hatred: Ethnic Cleansing in Twentieth-Century Europe*. Harvard University Press, Cambridge, MA.

Neal, A. G. (1998) *National Trauma and Collective Memory: Major Events in the American Century*. M. E. Sharpe, Armonk, NY.

New York Times (2009) Gaza: Cleric Denounces Possible Holocaust Education. September 1, A6.

New York Times (2001) For Nations Traumatized by the Past, New Remedies. July 29, A5.

New York Times (2000) Letters to the Editor, Sec. 1, December 19.

New York Times (2000) No Formal Apology by the US For Korean War Civilian Deaths. Foreign Desk, December 22.

New York Times (1994) Yeshayahu Leibowitz, 91, Iconoclastic Israeli Thinker. August 19.

Newman, D. (1985) *The Impact of Gush Emunim: Politics and Settlement in the West Bank*. Croom Helm, London.

Norich, A. (1998–9) Harbe sugyes/Puzzling Questions: Yiddish and English Culture in America during the Holocaust. *Jewish Social Studies* 1–2 (Fall/ Winter), 91–110.

Novick, P. (1999) *The Holocaust in American Life*. Houghton Mifflin, New York.

Novick, P. (1994) Holocaust and Memory in America. In J. E. Young (ed.) *The Art of Memory: Holocaust Memorials in History*. Prestel-Verlag, Munich, pp. 159–76.

Nudel, A. (1995) Prof. Moshe Zimmerman: The Children of the Settlers in Hebron are exactly like the Hitler Youth. *Yerushalayim*, April 28.

Nussbaum, M. (1992) Tragedy and Self-sufficiency: Plato and Aristotle on Fear and Pity. In A. O. Rorty (ed.) *Essays on Aristotle's Poetics*. Princeton University Press, Princeton, NJ, pp. 261–90.

O'Donnell, E. (2004) "Woman" and "Homeland" in Ritwik Ghatak's Films: Constructing Post-Independence Bengali Cultural Identity. *Jump Cut*, 47.

217

Ofer, D. (2000) The Strength of Remembrance: Commemorating the Holocaust During the First Decade of Israel. *Jewish Social Studies: History, Culture, Society* 6(2), 24–55.

Ofer, D. (1996) Linguistic Conceptualization of the Holocaust in Palestine and Israel, 1942–53. *Journal of Contemporary History* 31(3), 567–95.

Pandey, G. (1997) In Defense of the Fragment. In R. Guha (ed.) *A Subaltern Studies Reader, 1986–1995.* University of Minnesota Press, Minneapolis, MN, pp. 1–33.

Pappe, I. (1992) *The Making of the Arab–Israeli Conflict, 1947–51.* I.B. Tauris, London.

Perlez, J. (2001) *Milosevic Should Face Trial by Hague Tribunal, Bush Says. New York Times,* A6, April 2.

Perry, G. S. (1948) Your Neighbors: The Golombs. *Saturday Evening Post,* 36, November 13.

Podeh, E. (2000) History and Memory in the Israeli Educational System: The Portrayal of the Arab–Israeli Conflict in History Textbooks (1948–2000). *History and Memory* 12(1), 65–100.

Prager, J. (1998) *Presenting the Past: Psychoanalysis and the Sociology of Misremembering.* Harvard University Press, Cambridge, MA.

Rambo, E. and Chan, E. (1990) Text, Structure, and Action in Cultural Sociology: A Commentary on "Positive Objectivity" in Wuthnow and Archer. *Theory and Society* 19, 635–48.

Remnick, D. (2007) The Apostate: A Zionist Politician Loses Faith in the Future. *The New Yorker,* July 30.

Rogan, E. L., and A. Shalim (eds) (2001) *The War for Palestine: Rewriting the History of 1948.* Cambridge University Press, Cambridge UK.

Rohde, D. (1999) The Visitor: Wiesel, a Man of Peace, Cites Need to Act. *The New York Times,* A1, June 2.

Rorty, A. O. (1992) The Psychology of Aristotelian Tragedy. In A. O. Rorty (ed.) *Essays on Aristotle's Poetics.* Princeton University Press, Princeton, NJ, pp. 1–22.

Rosenfeld, A. H. (1995) The Americanization of the Holocaust. *Commentary* 90(6), 35–40.

Said, E. W. (2001) Afterword: The Consequences of 1948. In E. L. Rogan and A. Shlaim (eds) *The War for Palestine: Rewriting the History of 1948.* Cambridge University Press, Cambridge, UK, pp. 206–19.

Said, E. W. (1988) Identity, Negation, and Violence. *New Left Review* 171, 46–60.

Said, E. W. (1979) *Orientalism.* Vintage, New York.

Said, E. W. (1979) *The Question of Palestine.* Times Books, New York.

Schwartz, B. (2011) Rethinking Conflict and Memory: The Case of Nanking. In J. C. Alexander, R. Jacobs and P. Smith (eds) *The Oxford Handbook of Cultural Sociology.* New York, Oxford University Press, pp. 529–63.

Searle, J. (1969) *Speech Acts.* Cambridge University Press, London.

Segev, T. (1993) *The Seventh Million: The Israelis and the Holocaust (*trans. H. Watzman) Hill and Wang, New York.

Shamir, S., Yitzhaki-Verner, T. and Bar-On, D. (1996) "The Recruited Identity": The Influence of the Intifada on the Perception of the Peace Process from the Standpoint of the Individual. *Journal of Narrative and Life History* 6(3), 193–233.

Shapira, A. (1998) The Holocaust: Private Memories, Public Memories. *Jewish Social Studies* 4(2), 40–58.

Shapira, A. (ed.) (1968) Warriors' Discourse: Chapter in Listening and Meditation [Siyach Lochamim: Pirkey Hakshava Vehitbonenut]. *Kvutzat Chaverim Tzeirim Mehatnua* Hakibutzit, Tel Aviv.

Shapiro, E. S. (1992) *A Time for Healing: American Jewry since World War II*. Johns Hopkins University Press, Baltimore, MD.

Shejter, A. M. (2007) The Pillar of Fire by Night, to Shew them Light: Israeli Broadcasting, the Supreme Court and the Zionist Narrative. *Media, Culture and Society* 29(6), 916–933.

Shirer, W. L. (1969) *The Collapse of the Third Republic: An Inquiry into the Fall of France in 1940*. Simon and Schuster, New York.

Short, K. R. M. (1981) Hollywood Fights Anti-Semitism, 1945–47. In K. R. M. Short (ed.) *Feature Films as History*. Knoxville: University of Tennessee, Knoxville, pp. 157–189.

Silk, M. (1984) Notes on the Judeo-Christian Tradition in America. *American Quarterly* 36, 65.

Sitas, A. (2010) *The Mandela Decade 1990–2000: Labour, Culture and Society in Post-Apartheid South Africa*. UNISA PRESS and Brill, South Africa.

Sitas, A. (2008) *The Ethic of Reconciliation*. Madiba Press/Centre for the Study of Social Systems, New Delhi.

Sitas, A. (2006) The African Renaissance and Sociological Reclamations in the South. *Current Sociology* 54(3), 357–80.

Sledge, E. B. (1998) The Old Breed and the Costs of War. In J. V. Denson (ed.) *The Costs of War: America's Pyrrhic Victories*. Transaction, New Brunswick, NJ.

Smelser, N. (2004) Psychological Trauma and Cultural Trauma. In J. C. Alexander et al. (eds) *Cultural Trauma and Collective Identity*. University of California Press, Berkeley.

Smelser, N. (1974) Growth, Structural Change, and Conflict in California Public Higher Education, 1950–1970. In N. Smelser and G. Almond (eds) *Public Higher Education in California*. University of California Press, Berkeley, pp. 9–142.

Smelser, N. (1963) *The Sociology of Economic Life*. Prentice-Hall, Englewood Cliffs, NJ

Smelser, N. (1962) *Theory of Collective Behavior*. The Free Press of Glencoe, New York.

Smith, P. (2005) *Why War? The Cultural Logic of Iraq, the Gulf War and Suez*. University of Chicago Press, Chicago

Smith, P. (1998) Barbarism and Civility in the Discourses of Fascism, Communism, and Democracy. In J. Alexander (ed.) *Real Civil Societies*. Sage, London, pp. 15–37.

Spasić, I. (2011) The Trauma of Kosovo in Serbian National Narratives. In R. Eyerman, J. C. Alexander and E. Breese (eds) *Narrating Trauma: On the Impact of Collective Suffering*. Paradigm Publishers, Boulder, CO.

Spurr, D. (1993) *The Rhetoric of Empire: Colonial Discourse in Journalism, Travel Writing, and Imperial Administration*. Duke University Press, Durham, N.C.

Stannard, D. E. (1996) The Dangers of Calling the Holocaust Unique. *Chronicle of Higher Education*, B1–2, August 2.

Stannard, D. E. (1991) *American Holocaust: The Conquest of the New World*. Oxford University Press, Oxford, UK.

Stember, C. H. (1966) *Jews in the Mind of America*. Basic Books, New York.

Strenghold, L. (1988) Review of Back to the Source. *Holocaust and Genocide Studies* 3(3), 337–42.

Sztompka, P. (1993) *The Sociology of Social Change*. Blackwell, Oxford, UK.

Sztompka, P. (1991). *Society in Action: The Theory of Social Becoming*. Polity, Cambridge.

Taub, G. (2010) *The Settlers and the Struggle over the Meaning of Zionism*. Yale University Press, New Haven, CT.

Thompson, K. (1998) *Moral Panics*. Routledge, London.

Todorov, T. (1984) *Conquest of America: The Question of the Other*. Random House, New York.

Tse-Tung, M. (1967) *Quotations from Chairman Mao Tse-Tung*. Bantam Books, New York.

Tse-Tung, M. (1962) On Contradiction. In A. Fremantle, *Mao Tse-Tung: An Anthology of His Writings*. New American Library, New York, pp. 214–41.

Turner, V. (1969) *The Ritual Process*. Aldine, Chicago.

Tyler, P. E. (2003) A New Power in the Streets: A Message to Bush Not to Rush to War. *New York Times*, February 17, A1.

van Gelder, L. (1999) After the Holocaust, If There Can Indeed Be an After. *New York Times*, May 5, D-1.

Volkan, V. D. (2001) Transgenerational Transmissions and Chosen Traumas: An Aspect of Large-Group Identity. *Group Analysis* 34(1): 79–97.

Watson, P. (2001) War's Over in Yugoslavia, but Box-Office Battles Have Begun. *Los Angeles Times*, January 3, A1–6.

Weber, M. (1978 [1956]) *Economy and Society*. University of California Press, Berkeley, CA.

Weissberg, L. (1997) The Tale of a Good German: Reflections on the German Reception of *Schindler's List*. In Y. Loshitzky (ed.) *Spielberg's Holocaust: Critical Perspectives on "Schindler's List"*. University of Indiana Press, Bloomington, pp. 171–92.

Weitz, Y. (1995) Political Dimensions of Holocaust Memory in Israel. In R. Wistrich and D. Ohana (eds) *The Shaping of Israeli Identity: Myth, Memory and Trauma*. Frank Cass, London and Portland, OR, pp 129–45.

Welles, S. (1945) New Hope for the Jewish People. *Nation*, May 5, 160: 511–13.

Whitman, H. (1949) The College Fraternity Crisis. *Collier's*, January 8, 34–5.

Wiesel, E. (1978) Trivializing the Holocaust. *The New York Times*, 2(1), April 16.

Wieviorka, M. (2007) *The Lure of Anti-Semitism: Hatred of Jews in Present-Day France*. Brill, Leiden/Boston, MA.

Wines, M. (1999) Two Views of Inhumanity Split the World, Even in Victory. *New York Times*, June 13, 4–1.

Winter, J. (2006) *Dreams of Peace and Freedom: Utopian Moments in the 20th Century*. Duke University Press, Durham, NC.

Wistrich, R. and Ohana, D. (eds) (1995) *The Shaping of Israeli Identity: Myth, Memory, and Trauma*. F. Cass, London and Portland, OR.

Wittrock, B. (1991) Cultural Identity and Nationhood: The Reconstitution of Germany or the Open Answer to an Almost Closed Question. In M. Trow and T. Nybom (eds) *University and Society*. Jessica Kingsley Publishers, London, pp. 76–87.

Wu, Q. (2004 [1957]) *Hong Ri (The Red Sun)*. Youth Press of China, Beijing.

Wyman, D. S. (1984) *The Abandonment of the Jews: Americans and the Holocaust, 1941–1945*. Pantheon, New York.

Yablonka, H. (2008) The Holocaust Consciousness in the Third Decade: From "There" to "Here and Now" [Hebrew]. In Z. Zameret and H. Yablonka (eds) *The Third Decade*. Yad Ben Zvi, Jerusalem, pp. 264–78.

Yediot Aharonot. (2009) Rabbi Metzger Brings Peaceful Message to Yasuf Village. December 14.

Yediot Aharonot. (2005) The Settlers: We'll Greet the Soldiers in Auschwitz Uniforms [Hebrew]. July 28.

Yin, J. and Young, S. (1996) *Rape of Nanjing: An Undeniable History in Photographs*. Triumph Books, Chicago.

Young, J. E. (1993) *The Texture of Memory: Holocaust Memorials and Meaning.* Yale University Press, New Haven.

Zelizer, B. (1998) *Remembering to Forget: Holocaust Memory through the Camera's Eye*. University of Chicago, Chicago.

Zertal, I. (2005) *Israel's Holocaust and the Politics of Nationhood* (trans. C. Galai). Cambridge University Press, Cambridge and New York, NY.

Zerubavel, E. (2006) *The Elephant in the Room: Silence and Denial in Everyday Life*. Oxford, New York.

Zielinski, S. (1986) History as Entertainment and Provocation: The TV Series "Holocaust" in West Germany. In A. Rabinbach and J. Zipes (eds) *Germans and Jews since the Holocaust: The Changing Situation in West Germany*. New York: Holmes and Meier, New York, pp. 258–86.

Zimmermann v. Yedioth Communication (2005) 2313/00 (Tel Aviv-Jaff a District).

INDEX